THE CASE
AGAINST
RACISM

An Investigation into the Nature of
the Prejudiced Mind

ROGER NELSON

ISBN-13: 978-1544600369
ISBN-10: 1544600364

Cover Photograph: *'These Bandits Offered Armed Resistance'*: from the report prepared by SS Brigadefuhrer Juergen Stroop in 1943 after he destroyed the Warsaw Ghetto.

SS Brigadefuhrer Juergen Stroop was the officer commanding the demolition of the Warsaw Ghetto in which both Jews and ethnic Poles resisted with carbines and one light machine gun. Against them were arrayed 36 officers and 2054 men of the Wehrmacht, SS and Polish police backed up by a battery of artillery, possibly two. Germany was virtually defeated on the Eastern front and this was all they had by way of a victory.

Stroop won several military honours including the Iron Cross 1st Class and, because of his pure Aryan stock, he was able to visit the Lebensborn centres He believed Adolf Hitler had been placed on earth by a higher authority, perhaps Wotan himself, to fulfil a higher destiny. Juergen Stroop was tried and hanged in Warsaw in 1952.

Wikipedia and the Jewish Virtual Library.

ABOUT THE AUTHOR

The author was born in 1933 near Leeds, Yorkshire. He went to school in England and Switzerland and did his National Service in REME in Germany before going to Cambridge where he got a degree in Engineering. Since this is a book about racism it is only fair to say that he is, racially, a Jew married to a Catholic and both are white. They have been married for nearly 50 years and have two sons. The family have travelled a good deal and have lived in the Far East, the Muslim Middle East and Catholic Latin America. He has been left with a good impression of the people in all the countries he worked in. He obtained a legal qualification and prepared, with others, commercial cases for litigation.

CONTENTS

PREFACE

In 1818, Mary Shelley, a girl of 20, published her novel, *Frankenstein*. In it, Victor Frankenstein, armed with the knowledge gained from a university where he studied natural philosophy and chemistry, creates life from dead body parts. The creature he creates, also called Frankenstein, is bigger than a human being and, by human standards, monstrous. It escapes the control of Victor and kills everyone his creator loves. Victor's younger brother William is murdered by strangulation. His best friend, Henry, dies the same way. His fiancée Elizabeth is also murdered by the monster. His father dies of grief. Tellingly, Frankenstein tells Victor that if he could create a female companion for him, he would disappear, never to be seen again. Victor tries to provide the monster with someone who could love him but finds himself unable to do so. Victor travels by dog sleigh in the frozen wastelands of the North Pole where he dies on an icebound ship. Walton, the captain of the ship, finds the monster weeping over the dead body of his creator before he too disappears into the Polar darkness never to be seen again. The monster is the only creature to mourn the passing of Victor.

The monster was created on dreary night in

November when the rain pattered at the window, and the activity of the monster is related to fits of depression felt by Victor. The book is a brilliant allegory of the racist who creates his monsters out of his own depression and unhappiness. If someone could only love him he would disappear. But nobody can.

He kills or alienates everyone who might be a friend or companion and travels looking for someone who will cure him. He and Victor are one and the same and both end lonely creatures in a frozen wasteland. No matter how sorry one feels for Victor, the disasters he has suffered have been brought about by the monster he created.

The emotionally damaged man or woman will restore their sense of control by destroying possibly the only people who hold him in their regard, nor can he repent the damage he has done to their lives as well as his own.

Women are frequently made to suffer from this kind of unhappy man. In Britain today, 25% of women experience domestic violence and two women a week are murdered by their partners or ex-partners.[1] The male can be suffering from individual psychological problems, sexual frustration, unbearable life pressure, or some innate urge towards aggression.[2] Jack the Ripper was a man who desexed his victims by cutting out their wombs possibly because he was a man who could not enjoy sex in a normal way and had difficulty, or found it impossible, to have sex with a woman. When he killed them he was, at last, in

---

[1] MWR on internet.
[2] Feminist.com.

control and it gave him transient comfort to kill them. Equally horrifying was that his coachman, whoever he was, cleaned the blood in the coach without going to the police because the women were only prostitutes[3]. The same attitude of indifference has been displayed to all outside groups if one looks around the world at any time.

[3] Melvyn Fairclough, *The Ripper and the Royals.*

CHAPTER 1

RACE

Race, is defined here as the ability to recognise a stranger. It is so pervasive that it could well have been part of mankind's survival mechanism when people lived in tribes and when hunting, gathering and childbearing were the activities which ensured survival. It exists in every country and every nation so that it must, like a human ailment, be a primitive condition common to all mankind. For the purposes of this book it is taken to be primarily, if not entirely, a question of appearance and speech. The racist is a person in the throes of emotional unhappiness and is obeying his, or her, emotions but it always brings comfort to the sufferer though bringing misery to the victim, sometimes, even death.

Members of the same tribe can recognise each other, members of the same social class can recognise each other and, if there is any doubt, when they speak, their accent settles the matter. It is a question of genetics, a question of intermarriage and it carries no rational basis of good or evil, nor any attribute like intelligence or stupidity. Frequent attempts have been made to find a rational basis for saying one race is superior to another but there has never been any scientific validity in any of the many theories put forward. It is simply a question of appearance and it is only when the element of prejudice is added that race becomes an ugly matter. Again, for the purposes of this book, ethnicity is taken to be a question of culture and covers things like taste in music, schooling, love of learning, if any, so that people of different races can have the same ethnicity. The comfort which the racist obtains as he takes control is always at the expense of some innocent third party who is viewed as weak.

Like the ability to learn a language, the structure that the language can be built on is built into the child's brain but the language itself has to be taught.[4] The teaching of race causes many, sometimes amusing, stumbles but by the age of eight, it is established. A young Japanese woman came to England in 2004 and took a job as a teaching assistant in an all-white primary school. The children, aged three to four, noticed various things about her: that her hair was black, that her eyes were black and that she spoke with a slight accent. The results of her conversations with the children are blurred because the well-meaning class teacher introduced her as a visitor from Japan. The children were able then to put a label on her and any conclusions they might have drawn might have been given to them by their parents.

There have been many studies of children because children are the unspoiled building blocks of human beings. Children are observant and, quite indifferently,

---

[4] See for example Gomez Proceedings of the National Academy of Sciences 8 April 2014.

observe everything from the fact that the sky is blue to the grass is green and their skin is black, the same colour as their parents'. In multiracial schools they observe that other children might look different to themselves but that has no connotations either positive or negative. In an article based on a study conducted in southern California between 1978 and 1980[5] children of different ages were recorded as follows:

Two and a half-year-old child with a black father and a white mother upon seeing some black women in a restaurant, commented: "I didn't know women were black."

Upon seeing an interracial couple in church, a three-year-old said: "It's funny that the mummy and the daddy are different. They should be the same."

Frequently reported question asked by white children about black children: "Will the colour come off in the bath?"

When T was between three and four he often asked his mother what her favourite colour was. When she said 'red' the first time he became angry and said that she didn't like him. T's mother was careful to say next time that brown was her favourite colour.

The last quotation is beginning to show that, in contrast to the others, the child is beginning to understand that some skin colours are liked and other colours are not so liked. The earlier quotations are completely innocent but somebody, somewhere has introduced into the child's conscious mind the idea of

---

[5] The authors of the Article were Louise Derman-Sparks of Pacific Oaks College, Carol Tanaka Higa, and Bill Sparks, teachers in the Los Angeles school system.

racial inequality which was probably not there previously. Some of the racial ideas come from television:

C asked: "Do I have to be black?" To the question of why he had asked, he replied, "I want to be chief of paramedics." His favourite TV shows at the time showed all the paramedics and fire fighters were white.

When D, a black child aged four, met a Native American man dressed in jeans and shirt, he refused to believe the man's race because he wasn't wearing feathers and 'Indian clothes', as the Native Americans did on TV.

At an older age children become confused between nationality and race:

Teacher: what are you?

Seven-year-old child: Chinese American.

Teacher: How do you know you are Chinese?

Child: Because I talk Chinese.

Teacher: Where were you born?

Child: In this country.

Teacher: What country is that?

Child: America.

Teacher: Does that mean you are American?

Child: Yes.

Teacher: Is everybody an American?

Child: No. Some are Chinese and some are not.

Teacher: What does it mean to be Chinese?

Child: You talk Chinese and you eat Chinese food,

but I don't like Chinese food.

As they get older the child's responses become more and more complex and they learn more and more that, for example, in a white society, all colours are not treated equally so that a white mother heard a group of her seven-year-old's friends, also white, talking about how they were glad they were not black. Whilst the ability to see differences in the appearance of human beings is innate, the rating of those appearances as 'better' or 'worse' is learned. What is more, experience has shown that for many people, it is difficult to unlearn.

In a test reported by CNN a little five-year-old girl in Georgia, USA, is asked to answer a series of questions in her school library. The girl who is white is looking at pictures of five cartoons, girls, all identical except for the skin colour ranging from light to dark. When asked who the clever girl is, she points to a light-skinned girl. When asked who the nasty child is she points to a dark-skinned girl... She says that child is good because 'she looks like me' and she says the black child is ugly because she's a lot darker. The mother who is watching assumes that she, herself, is guilty of not protecting her daughter from racist attitudes. Clearly, the mother, who began to cry, believes that she is guilty of some sort of negligence, but she is clearly of the view that the child learnt her attitudes outside the home. It must be remarked that the guilt shown by this mother in the 21st century is a vast improvement over the attitude of older white people, born in the 1930s and 1940s, who consider racial prejudice to be completely normal and justified.

There are probably several sources of imagined

white, racial superiority among white dominant populations: The home and the parents, school and entertainment in the media for example. Proshanski (1966)[6] concludes that racial awareness appears at about the age of three in both black and white children, increases rapidly for the next several years, and is pretty well established by the time children are eight years old. The basis of this completely fictional idea of racial superiority is almost laughable were it not for the fact that it causes so much damage. It is to be found in people's idea that there is a racial hierarchy. There is no scientific basis for such a belief but the idea that there is such a hierarchy finds a ready home in the emotional makeup of most people, possibly more so among the less thoughtful. Religion is also a dividing marker, particularly so, if special clothing has to be worn as part of the faith such as skullcaps or veils. The people who wear them in Western society are, effectively, making a statement which says: I am proud of my religion and my race. Such apparel, in most countries is, quite correctly, perfectly legal but the wearer, in a Western society, is set apart.

It follows then that children are not born racist but have to be taught, and are ready to learn, that some racial appearances are considered inferior to others. The ways in which they are taught comes from a widely held belief in the existence of a racial hierarchy. In its most primitive form, the controlling population make the racial ideal the same as they believe themselves to be, while anyone who varies from that

---

[6] Quoted in *Development of Children's Racial Awareness and Intergroup Attitudes* by Phyllis A. Katz.

ideal is beneath them. A typical melange of characteristics might be: White; fought for his country; heterosexual; churchgoer; privately educated; rich, and anyone who does not score 100% on these characteristics can, to some extent, be looked down on.

On a nation state basis, much kudos is gained by victory in war while defeat has the opposite effect. The winner in a war is normally the one who has invented a superior strategy, comes from a more advanced industrial society and has superior armaments. Shakespeare's Henry V is a wonderful play but the cry of the King: *"Once more unto the breach, dear friends, once more; Or close the wall up with our English dead!"* is heroic but grossly misleading. The army was decimated with typhus and only the longbow, manned by Welsh archers with a superior rate of fire, saved the day. The facts of history do not generally support racial superiority or the prevailing power of raw courage, though some courage, training and discipline play their part. History emphasises the role played by the host race and/or the winners. The presence of the Dutch and Austrians at Waterloo and the presence of a wire cattle fence at Cemetery Ridge were both significant factors in gaining victory but frequently go unmentioned.

CHAPTER 2

RACIAL HIERARCHY

An essential element of racism is the formation in many minds of a racial hierarchy. Only the most enlightened are truly immune from the belief that such a hierarchy exists though, in fact, there is no rational basis for such a belief. Those who harbour this belief always place their own race at the top and everybody else of different appearance to them, below. Most people take this to be absolutely normal and establish a racial norm which they believe in and even they feel guilty if they fall short of it. It has been asserted to the author that, in Britain, the racial ideal is a white male with blue eyes. English, not Welsh or Scottish or Irish. Religion: Protestant, not Catholic and certainly not Jewish. A warrior who has fought for his country as an officer in a front-line regiment. A heterosexual married man who has brought up children and educated them to be members of the officer class. In the mind of a significant number of British people this amazing list still represents an ideal against which anyone who does not attain it is looked down upon and, more pertinently, has been internalised so that those looked down upon themselves sometimes internalise a sense of inferiority. This acceptance is, quite rightly, becoming rarer.

When a 'racially inferior' person does not accept his position then a racist loses control and becomes angry. When a black boy runs away after being challenged by a white policeman who is armed and in uniform, it is like an insult to the policeman and he might fire.

The Encyclopaedia Britannica 15th Ed 25.551.1b sets out the position on racial superiority and whether it exists at all, as follows:

The debate-whether the variation in intelligence levels is a product of the conditions into which people all having the same initial potential are born, or whether it is a reflection of variations in the capacity with which they are born-is very closely related to the question of whether there is such a thing as human nature common to all human beings, or whether there are intrinsic differences among those whom we recognise as belonging to the biological species Homo sapiens. This is because, as the name Homo sapiens suggests, man is traditionally thought to be distinguished from and privileged above other animals by virtue of his possession of reason, or intellect. When the intellect is positively valued as that which is distinctively human and which confers superiority on man, the thought that different races of people differ by nature in their intellectual capacities has been used as a justification for a variety of racist attitudes and policies. Those of another race, of supposedly lesser intellectual development, are classified as less than fully human and therefore as needing to be accorded less than full human rights. Similarly, the thought that women are by nature intellectually inferior to men has been used as a justification for their domination by men, for refusing them education, and even for according them the legal status of property owned by men. On the other hand, if differences in adult intellectual capacity are regarded as a product of the circumstances in which potentially similar people are brought up, the attitude is to consider all as equally human but some as having been more privileged when growing up than others.

More radically, the evidence for variations in intelligence levels may be questioned by challenging the objectivity of the standards relative to which these levels are assessed. It may be argued that conceptions of what constitutes a rational or intelligent response to a situation or to a problem of themselves culturally conditioned, a product of the way in which the members of the group devising the tests and making the judgements have themselves been taught to think. Such an argument has the effect of undermining claims by any one human group to intellectual superiority over others, whether these others be their contemporaries or their own forebears. Hence, they may also be used to discredit any idea of a progressive development of human intellectual capacities.[7]

If what the distinguished authors quoted above are saying is that because human beings are of one race and any attempt to talk about racial superiority or inferiority must be suspect, then no one could disagree with them. What follows is a series of attempts by others to show that a racial hierarchy really does exist but the examples quoted were all carried out by white Christian men who already had a hierarchy in their minds and were merely choosing 'facts' to support what they already believed to be true. Nevertheless, the fiction of racial superiority

---

[7] George Paul Gusdorf (Former Professor of Philosophy, University of Strasbourg, France) and Mary Elizabeth Tiles (Associate Professor of Philosophy, University of Hawaii at Manoa Honolulu) writing in the Encyclopaedia Britannica 15th Edition 25.551.1b.

held by the great majority of individuals is powerful and is the basis of racial hatred.

There has been a tendency since the days of Plato and Aristotle to rank objects from the most glorious at the top to the most insignificant at the bottom and in this way what is known as the Great Chain of Being came into existence, starting with God who possesses spiritual attributes outside the realms of creation and then going on to angels, starting with a superior kind of angel called a Seraph and going onto Cherubim and ending up with archangels. Human beings, it has been noticed since the days of St Thomas Aquinas, have a spiritual side and an animal passions side with their vulnerability to pain, hunger, thirst, sexual desire, just like the animals that inhabited the lower part of the chain. The larger mammals came next, like the elephant and the lion, ending with less dangerous animals like the domestic cat. Birds began with birds of prey, hawks, owls and so forth, ending with seed-eating birds that you can see in the garden, and offer no threat to mankind. Aquatic creatures begin again with the largest, the whale, and end with tiny fish and then the Chain of Being goes on to plants and trees down to fungus at the end. Followed finally by stones, beginning with diamonds and ending with less precious stones. The metals come next, gold down to copper, but curiously iron and bronze from which weapons are made are rated higher. Last of all come stones, finishing with gravel and sand.

This idea that everything around us is ordered from the most powerful to the weakest somehow lies at the heart of a progression of life forms from the simplest creatures to the more complex.

Following the formation of the Royal Society after a lecture by Christopher Wren in 1660 with the motto 'Nullus in Verba' (take nobody's word for it), scientific investigation spread across Europe consisting of the establishment of facts based on experiment. Modern racism, a cardboard imitation of the scientific method, began with Count Arthur de Gobineau whose essay: *The Moral and Intellectual Diversity of Races with Particular Reference to Their Respective Influence in the Civil and Political History of Mankind*, the American edition of which was published in Philadelphia in 1856. The American edition contains an appendix which has, in its own opinion, the latest scientific facts bearing upon the question of unity or plurality of species by JC Nott, MD of Mobile Alabama.

His essay begins from the premise that the races are mentally unequal because the Negro, for example, has been endowed with the richest land but is the most feeble intellectually. He then goes on to the following tables:

	Black Races	Yellow Races	White Races
Intellect	Feeble	Mediocre	Vigorous
Animal Propensities	Very Strong	Moderate	Strong
Moral Propensities	Partially Latent	Comparatively Developed	Highly Cultivated

The Russians, Poles and Serbs, he goes on to say, are only superficially civilised. None of this is supported by fact and certainly no experimentation. Many people were very impressed with Gobineau's racial theories because they were easily understandable even though unsupported by evidence. Adolf Hitler, as part of his war aims, intended to reduce the Russians, the Serbs and the Poles to slavery in the service of the ethnically pure German people.

Gobineau placed enormous faith in the Aryan race and the Teutons, but in passing, he is very impressed with the work of Dr Morton who measured the volume of skulls by pouring peppercorns into them and weighing the result. His premise was that the greater the volume of the skull, the more civilised the owner had been in life. On this basis he placed the races in the following order:

White races – Yellow races (Mongolian and Malay) – Copper-coloured races, and finally, in last place, Negroes.

The upper classes of each race have larger skulls and even Gobineau wonders how Dr Morton knew which class each skull came from and whether his selection of skulls was not biased in some way. He attacks J C Prichard, author of *Researches into the Physical History of Man*, 1851, who argues in favour of the uniformity of human races. Gobineau is vaguely aware of genetics but argues that when Jews have light hair and blue eyes they are still inferior because this is purely due to climate. He asserts that Jews keep themselves racially pure and therefore cannot have mixed in the superior Teutonic Aryan race. Gobineau therefore starts from the proposition that a racial hierarchy headed by the Teutonic race exists in order to prove that a racial hierarchy exists headed by the Teutonic. This is a common human fallacy but it ends at the starting point having gone nowhere.

Finally, he looks at the world as he sees it in his day, relying on the idea that the most well researched and obvious civilisations were the most advanced because, and here he has no evidence whatsoever, they had the sacred admixture of Aryan and Teutonic racial element. In chronological order he places them as follows:

1. The Indian civilisation. It spread among the islands of the Indian Ocean, towards the north, beyond the Himalaya Mountains, and towards the east, beyond the Brahmaputra. It was originated by white race of the Aryan stock.

2. The Egyptian civilisation comes next. As its satellites may be mentioned the less perfect civilisations of the Ethiopians, Nubians and several other small peoples west of the oasis of Ammon. An Aryan colony from India, settled in the upper part of the Nile Valley, had established this, were all branches of the Aryan family.

3. The Assyrians, around whom were allied the Jews, Phoenicians, Lidians, Carthaginians, and to whom they were indebted for their social intelligence, were due to repeated invasions of white populations. There are the Iranians, who flourished in further Asia, under the names of Medes, Persians and Bactrians. They were all branches of the Aryan family. (The reader will notice that white invasion improves the culture of the people thus invaded.)

4. The Greeks belonged to the same stock, but were modified by other elements, which, in course of time, totally transformed their character.

5. China presents the precise counterpart of Egypt. The light of civilisation was carried thither by Aryan colonies. The substratum of the social structure was composed of elements of the yellow race, but the white civilisations received reinforcements of their blood at various times.

6. The ancient civilisations of the Italian peninsular (the Etruscan civilisation), was developed by Mosaic population of the Celtic, Iberian and other stock, but cemented by Aryan element. From it emerged the civilisation of Rome.

7. Our civilisation is indebted for its tone and character to the Germanic conquerors of the fifth century. They were a branch of the Aryan family.

8, 9, 10. Under these heads he classes the three civilisations of the Western continent: the Allegheny, the Mexican and the Peruvians.

Gobineau simply places at the top of his hierarchy white-skinned aristocrats, which is all he is left with of his ideal. His father was a royalist, an aristocrat and a military officer. His wife left him and ran off to Switzerland with her lover, taking the seven-year-old Arthur Gobineau with her. Arthur returned to his father and failed the military examination. Arthur earned a living writing fiction. In 1846 he married Clemence Monnerot, mistress and model for Theodore Chasseriau, an artist of considerable ability. Clemence herself was born in Haiti into a rather racy family of uncertain means. She bore Arthur two daughters. Thus, all Arthur was left with was his white skin and his aristocratic father. His entire racist edifice was nothing more than a pseudoscientific form of boasting which put him, and people he aspired to be like, at the top of a pyramid.

The author of the appendix to Gobineau's essay, J.C. Nott, M.D, of Mobile, Alabama develops Dr Morton's work, of the peppercorn-filled skulls, and comes to the following conclusions with regard to racial hierarchy starting at the top:

Germans – English – Anglo-Americans – Persians, Armenians, Circassians – native Irish – Bengalis – the Semitic family which, since Shem was the grandfather of Abraham, must include Arabs and Jews – Felah from the Nile – Greco-Egyptians – Egyptians – Chinese – Malays – Polynesians – Peruvians – Mexicans – barbarous tribes including the Iroquois League – Cherokee and Shoshone – native African family, American Negroes – Hottentots – aboriginal Australians.

Dr Nott provides no evidence for this hierarchy being related to skull size or even that such a hierarchy exists at all. Whilst Nott did some valuable work on the transmission of Yellow Fever and Malaria, Darwin in his *Descent of Man* did not agree with his anthropology.

A little later Alfred Binet (1857-1911) invented the IQ test which purports to measure the inherent intelligence of a child. Clearly, the children he was testing were French children speaking French and the test included following a beam of light or a line of chalk back to the examiner, naming body parts, repeating a series of two digits, repeating simple sentences, defining words like 'house', 'fork', and 'Mama'. They continued with increasing complexity up to a question like: "My neighbour has been receiving strange visitors. He has received in turn a doctor, a lawyer and then a priest. What is taking place?" This last question might be comprehensible to a middle-class French child who came from a Christian family but a child living in the slums of Paris would have been baffled by it. Similarly, a child living in the Australian bush would also have never come across any of these people before. Nevertheless intelligence tests became very popular and well accepted for many years and particularly Binet's dictum: That an intelligence quotient test which was below 25 would describe the child as retarded. This has now fallen into complete disrepute.

Sir Francis Galton, a fellow of the Royal Society, took intelligence tests very seriously and between 1884 and 1890 carried out his own tests in which he related sensory discrimination to intellectual prowess. He therefore measured grip strength and reaction time so that he was concentrating on the physical attributes which a child of any nationality or background could exhibit. Unfortunately there is no correlation between sensory ability and innate intelligence. Sir Francis Galton, a cousin of Charles Darwin, forgot entirely about the environment which the child grew up in. Ibn Khaldun's work (1332-1406) has stood the test of time because he said that a major factor in any work was to discover how people earned a living. That is, you cannot divorce the study of an event from the environment in which it took place. Galton did however understand that genetics played an important role in inherited intelligence. He therefore suggested that girls below an IQ of 25 or, possibly, 12 should be sterilised so that there would be a very gradual improvement in the race. Adolf Hitler and the Germans took this one stage further and erected gas chambers in the grounds of mental homes and gassed young people who were deemed to be of sub-normal intelligence[8]. The T4 programme, as it was called, continued until 1945 at which stage 250,000 victims had been murdered.[9] The Catholic Bishop, Clemens Graf von Galen, spoke out against this practice and it was partially stopped. Galton, in his will, endowed a chair of eugenics at University College London.

The first occupant of the chair of eugenics was Karl Pearson (1857-1936) a mathematician of considerable repute whose work on statistics is still respected. Pearson, for all his intellectual ability, strayed into racism and believed that the survival of the fittest was arrived at by fighting for your country. The English who had fought the Saxons, the Norsemen and the Danes were the fittest people in the world. There is no sign that Pearson himself had ever served in the Armed Forces. He was considered, in his day, a left-winger and a freethinker. With Margaret Moul, he did a study of Jewish immigrant children: *"The problem of alien immigration into Great Britain by an examination of Russian and Polish Jewish children."* He came to many conclusions notably that those immigrants born in England were more intelligent than those born abroad. 'This country has no place for aliens whose religion, social habits will

---

[8] Ian Kershaw, *Hitler Nemesis*, pp426-427.
[9] Holocaust Memorial Day Trust/Action T4.

forever keep them as a caste apart. They will not be absorbed but will develop into a parasitic race because Jews have less intelligence than Gentiles,' he concluded.[10] He found that their lack of intelligence did not depend on physical size or hair colour, eye colour, or on domestic ventilation, nor did he make any allowance for their command of English and the fact that they lived in overcrowded tenements in the East End. His final words on the subject were that taken on the average, and regarding both sexes, this alien Jewish population is somewhat inferior physically and mentally to the native population. In case anybody thought he was anti-Semitic he professed a great admiration for the composer Felix Mendelssohn. Some of his best friends were Jews. His conviction that Jews were inferior because they had no country for which they had fought and been naturally selected was something which rang a bell in the hearts of many of his fellow citizens and even convinced the Jews themselves who heard it. It could be that it was this sentiment that gave birth to Zionism. There was a belief at the time that if Jews had a country of their own persecution of Jews would cease. Reading his work one is left with the impression that he began the paper and the investigation with a dislike of Jews and was carrying out the tests in order to demonstrate that his dislike of Jews was founded in reason, i.e. he was rationalising an emotional attitude. This belief is not without foundation. Whilst studying at Heidelberg, Pearson had visited a Passion Play near Innsbruck in

---

[10] He had 'an intense personal friendship' with Raphael Weldon, another brilliant mind, according to H M Walker in Karl Pearson American Statistic Association, Vol 53 1958 11-22.

1879. In the same year he recorded that he longed to believe. In 1881 at Cambridge he was reading Passion Plays and, in about 1882, he wrote a Passion Play for the 19th Century.[11] The Wikipedia entry on Passion Plays says: *Many Passion Plays historically blamed the Jews for the death of Jesus in a polemical fashion, depicting a crowd of Jewish people condemning Jesus to crucifixion and a Jewish leader assuming eternal collective guilt for the crowd for the death of Jesus...*

What Pearson and others forget is the respect which Jewish culture has for academia. Modern research is very conscious of eliminating, so far as is possible, the bias, if any, of the researcher.

In spite of the lack of obvious merit in intelligence testing, people continued to hold that some races were superior to others. A woman in Los Angeles writing in 2005 was good enough to post her prejudices on the web as follows:

English – German – French – North-West European mixtures – Spanish or Portuguese – multiracial South and East European mixtures – Italians – other eastern or southern Europeans – Irish – multi-ethnic half white "good Asian" and "white tribe Native American" – multiracial mixed with dark-skinned people – multiracial half white with light-skinned people – Asians, Chinese, Japanese, Vietnamese, Korean, other good light-skinned Asians – multiracial, less than half, black with any other race providing they were light-skinned – multiracial of mixed heritage with not more than half black, brown

---

[11] Theodore M Porter: *Karl Pearson The Statistical Life in a Statistical Age,* pp. 71, 85, 119.

skin – Pacific island – all other Native American – African, northern or eastern and light-skinned – Middle Eastern, Iraqis, Arabs – Sephardic Jews from Spain, Italy, and South Europe – any other Jews with darker skin – Russian Jews – Ethiopian Jews – Ethiopian Somalis – blacks from Africa and those in the African Diaspora – black African-Americans, descendants of slaves.

This is a remarkably detailed list which is based mainly on her idea of skin colour.

A correspondent writing in the Guardian newspaper suggested, with some bitterness, that there was a global hierarchy of race from his experience in Hong Kong which went as follows:

White – Chinese – Japanese – Malay – Arab – Jew – African.

There is no doubt, and he is explicit on the question, that colour is the salient factor.

Jews have lived in Japan since the 16th century but presently amount to no more than 2,000 people mainly because there is so little animus against Jews that intermarriage[12] has maintained the Jewish population at a very low level. Nevertheless, during a survey of anti-Semitism in Japan in 1988 by the Nippon Research Centre the author of the survey, Akito Hikayushi, collated the results as follows:

Before the second Sino-Japanese war (1937-1945): Japanese – Germans – Italians – Koreans –

---

[12] With regard to intermarriage only, this is the opinion of Daniel Ari Kapner and Stephen Levine writing in the Jerusalem Center for Public Affairs in 2000.

Americans – English – French – Indians – Chinese – Africans – Jews – Russians.

In 1962: Japanese – Americans – English – French – Germans – Italians – Indians – Russians – Chinese – Jews – Africans – Koreans.

The author of the survey himself believes that, with regard to Jews only, the students he interviewed were influenced by the treatment of Jews in Europe but the remainder of the racial groups they listed were their own opinion.[13]

In the days of Kublai Khan (1260-1294), when he ruled of China, he divided the Yuan Dynasty into the following races:

Mongols (at the top) – Semurem (immigrants from the West), some clans of central Asia including Muslims, Christians, Jews, Buddhists – North Chinese, Khitan (Nomadic Mongolian people), Jurchens (people who inhabited North-East China/Manchuria) and Koreans – southerners, subjects of the former Song Dynasty. Jews and Arabs were discriminated against to the extent that attempts were made to force them to eat Mongol food and not Kosher or Halal slaughtered meat, and to desist from the circumcision of infants. Muslims were further discriminated against to such an extent that they joined the Han rebellion.

The Chinese generally are as xenophobic as any

---

[13] Quoted in *Jews in the Japanese Mind* by David G. Goodman and Masanori Miyazawa, p4. With regard to intermarriage the authors did not agree with what is stated in the above text. It may be that what people say and what they do are two different things.

other race so that they are prejudiced against Europeans and Westerners, against Arabs, against the indigenous people of China, against Japanese, against Koreans, against Africans, against Indians, against Uyghurs (a racially Turkish people living in East Asia), and against mixed races. The only major difference between them and other races from Europe and the West is that in the first place they seemed to have no antipathy towards Jews, especially because Jews intermarried and became part of the native population. They seem to have no racial hierarchy but dislike everybody who is foreign, equally.

There is a hugely detailed list imputed to the Metropolitan Police of London available on the Internet but it can be paraphrased into: White – mixed race – Asian – black – Chinese – other.

No credence can be placed on any of these groupings except to say that any population holds the view that their race is superior to other races, and the hierarchy popular with any race varies round the globe with the race of the person talking. With the ubiquity of television, people in Japan pick up the prejudices of the USA through TV dramas and, while they enjoy African-American culture, they take black people less seriously than white because they are portrayed in the media as poor and illiterate. The stereotype of Jews portrayed in Europe has been converted in China to a feeling of kinship because they too respect education, close family relations, and are careful with money (the Talmud has been consulted as a source of business advice). They admire the great intellectual achievements of Karl Marx but they also admire Adolf Hitler because he was a strong leader.[14]

The history of the IQ leaves a great deal of doubt as to its value. During the First World War Colonel Robert Yerkes and his team gave one million tests to US Army recruits: Alpha for the literates, Beta for the illiterates. Each test took an hour and, it was intended to use Yerkes's grading to place recruits in a suitable arm of the services. The Army seems to have paid little attention to it. One of Yerkes's aides took 160,000 of these results to make racial comparisons and place races in a hierarchy. Because many could not speak English fluently, and Yerkes made no allowance for this, Russians, Italians, Poles and Blacks were graded moronic or near moronic to such an extent that non-English speaking nations were referred to as 'low-IQ nations'. It seems the results were widely believed for a time.[15]

Almost as a last resort, one of the only remaining ways of demonstrating the inferiority of any particular minority race is to quote the greatest in the land to prove the point. In pursuit of this goal, Abraham Lincoln, who emancipated the slaves is much quoted among white racists, apparently saying that the black population is inferior:

'Negro equality. Fudge! How long in the government of a God great enough to make and maintain this Universe, shall there continue knaves to vend, and fools to gulp, so low a piece of demagoguism as this.'

---

[14] Clarissa Sebag Montefiore in the New York Times.
[15] Gavin Evans, *Black Brain, White Brain: Is Intelligence Skin Deep?*, Location 2273.

Fragments. Notes for Speeches, September 1859[16]

The date, 1859, is noteworthy. The attack by confederate forces on Fort Sumter took place in April 1861 when ten states had seceded from the Union leaving Delaware, Maryland, Kentucky and Missouri undecided as to which side to support. They contained 400,000 slaves and a white population of 2,600,000 as well as considerable manufacturing capacity. Lincoln had to keep them neutral at the very least. It was clear that the emancipation of the slave population would be of strategic advantage because it would rob the South of their labour force and reduce their capacity to put white soldiers in the front line. Lincoln took a slow, gentle approach. Maryland came under military rule with Unionist candidates elected. Kentucky was pro-Confederacy and again a soft approach was adopted until Union candidates won nine out of ten seats so that, by 1863 Kentucky was solidly Unionist. Missouri was plunged into civil war by Unionist aggression. The sentence quoted above, like statements from the bible or the gospels, is taken not only out of context but out of the environment in which it was made.

In spite of having no reasonably based validity, the hierarchy of their race has taken on a solidity and is believed as though it were a scientifically proven fact. It is always, as in warfare, accompanied by reification so that people of another race can be treated as an enemy. An attempt will be made in the next chapter to show how this comes about.

---

[16] *The Collected Works of Abraham Lincoln* Volume 3, p.399.

CHAPTER 3

REIFICATION

Reification is the reduction of a human being into a non-person and the first stage is to deprive him or her of a name. At the most innocuous level it might simply be 'mon cher' or 'young man'. Further along it might be a word of unsolicited advice such as 'you should find your proper name' or 'do we know you?' or 'you will have to remind me of your name'. Much more purposeful and further down the process of depersonalising somebody is to refer to a whole class as though they were all identical. The 'Working Class'. 'The Rich'. 'The Muslims' or 'the Jews'. Much more purposefully is to give somebody a number as well as allowing them to keep their name. This is done in most armies in order to enhance discipline and make the soldier understand he is a member of an anonymous fighting force. A soldier who survives battle, if any, can always remember his number and it can, at times, provide a bond with others who had the same experience. German SS men kept their names but had their number tattooed under their armpits. Finally, approaching horror, those who were too old to work or children too young to work, were sent directly to the gas chambers. Those who were neither old nor children who were capable of being used as slave labour, had their numbers tattooed on their wrists and had no name.

The term reification was first coined by Karl Marx when he noticed 'the working class' were reduced in the middle-class mind to 'things' because during the industrial revolution they were made to disappear into factories and the goods they made were made by an invisible hand. Many goods were made, in popular conception, according to their make without considering in the slightest, the people who made them. The sense of alienation from the product was also accompanied by alienation from decision making of the work force, leading to social injustice which is still evident. This process has been described as follows:

The sense of alienation also concerned the hierarchy of the work place, the customary practices of large disciplinary units such as factories, major operations where all decisions were made elsewhere, by others and in an opaque fashion. To maintain a psychological balance under these Fordist industrial labour conditions, the worker had to mentally travel: she had to dream. Fordist workers severed their labouring bodies from their dreaming minds, which drifted elsewhere while their hands, here, tightened screws and stamped sheet metal...[17]

From the consumer's point of view, the worker who produced the Ford motor car disappeared and was replaced by the brand. Under these circumstances the 'worker' could be vilified. This was true in Britain in the 1920s during the general strikes which followed the Wall Street Crash when the workers were accused

---

[17] Diedrich Diederichsen, *Animation De-reification and the New Charm of the Inanimate.* Essay on the Internet.

of laziness and a ditty which contained the line 'the dirty shirking working class' was commonly sung by middle-class schoolboys to the tune of the Red Flag. In the 1920s Britain was taken onto the gold standard and British coal became too expensive to sell overseas. The 'coal owners' cut wages and after years of struggle the miners came out on strike followed by textile workers. Middle-class volunteers kept some trains and buses working and some electricity in supply. A schism opened between the classes. Violence broke out, put down by the police, and there was wild talk of a communist plot contrived by Zinoviev. The working class became people who lived on the dole and would not do a proper day's work when the real problem was the handling of the money supply and lack of investment in mechanising the coal industry. This is an example of reification and the working class were reified.[18]

A further example is the belief that alleviating inequality is featherbedding those who refuse to do a proper day's work. In 1942, during the war, William Beveridge (1879-1963) wrote a report which guaranteed a minimum subsistence standard of living to everyone in Britain. In spite of their obvious suffering, the working class had been so alienated that many people believed that helping them would turn them into spongers who would exploit the nation. Some newspaper reports illustrate this attitude:

Turning Britain into a machine that carries us safely from one end of life to the other in a very

---

[18] GCSE Bitesize.

comfortable life style.[19]

The author of this report is an economist turned spendthrift...destroying every vestige of self reliance and self help...if this becomes law then Ribbentrop might truly allege the Anglo Saxon race was decadent. (Ribbentrop, 1893 to execution in 1946, was the German minister for foreign affairs and mentioning him in time of war was an implication of disloyalty.)[20]

The land will become a nightmare of paternalism or Totalitarianism. Men and women will be stripped of responsibility.[21]

Though the opposition to the report demonstrates the existence of reification among some sections of the community, most people were in favour of the establishment of a welfare state. However, many felt that a Conservative government would never implement the report and this alone is given as one of the reasons for the resounding victory of the Labour Party in 1945.

During wars the enemy have to be reduced to the level of sub-humans capable of any bestiality, otherwise it would be difficult to fight and kill a fellow human being. Arthur Ponsonby (1871-1946) was opposed to Britain's entry into the First World War and, in his book *Falsehood in War-time* he quotes Lord Roseberry, Asquith and Lloyd George to the effect that there was no agreement, secret or otherwise, which constituted a binding obligation, moral or legal, to go

---

[19] Daily Telegraph, 2.12.42.
[20] Percy Rockliff, Secretary of the National Union of Friendly Societies.
[21] Truth, 4.12.42.

to war with Germany. Commencing in 1906 the British and French military commanders worked out a plan for transporting and positioning 100,000 men in France. There were telegrams from German sources, with what seniority is not known, to the effect that this would be a limited war between Austria-Hungary, Serbia and Russia.

In 1913, Mr Asquith, the Prime Minister, when asked by Mr King: *'(1) Whether the foreign policy of this country is at the present time unhampered by any treaties, agreements, or obligations under which British military forces would, in certain eventualities, be called upon to be landed on the Continent and join there in military operations; and (2) whether in 1905, 1908, or 1911 this country offered to France the assistance of a British army to be landed on the Continent to support France in the event of European hostilities.'*

Mr Asquith, the Prime Minister, replied: *'As has been repeatedly stated this country is not under any obligation not public and known to parliament which compels it to take part in any war. In other words, if war arises between European Powers, there are no unpublished agreements which will restrict or hamper the freedom of the Government or of Parliament to decide whether or not Great Britain should participate in a war. The use that would be made of naval and military forces if the Government or Parliament decided to take part in a war, is, for obvious reasons, not a matter about public statements can be made beforehand.'*

The reply was ambiguous because he knew that there had been secret negotiations between Sir Edward Grey and his French counterpart. A year later, using the Royal Prerogative, Asquith declared war in which five million combatants and seven million civilians died. Had the decision been taken by parliament it is by no means certain that the country would have gone to war because four cabinet ministers and one junior minister resigned when the king, acting on the advice of his Prime Minister, signed the declaration of war with Germany. Almost at once a campaign of propaganda started in order to paint the Germans as unprincipled monsters. A nurse called Grace Hume was mutilated by a German wielding his bayonet until it was discovered that her sister, living in the UK had forged a letter and made up the story. The magazine, Punch, stated that 4,000 British soldiers had been mutilated on the Kaiser's direct orders. The Kaiser scoffed at the British army which he described as 'contemptible'. German soldiers were said to chop off the arms of babies and impale them on their bayonets. The Times reported that the Germans had a marching song contained the lines 'He shot the wives and children. The wives and little children and laughed to see them die.'

Germany tried to sew discontent among the entente allies by dropping pamphlets on the French trenches saying that Germany was blameless and showing the English bombing French churches. There were forged documents designed to show the English were going to occupy Belgium. There were anti-Catholic stories saying that priests were concealing machine guns behind the altar and betraying the position of German soldiers from the top of church towers. This last story was exposed as false in the Frankfurter Zeitung in September 1914.[22]

Ponsonby set out many more propaganda claims

---

[22] Arthur Ponsonby, *Falsehood in Wartime, Containing an Assortment of Lies Circulated Throughout the Nations During the Great War.*

showing that it was a propaganda procedure followed in France, the USA and Italy. Anne Morelli, a Belgian historian working at a centre for the study of religion and secularism, has summarised Ponsonby's work as follows:

1. We do not want war.

2. The Opposite party alone is guilty of war.

3. The enemy is the face of the devil.

4. We defend a noble cause, not our own interest.

5. The enemy systematically commits cruelties; our mishaps are involuntary.

6. The enemy uses forbidden weapons.

7. We suffer small losses, those of the enemy are enormous.

8. Artists and intellectuals back our cause.

9. Our cause is sacred.

10. All who doubt our propaganda are traitors.[23]

Whilst the general public believe these stories and have to believe them otherwise they would not hate with sufficient intensity to withstand the privations of war and send their children to die believing them, whilst very brave to face death, to have died in an honourable cause. Those in power do not believe the stories they have put about. In December 1920 Lloyd George said, 'I cannot say Germany and her allies were solely responsible for the war which devastated Europe.' The 21st-century interventions by Western

---

[23] Anne Morelli 'Ten Commandments of Propaganda' quoted in Wikipedia.

countries in Afghanistan and Iraq have left many wondering whether their young people died fighting an effective war.

Anti-black prejudice is the most persistent in white-skin majority countries for no other reason, possibly, than that black skin stands out more.[24] What further operates in favour of prejudice is that the black population of the Caribbean and the USA were transported from Africa, mainly in English ships, as slaves in the most inhumane conditions. Slavery is recorded in the Mycenaean period (1600-1100BCE) though the slaves were mainly women, used as concubines and servants, and unions between slaves and free men were common. Men taken in battle were usually killed. By the time of Xenophon (430BCE) male slaves were being kept and used on the land in agriculture. The use of free or cheap labour was seen as absolutely essential to the wealth of both landowners and the nation. The peasant revolts in Europe between 1381 and 1524 bear witness to this. The advent of steam-driven machinery generated by coal slowly eroded though faith in cheap labour persists to this day (2016). The continent of Africa was no exception and wealth depended on slaves particularly as the arrival of Arab trade ships massively increased the volume of trade and wealth of the tribal kings.[25]

Slavery was legitimised in the minds of the religious by its inclusion in the Bible in the book of Leviticus:

---

[24] John Hope Franklin, *From Slavery to Freedom.*
[25] Franklin, p.7 et seq.

Such male and female slaves as you may have-it is from the nations about you that you may acquire male and female slaves. You may also buy them from among the children of aliens resident among you, or from their families that are among you, whom they begot in your land. These shall become your property.[26]

This unfortunate phrase has been used to justify slavery leaving aside that three millennia ago, slavery was widespread when, even then, the exploitation of human beings was not justified. Animals were a better source of power.

Nevertheless, this and much more was used to justify continuing to hold the African-American in slavery in spite of the obvious pain and humiliation of their position. The certainty that they were inferior held by white Americans who were, in every other respect, perfectly decent people, allowed them to justify what was in reality sinful behaviour.

After the South lost the civil war there were senior, authoritative figures preaching the inferiority of the black man. One such was Jefferson Davis (1808-1889), a colonel in the US Army who rose to be a congressman, senator, Secretary of State for War and, finally, President of the Confederate States. In 1881 he wrote his memoirs, *The Rise and Fall of the Confederate Government*, in two volumes with copious references to black Americans, a few of which are paraphrased as follows:

The abolitionists were a corrupting influence. – p.3 et seq.

---

[26] Leviticus 44-45 referred to in The Religious Defence of American Slavery before 1830, Larry R Morrison.

Those who associated themselves with the abolitionists were guilty of hypocrisy and political cant but not the abolitionists themselves. – p.29 et seq.

Those of the African Race could not be considered as 'part of the people' or citizens under the Constitution of the United States. – p.70 et seq.

Slaves in the South are comfortable and happy and the kindest relations exist between them and their masters. – p.458 et seq.

They increased from a few unprofitable savages to millions of efficient Christian labourers. – Vol 2, p.161 et seq. (Presumably, this was their reward and they should be grateful.)

They were dehumanised, which is what reification does.

The loss of the civil war followed by the deep economic recession of the reconstruction period left the Southern White trying to regain control of his life and future. In pursuit of control they resorted to denial of the black's right to vote, terrorism and lynching. The main perpetrators of anti-black violence was a white supremacy organisation called the Ku Klux Klan who operated as a large vigilante group carrying on above the law and outside legal restraint. They hanged black human beings because they were black. It was not until President Grant proposed the Ku Klux Klan Act which passed into law in April 1871 supported by the Republican Party that allowed the Klan to be investigated by Federal agents. The minority Democrats did all they could to frustrate the operation of the act and discredit the findings made under it in spite of the undoubted fact that the agents were investigating criminal and fraudulent behaviour.[27] There was, of course, money and status in being a Klansman. Black equality was growing after emancipation. Work was available for labourers on the railroads, agriculture and munitions and in 1900 80% of blacks were labourers and 22% owned their own homes. Some grew their own cotton and in manufacturing they were paid similar wages.[28] Adding to this was the fear of 14 million new immigrants coming to the United States. An unemployed, unmarried, middle-class drifter, William Joseph Simmons, saw his opportunity to become rich and resuscitated the white supremacy, KKK, and led a group of white men up Stone Mountain on the night of Thanksgiving, 1915. He had burning crosses, wearing white robes with pointy tops, and gave a grandiose lecture on patriotism, white supremacy and the virtues of racial segregation.[29] He employed two publicists and, at its peak, the Klan had 5 million members made up of substantial people of decent standing paying $10 each.[30] One might think this was simply a fraud played on gullible people but lynching continued and in 1919, for example, 7 Whites and 76 Blacks were assassinated.[31] Simmons was finally deposed for appropriating too much Klan money.

The imitation and support of the words of

---

[27] Nigel Sutton, *Ku Klux Klan: The Rise and Fall of the Three Klan Movements*, Loc 122 et seq.

[28] EHnet Economic History Association, Thomas H Maloney, *African Americans in the Southern States*.

[29] David B McCoy, *The 1920s: The Invisible Empire of the Ku Klux Klan*, Loc 49.

[30] McCoy, Loc 21.

[31] Lynching by Year and Race on the Internet.

admired senior people, frequently taken out of context provides justification for acts which, taken at face value, are clearly criminal even bearing in mind the law when the acts were carried out. Simmons, for example, as part of his harangue on Stone Mountain in 1915 used the Epistle to the Romans, said to be one of the most influential documents in Christian theology: *Beloved, never avenge yourselves but leave room for the wrath of God; for it is written "Vengeance is mine, I will repay, says the Lord" No, "if your enemies are hungry, feed them; if they are thirsty, give them something to drink; for by doing this you be heaping coals on their heads." Do not be overcome by evil, but overcome evil with good.* It seems his listeners saw themselves as the deity and took the lives of innocent people. They chose to misunderstand.

Even today, Blacks in America are depersonalised by stereotype. In the 19th century they were portrayed as superstitious, ignorant, and musically inclined. Today they are portrayed as having violent, quick tempers, overtly lethargic and very religious and, at the same time superstitious.

The unemployment among the black population is consistently double that of the Whites.

CHAPTER 4

DEPRESSION AND CONTROL

It will come as no surprise to anyone to find that those who find it hard to occupy an equal place in society feel, sometimes unconsciously, depressed, and some of those seek to bring their lives under control by denigrating, or even killing, someone who is a member of a weaker group. The reason is not hard to find. While they are, bullying or even killing a weaker person, they are in charge, if only fleetingly. They often kill, like the monster, Frankenstein, someone they love. This might be similar to the rejected stalker who once enjoyed an intimate relationship with the victim, not always sexual, and now wishes to do them harm.[32] Of the five types of stalker, the rejected stalker is the most likely to become violent.

In a modern, 21st-century society in the Western world, the most common cause of mild depression is economic. Just about managing for many years or being unemployed. In Britain, poverty is defined as a family who have less than 60% of the median wage to live on. Indeed, it does not require a great intellectual

---

[32] Stalking Risk Profile which divides the kind of stalker into five types depending on the relationship they had with the victim.

leap to understand that having paid the rent and travel, if there is insufficient money left to feed a family, this would render the wage earner feeling inadequate. For Freud and his followers the unconscious is the great bulk of a person's psychic life and conscious acts are merely isolated acts and parts of the total.[33] It is the operation of the unconscious mind attempting to restore control which causes the victimisation of weaker groups and among these are foreigners, immigrants and women. For example, following the banking crisis in 2008, among couples under economic stress, domestic violence was 9.7% rising to 12.3% when the male was unemployed, compared with 2.7% among couples who did not feel under economic stress.[34]

There are many forms of depression but in an extensive survey of the subject, Paul Gilbert said the following of two types of depression: Exogenous (reactive)-Endogenous: '*Exogenous has sometimes been used to describe precipitated disorder (e.g. life events), endogenous being unprecipitated. At other times reactivity has been used to denote patients who can react to events even though depressed. More recently it is the pattern and type of symptoms which trigger the diagnosis endogenous.*' [35]

Reactive depression is the most common form of depression, i.e. that is caused by life events. Even the Reactive Depressives who have been subjected to the same life events, can be further divided into those who maintain their locus of control and those who do

---

[33] Sigmund Freud, *A General Introduction to Psychoanalysis*, p.10.
[34] Claire M Renzetti, National Online Resource Center on Violence Against Women 2009 in USA.
[35] Paul Gilbert, *Depression, The Evolution of Powerlessness*, 1992, p.28.

not and become hopeless and easy pickings for a strong leader who offers xenophobia as a way of regaining control. Hopelessness depression is caused by negative life events or stress. '*An individual might not see themselves as having caused the bad event but coping with the event may show up personal deficits. These two links (e.g. negative events and perceived implications) give rise to hopelessness.*[36] When this stage is reached, any strong figure who can bring hope and control into the depressive's life is greeted like a messiah and in extreme cases, anyone who does not support him is condemned as a traitor. Those with high self-esteem but depressed, might well adopt an interpersonal style which is hostile dominant, whilst those with low self-esteem are hostile submissive. The former might be exemplified by Adolf Hitler whilst the latter might be closer to Uriah Heap, a Dickens character. Stalin was, on the surface, friendly dominant but below it was paranoia.[37] An example of hopelessness was Mussolini, the Italian dictator. At the end of the Second World War he was an example of utter hopelessness but he accepted death with honesty. He was a classic case of pure depression. He, at the end of his life, watched with resignation as Anglo-American troops advanced over the Apennines and when a woman journalist called Mollier came to take his photograph: "*she found him looking like a man in jail, with lifeless eyes and a shaven head, dressed in a braidless tunic and a black shirt with a low collar. He appeared humble and sincere in the interview and said to the journalist, "I am finished, my star has set. I no longer feel like an actor in the*

---

[36] Paul Gilbert, p.374.

[37] After Paul Gilbert, p.93.

tragedy, but like the last spectator waiting for it to end. I have been wrong and I will pay the price, if my wretched life can serve as atonement". But even in these circumstances he could not resist showing off and drew the lady's attention to his bookshelves bearing the works of Goethe, Kant, Schopenhauer, Eichendorff, Sappho, Homer, Aeschylus and Aristotle.

When she asked him if he read Greek, he answered with pathetic boastfulness, *"Oh yes, I have studied it."*[38] It will be noticed that he took the blame for the tragic circumstances he had brought upon Italy, upon himself and a short while later when the partisan, Colonel Valerio, caught up with him, he and his mistress Claretta Petacci were placed against the wall of the Villa Belmonte. He tore his shirt open to receive the bullet and was duly shot, as was Claretta. He expected death and thought he deserved it. His mistress wanted to die with him because he was the greatest man she had ever known and her life, the remainder of which would have been a wasteland without him, was worth nothing. The partisan who found him huddled in the back the back of a German lorry said that Mussolini was exhausted, glassy-eyed but not afraid.

Many experiments with human beings are based on the expectancy of success depending on whether they believed they were using skill rather than chance. The ones who believed they were using skill had a higher expectancy of success because they felt they were in control of what they were deciding.[39] In a further test of control, subjects showed a preference

---

[38] Quoted in *Mussolini an Intimate Life* by Paolo Monelli.
[39] E Jerry Phares *Locus of Control in Personality* pp.27-28.

for predictable over unpredictable punishment. Each type of control is related to stress in a complex fashion, sometimes increasing, sometimes reducing it, and sometimes having no influence at all... The stress-inducing or stress-reducing properties of personal control depend upon such factors as the nature of the response and the context in which it is embedded and not just upon its effectiveness in preventing or mitigating the impact of the potentially harmful stimulus.[40] In short, given the same life events some people believe that they themselves remain in control of their lives whilst there are others, possibly a majority, who believe that external forces are too great for them to control. Understandably, the latter give way to anger or despair. Those who maintain internal control do more research to justify and support their feeling of control. Those who feel they are subject to powerful external events feel out of control[41] but previous experience decides more than anything else whether they maintain internal control or adopt the feeling that external events are controlling their lives.

Politicians have discovered the power of offering to those suffering economic inequality, unable to make ends meet, the possibility of taking control by stopping immigration and taking Britain out of the control of foreigners: '...*Nigel Farage beaming in front of a poster depicting a sea of refugees worthy of Josef Goebbels himself, promises made during the campaign cheerfully revoked within hours of the votes coming in-yet Leavers found language with a power and cogency that eluded their adversaries. Take*

---

[40] E Jerry Phares, pp.31-33.

[41] Phares, p.23.

back control. Independence Day. Both these phrases offer the listener agency and at least the prospect of opportunity and hope. Dismissed as absurd, not just by the opposing politicians but by much of Britain, they nonetheless pushed Brexit over the top. [42]

Brexit was a campaign to take Britain out of the trading group called the European Union which was seen by some as foreigners dictating British decisions. This is not to say there might not be other arrangements which would suit Britain better and there was what might yet be a valuable debate.

As an example of what might be the deadly effect of helplessness, people in prison, more than any others, are subject to powerful external forces and suicide attempts are very common. In Guantanamo Bay, where a judicial trial is withheld, there were 350 self-harm and/or suicide attempts as revealed in 2003.[43] In Britain with declining prison staff and increased smuggled drug use, inmate suicides reached one every three days in 2016.[44]

When a subject is depressed, control can be gained simply by making downward social comparisons. These can be quite harmless particularly if the object of the unfavourable comparison does not know the comparison has been made. Social research on cancer patients consistently shows that they evaluate their condition by comparison with people who are less fortunate than themselves. This, presumably, gives them some comfort. It can also bring comfort to

---

[42] The Guardian, 27 August 2016.

[43] Guantanamo Bay Detention Camp Suicide Attempts, Wikipedia. In 2006 US Department of Defence released the names of 558 detainees.

[44] The Telegraph, 28 November 2016.

evaluate their condition against someone who is recovering, particularly if the other patient is stated to be in a similar condition to themselves.

In a further example of downward social comparison: in a random trial in Holland 632 married people were chosen; 304 men and 328 women were asked how often they made upward and downward social comparisons and whether this had a positive or negative emotional effect on them.

"...the level of marital dissatisfaction was significantly and strongly related to the frequency with which downward negative affect comparisons were made for men...The frequency of upward negative effect comparisons was even more strongly related to the level of marital satisfaction...the higher the level of marital dissatisfaction, the more often individuals felt unhappy and bad when they compared themselves with couples who had better marriages, and the more often marriages worse than their own evoked negative affect.

In contrast, marital dissatisfaction had little influence on the frequency with which comparisons to other couples evoked positive affect...There was no significant difference in the frequency with which positive affect upward comparisons were made...People in less happy marriages felt less positively in response to downward comparisons that those whose marriages were more satisfying."[45]

It will be noticed that, generally, the more unhappy the subject the more frequently they made downward social comparisons because they felt better for doing so. It alleviated their unhappiness.

Abraham Tesser put forward a Self-Evaluation

---

[45] Bram P Buunk et al, pp.137-138.

Maintenance Model based on the belief that people will behave in a manner which will maintain or increase self-evaluation and that relationships with others have a substantial impact on self-evaluation.

The ambit of the model may be illustrated as follows:

Suppose A and B are both friends who are amateur musicians at school. They both audition for the school orchestra but only B is chosen. Depending on how important to her this failure is, A can react in one or more of the following ways.

A can distance herself from B. The friendship could become cooler or even non-existent because, to A, B's success could be like an insult depending on how important and central to her sense of self her failure to get into the school orchestra was.

A can hinder B's performance. In real life this could take the form of belittling her musical performance and making unpleasant references about her to others in her presence. This corresponds with those with high self-esteem belittling the achievements of more successful people.

A can believe that B was merely lucky and that time would reverse her success.

A could remain friends and use B as a standard to be attained and take pride in the success of her friend. This last would be an ideal condition which can only be attained by those who have reached a certain level of contentment themselves. Anyone fundamentally unhappy would adopt one of the more antagonistic models.

A study which begins to show the improvement in sense of self-worth by making downward racist social comparisons was made at the University of Michigan to measure the rise in self-esteem after making a downward social comparison following failure. This was carried out in the 1990s when 196 students of psychology volunteered to take what they thought was a genuine intelligence test which measured their intelligence against the average intelligence of young men in the USA and in Canada. In fact, that test was completely bogus and the questions were designed to be both difficult and ambiguous. The participants were divided into two groups of equal numbers selected on a random basis. Both groups were asked to watch a video of a woman applying for a job. One group were informed her name was Julie Goldberg. Round her neck was a necklace which included amongst the ornaments a Star of David. The other group watched the same video of the same woman but this time they were told that her name was Maria D'Agostino and the necklace was hidden out of sight in her jumper. The participants would have assumed, wrongly, that one was Jewish and the other was Italian, probably Catholic.

The participants then filled in the intelligence test and were, arbitrarily allocated marks which in general showed that half of them were well above average intelligence in the 93rd percentile. The other half were told that they were somewhat below average intelligence in the 47th percentile. Those who had had positive feedback rated the suitability of the Italian woman at 82 and the Jewish woman at 84. Those who had had negative feedback rated the Italian at 82 again but the allegedly Jewish candidate had been rated 62. After this, the change in self-esteem of all the participants was measured. Those who had been given positive feedback and rated the Italian woman had an increase in self-esteem of 2.2 and those who had rated the Jewish woman had an increase of 2. Those who had been given negative feedback and had preferred the Italian woman over the Jewish woman had an increase in self-esteem of 4.5. i.e. making the 'Jewish candidate' the loser, improved the self-esteem of those who thought they had done badly in the test.[46]

One explanation for this limited but telling result is that participants who had been given a poor test result were taking back a sense of control by making a downward social comparison though they might never have made any such a remark to 'Julie Goldberg' to her face.

---

[46] This test was reported in "Stereotypes and Prejudice" edited by Charles Stanger and was carried out by Steven Fein and Steven J Spencer.

CHAPTER 5

DEFENCE MECHANISMS
PROVIDING CONTROL

The most innocuous of the defence mechanisms is daydreaming, which harms nobody except, possibly, the dreamer himself because they take the place of real achievement and compensate the dreamer for his lack of success. The most famous of the daydreaming books is *The Secret Life of Walter Mitty* by the humourist James Thurber. Mitty is locked into a childless marriage with a discontented woman of means who vents her own unhappiness on him by constant petty criticism. Mitty escapes into his daydreams in which he is a powerful, heroic figure who succeeds where others fail. Thus he is the icy calm figure who propels his navy hydroplane through enemy defences by turning on every ounce of shrieking power followed by his devoted crew. As the brilliant surgeon he saves the life of the millionaire, Wellington Macintosh, by repairing an immensely complicated piece of surgical equipment and performing 'the tertiary' before the patient expires. Finally, in a light fall of snow, he flattens his shoulders against a wall, lights a cigarette and brushes aside the blindfold as he faces the rifles before execution fighting for justice.

In real neurosis, the subject substitutes a version of the truth which leaves him, the victim of failure, stabbed in the back by external, malevolent forces beyond his control. Thus, one subject lost his small business when his backers, members of his wife's family, refused to continue guaranteeing his overdraft after his wife divorced him. Joseph Goebbels, the German propaganda minister during the Second World War blamed the destruction his government had brought upon Germany on a conspiracy of International Jewry who had mobilised the whole world against him.[47] This invented reality replaces what really happened as much for the petty business man as it did for Joseph Goebbels, who forgot that Germany invaded Poland, Germany invaded Russia and Japan bombed Pearl Harbour. Nobody wanted war in 1939 except the Germans themselves.

The need for this particular form of distortion of the facts is described as follows: so powerful and pervasive is denial that Nathaniel Branden in his book *The Psychology of Self-esteem* says in Chapter IV: *"so intensely does a man feel the need for a positive view of himself, that he may evade, repress, distort his judgement, disintegrate his mind-in order to avoid coming face-to-face with fact that would affect his self appraisal adversely."* Thus the need for a positive opinion of oneself, for some people, is so strong that it displaces reality.

Adolf Hitler, the Dictator of Germany, helped by the German people who voted for him, between 1933 and 1945 brought Europe to ruin with, possibly, more

---

[47] German Propaganda Archive, Calvin College.

than 40 million dead, nobody knows, and Berlin a heap of rubble, in a war triggered, finally, by Germany's invasion of Poland. The total disaster of his decision to invade Poland in 1939 followed by his invasion of the Soviet Union in 1941 might be thought to be a difficult series of facts to deny but Adolf Hitler managed it. In his last will and testament, dictated to the youngest of his three secretaries, none of whom had any work to do, Traudl Junge, he made the following declarations: *"in these three decades love and loyalty to my people have guided all my thoughts, actions and my life. They gave me the strength to make the most difficult decisions ever to confront mortal man. In these three decades I have spent my strengths and my health.*

It is untrue that I or anyone else in Germany wanted war in 1939. It was wanted and provoked solely by international statesman either of Jewish origin or working for Jewish interests. I have made too many offers for the limitation and control of armaments, which posterity will not be cowardly enough always to disregard, for responsibility for the outbreak of this war to be placed on me. Nor have I ever wished that, after the appalling First World War, there would ever be a second against England or America. Centuries will go by, but from the ruins of our towns and monuments the hatred of those ultimately responsible will always grow anew against people whom we have to thank for all this; international Jewry and its henchmen."

His final words were: *"Above all, I enjoin the government and the people to uphold the race laws to the limit and to resist mercilessly the poisoner of all nations, international Jewry."* Dated Berlin, 29th of April, 1945, 4 AM and signed 'Adolf Hitler'.

A second form of denial is the imposition by an admired third party of a personal fantasy into a real world where real people do not behave that way. Thus, Voltaire's *Candide* in which Dr Pangloss tells the eponymous protagonist that: *everything is for the best in the best of all possible worlds.* Episode after episode in the book demonstrates that this is simply not true but Candide continues to believe it.[48] This was a way of maintaining order in a chaotic world. It was in fact a satire on optimistic determinism which stated that there was only one possible outcome of any event. It was proposed by Spinoza and adopted by the Calvinists and since God was good, everything was for the best. This question, the one posed by Voltaire: *Where was God during a disaster?* has been agonised over by the faithful over hundreds of years with no universally accepted answer. Nevertheless an article of faith which brings order into people's lives will be believed against all the evidence to the contrary.

In a refreshingly frank interview with Thomas Hornall on October 8, 2015 published on the internet, Sohail Ahmed, brought up in an ultra observant Muslim household in London's East End, was, from the age of 14, a closet gay. He became homophobic to the outside world and considered suicide and, at the age of 16, considered becoming a suicide bomber. Homosexuality is anathema to the devout Muslim. His family tried having him exorcised of the demons which must, by definition, possess him. Now that he has come out, all phobias have dropped away from him and he has chosen life.

A far more complex and pervasive psychological method of feeling good about oneself is 'Projection' in which someone who suffers from a defect projects an

---

[48] Phebe Cramer, *Protecting the Self*, Kindle Location 566.

evil characteristic on someone else. Not necessarily the same defect but a defect accepted as such by society generally. The sufferer's defect is frequently sexual and in itself completely innocuous other than it attracts society's disapproval. *In the broadest sense projection protects the child from disruptive anxiety by attributing the unacceptable feelings, wishes and impulses to someone else; the disturbing thoughts are placed outside of the self-"ejected" into the external world and attached to some other object.*[49]

The attribution of aspects of the self to others is something which remains into adult life for those who do not mature to the extent they might do. When they attribute the defect it remains with them but it gives relief for a time to endow the defect on someone else. The psychological process is known as 'splitting' and lies at the heart of projection and is covered more fully in most psychology texts. A neat example might be given by the following distressing example:

Abby, a Jewish girl, when studying medicine met, and fell in love with, a fair-haired fellow student who was Catholic. Abby's father, a doctor, was vehemently opposed to any marriage to a fair-haired Catholic and made racist remarks. When they did marry her parents did not attend the wedding and did not communicate in any way whatsoever in spite of her modest overtures. Eighteen years went by when, without warning, she got a call from her mother to say that she and father were getting a divorce. It seems that for 25 years the father had been having an affair with his secretary, also fair-haired and also Catholic.[50]

---

[49] Phebe Cramer, Kindle Location 985.
[50] Stephen Grosz, *The Examined Life*, pp.67-68.

In the broadest sense, in abusing his daughter and causing her undoubted distress, her father was projecting onto her punishment for his own defects. But the most important difference between father and daughter, was that father was an adulterer and daughter was not.

As Abby herself said: *The bigger the front the bigger the back.*

While splitting is easily understandable, the way in which a person who suffers from a defect of which he, unconsciously, feels ashamed is to project his feeling of guilt on to someone else, again unconsciously, without realising what he is doing. Thus, one subject who was found in bed with a fellow soldier, when such an act was criminal, had a lifelong contempt for homosexuals without realising why.

There is a further form of defence called paranoia in which the sufferer says: 'It is not I who hate, it is people who hate me.' Whilst many practitioners find this unconvincing it is accepted that paranoia occurs with mania and depression.[51]

Altruism is a noble sentiment which is rightly espoused by many faiths but it depends on the aid given to someone who is weaker. The act of helping someone who is weaker enhances the donor though the great majority of donors see it as nothing more than a humanitarian duty. One politician, a former mayor of London said on a Vanessa Feltz interview in 2016 that *Adolf Hitler was supporting Zionism.* In saying this he was equating Zionists with the racist Nazi Party and showing the Israelis treatment of the Palestinians

---

[51] Dr Peter Chadwick, *Understanding Paranoia*, pp.21-24.

was no better. The former mayor then emphasised his remarks by saying to the Evening Standard (a London newspaper) that he stood by his comments: What's wrong with the remarks I made? Is it insensitive to look at history? This poor man thought he was behaving in an altruistic manner helping the Palestinians. In the uproar which followed, the source of his remarks was lost. He was presumably referring to the Transfer Agreement whereby Jews in Germany gave a minimum of £1,000 (a year's salary of a man in a good way of business in 1929) to a Jewish company importing citrus fruit to Europe. They bought German goods, sold them in Palestine and gave the money to the original donor when he arrived. It was like a letter of credit by barter. If the original donor did not want to go to Palestine the money was given to Yishuv, Ben Gurion's party to help them house Polish Jews fleeing the anti-Semitism in Poland. When Hitler came to power in 1933, he did not stop the transfers but this hardly makes him a Zionist. He was a populist appointee who did not want to be seen damaging Germany's export trade at a time of world recession. Nevertheless this act of appearing to help the distressed Palestinians gave more help to the former mayor than it gave to the Palestinians.

David Irving, the historian (born 1938), said, in an interview with Ron Rosenbaum that, as a child during the war, he thought Hitler was portrayed very unfairly, particularly in cartoons. His father, a career naval officer had abandoned his family. Irving felt deprived. He went on to become a holocaust denier but found guilty in a subsequent trial, when he sued

Penguin Books, of distorting the facts.[52] It is over simplistic to describe Irving as anti-Semitic, it might be more accurate to describe him as anti-British, the side his father fought for.

During the European recession of the 1930s following the bank crash of 1929, there was an anti-Jewish conspiracy theory called The Protocols of the Elders of Zion which became very popular because it explained the threat to civilisation. The Protocols of the Elders of Zion was a convincing description of a totalitarian state controlled by rich Jews. It contained the principles for maintaining power by a select few over many, which may be paraphrased under the following headings:

Might is right; Money can be made out of wars; Abuse of power becomes the rule; An appearance of justice must be maintained but it must not be allowed to imply equality; Remove land from the aristocracy and establish monopolies[53]; Intensified armaments production. Control of the press and public opinion; Everyone will have a right to liberty, the duty of equality and the ideal of brotherhood but they will all be kept out of their grasp; Constitution to create law by decree of the president, freedom will then become the right to do what the law allows; The Jews will introduce measures which keep them in power; Arrest will be made on suspicion only; A progressive tax so that the rich will pay more; Even though insolvent the state would go on issuing paper money and bills of

---

[52] Wikipedia David Irving.
[53] The Protocols were written to influence the Czar and the aristocracy under the threat of Bolshevism.

exchange[54]; The maintenance of a high level of unemployment; The irreproachable morality of the King of the Jews.

The Protocols of the Elders of Zion describe a totalitarian state. It is ironic that it was the Russians themselves who first produced the totalitarian state under the dictatorship of Joseph Stalin. The Protocols are subtle and against the freedom of the common man. They are not an original work of fiction but were based upon the book by Maurice Joly called *The Dialogue in Hell Between Machiavelli and Montesquieu* written at the end of the 19th century. They had a profound effect on anti-Semitism for the next 50 years and are still mentioned in connection with Israel and as a justification for anti-Jewish prejudice. They are a complete fabrication and their original, *The Dialogue in Hell*, was written by Joly as a satire in about 1880 on the political manoeuvrings of Napoleon III. The Protocols' primary target was to persuade Nicolas II that the murder of Jews in the pogroms was not only beneficial for his reign but justified in order to avert a terrible danger for Russia from a Jewish conspiracy.

After any disaster there are a spate of conspiracy theories. After the fire of London in 1666, there was a theory, based on the perjured evidence of Titus Oates, that it had been started by Jesuit priests and 22 innocent people were executed. The Monument in London said as much until 1830 when the words: *Burning of this*

---

[54] This might be a reference to Keynsian economics, then considered very left wing.

protestant city begun and carried out by the treachery and malice of the popish faction.' were chiselled out. In the meantime the Popery Act 1698 was enacted which was an Act for preventing the Growth of Popery.

Peter Sutcliff, the Yorkshire Ripper, was shy with women and this made him feel inferior in the macho society of his day. He boasted that he had tremendous success with prostitutes but on one occasion having agreed the price at £5 he gave the girl £10 expecting change. Upon being taken to a hotel he changed his mind and wanted his money back. The girl had two protectors who told him to shove off. Shortly afterwards he found her, plying her trade, in a bar and demanded his £10. She laughed in his face and described to all the people in the bar what an idiot he had been. This humiliation in public was something he was unable to bear and whilst still boasting of his success with prostitutes (completely imaginary), he took to kerb crawling and shouting humiliating remarks at the women standing there. With no internal control the life events he had experienced had provided him with a deep layer of depression. Thus began his career of murdering prostitutes and any woman he found walking at night. He was taking back control. In all he murdered 13 women in Yorkshire towns including the Chapeltown Road area of Leeds. He was finally caught, almost by accident, with a prostitute in his car, at night. The thing that gave him away was that he had taped stolen number plates onto his car and after a long cross examination he confessed to being the Yorkshire Ripper.

His murder of women alone at night had a strong

sexual message in that he stripped them post-mortem then stabbed them 50 to 60 times with a sharpened screwdriver. His method of killing was to beat them over the head with a hammer. In every other respect he was well liked and was kindness itself.

The maintenance of high self-esteem does not have to involve murder but merely making public downward comparisons which embarrass the victim of the comparison. Crocker and Schwartz 1985 *"...found that individuals high in self esteem are more likely to make self enhancing downward comparisons than those with relatively low self esteem. They argued that high self esteem individuals have positive self concepts, in part, because they engage in these self enhancing strategies....A more general version of the hypothesis would be that individuals high in self esteem make comparisons favourable to themselves regardless of their objective standing relative to the target. Thus, high self esteem individuals may be more likely to make self enhancing downward comparisons than low self esteem persons and more likely to interpret upward comparisons as self enhancing as well.*

Conversely, those with low self esteem may be less likely to interpret either an upward or downward comparison as favourable to themselves."[55]

The exercise of control is normally exerted over someone weaker than the person in need of control but when someone with high self-esteem exerts control and the intended victim answers back, it promotes anger. Few targets can be weaker than a woman walking alone at night but there are many levels of humiliation before murder is arrived at.

---

[55] Bram P Buunk et al, *Downward Comparison Theories* eds Diederick, A Stapel, and Hart Blanton, Reading 7 p.129.

CHAPTER 6

EXAMPLES OF RACIST LEADERS

The racist leader is a man with high, damaged self-esteem. It is the damage that makes him a racist. The damage can be varied as, hopefully, the following studies will reveal, but they are never very exotic. They may be economic or physical or sexual. They are always banal, neurotic rather than psychotic. In the modern world such people may be elected during the period following war or during periods of severe economic depression when the run of the people need an, apparently, strong leader who can explain the way forward and promises national success. The difficulty arises when they select a neurotic, and many of us are neurotic, who does no more than tell the public what many of them want to hear. 'I have suffered like you' or 'I, like you, am not a member of the political establishment'. This start appeals to many people who have suffered economic or other difficulty for years, whatever it may be, but the racist goes on to say that a racial minority or immigrants of a certain kind are a major contributory factor to the nation's suffering. The loss of the First World War followed by hyperinflation in the 1930s made Adolf Hitler and the party which manipulated him powerful, and this completely inadequate man was seen as an acceptable leader. At the present time (2015) seven years of economic stagnation has seen the rise of right-wing leaders in Europe and the USA though at the time of writing, none of them have been elected to power.

6a Joseph Goebbels

Joseph Goebbels (1897-1945) was the Reich minister of propaganda from 1933, when Hitler took power, to 1945, when he took his own and his family's lives. Goebbels preached racism against Jews in particular. He had a fine sense of his own importance from being his mother's favourite and a flaw, of which he was made, by his mother's shame, to feel ashamed. He had a club foot and was turned down for military service because of what the army called a 'deformity'. He started life as a Catholic and Catholicism, in particular, has always taught the culpability of Jews for the death of Christ.

Goebbels came from an observant Catholic home and the catechism then in use might have been similar to the Baltimore Catechism since the Plenary Council of Baltimore was given the task of revising the German Catechism in 1852.[56] The Baltimore catechism is very plain on the question of Jews: *Q1089. To what may we attribute the desire of the Jews to put Christ to death? A. We may attribute the desire of the Jews to put Christ to death to the jealousy, hatred and ill will of their priests and the Pharisees, whose faults he rebuked and whose hypocrisy he exposed. By their slanders and lies they induce the*

---

[56] Catholic Encyclopaedia online.

people to follow them in demanding our Lord's crucifixion.

His birth had almost cost his mother her life and, possibly because of this, she idolised him. The Goebbels family form of devotion was more ritualistic than most. Mass was celebrated on a daily basis together with confession, devotions at home and, after this, mother made the sign of the cross on the children's brows with holy water.[57] As a child Goebbels almost died of pneumonia. He then contracted osteomyelitis and for two years a doctor and a masseur tried to rid the child of intermittent paralysis until, finally the doctor had to tell the parents that the boy would be lame for life and would eventually become a club foot. The parents sought high-level advice, presumably at great expense, until finally the Maria Hilf Hopital in Munchengladbach operated on the ten-year-old. The operation was a failure. Most importantly, his mother was ashamed of his foot and attributed it to an accident, saying he had caught his foot between two slats.[58] It was important in those days, and later, to show there was no 'bad blood' in the family and these traits were not hereditary. The pitying looks and bullying at school made a deep impression in the child Goebbels.

Upon the outbreak of war in 1914 he felt inadequate in not being able to go to war like his brothers. Loaded down with this inadequacy his life became one of compensation and making up for failure: dominating women or dominating Jews even though some Jews were people he greatly admired. This ability to separate the people of a certain race but

---

[57] Ralf Georg Reuth, *The Life of Joseph Goebbels*, p.7
[58] Reuth, p.8.

whom one knows as human beings whilst at the same time regarding the others of the same race as 'things' is very common among racists. With regard to women, he made advances to the stepmother of one of his school friends when he was no more than sixteen. He wrote her poems but his feelings were not reciprocated. His desire for Anka Stalherm is mentioned in most biographies. Her parents absolutely rejected him. In 1920 he met and had a long-term relationship with a young teacher called Else Janke who had a Jewish mother though, initially, he did not know this. In 1922 Else revealed that she was half Jewish. Nevertheless, the relationship continued and was described by Goebbels in the most ecstatic manner in 1925: *I am yearning for Else. When shall I have her in my arms again. Else dear, when shall I see you again? Alma, you dear featherweight! Anka, never can I forget you!* In September 1925: *Else is here! On Tuesday she returned from Switzerland-fat, buxom, healthy, gay, only slightly tanned. She is very happy and in the best of spirits. She is good to me and gives me much joy.*[59]

There can be little doubt that he was enjoying some sort of sexual relationship with Else. His 'love' for Else did not stop him pursuing other women: Lena Krage; two sisters called Liesl and Agnes in Bonn; while rising and achieving importance in the Nazi Party under Hitler the names Xenia, Charlotte, Erika, and Julia are recorded[60] when he became Gauleiter of Berlin between 1926 and 1928. In 1931

---

[59] Quoted by William L Shirer who knew Goebbels before 1939 in *The Rise and Fall of the Third Reich*, p.125.

[60] Revue by Alan Hall of a biography of Goebbels by Peter Longrich in the Telegraph, 8 January 2011.

he met Magda Quandt, a divorcee, and married her in 1932. They had six children, five girls and a boy. After marriage he continued filling his life with affairs, notably, one with the actress Lida Baarova which was so blatant Magda was distressed and went to Hitler who ordered Goebbels to end it, which he did. Baarova got no more work in Germany.

America was giving massive aid to the United Kingdom, the German advance into the Soviet Union stalled in front of Moscow by October 1941, and in spite of being invaded the Soviets were bombing Berlin from August 1941. The RAF were bombing Berlin from August 1940 and were able to disperse a large German raid on 15 September 1941. On 7 November 1941 160 RAF bombers attacked Berlin. The initial successes of the German army were ending and the German advance had stalled.

In his capacity as Propaganda Minister Goebbels wrote an essay which was read over the radio on 16 November, presumably in response to that raid, and, according to Howard K Smith's book *Last Train from Berlin*, was distributed with the monthly ration cards. Entitled 'The Jews are Guilty!', it runs to four pages and goes as follows: The Jews are responsible for this war but the German Reichstag are going to exact revenge by destroying the Jewish community in Europe. They are perishing and every Jew is our enemy in this historic struggle (the German Army had started murdering Jewish peasants in Poland). They will never give us rest in their search for financial domination and anyone who feels sympathy for them should remember there is a Jew, sitting in New York, plotting the death of a German soldier. And so it goes on. It ends with a cry for loyalty and the operation of '...an unforgiving cold hardness against the destroyers of our people...' Some doubt is creeping into Goebbels' mind because he ends his piece with the words: '...if we win.'[61]

America entered the war a month later and one of the last Americans to speak to German soldiers in Belgium at about the same time reports soldiers saying that Hitler was a sincere and honest man but Goering, Goebbels, Hess, Himmler, and Von Ribbentrop were corrupt and unscrupulous. They did not mention the Jews. Goebbels had started appealing to an audience who had begun not to listen.

Goebbels himself corresponds to the racist with very high self-regard but flawed by shame of being physically imperfect and with a lack of feeling for his fellow human beings.

In 1945, after Hitler wrote his Will and poisoned or shot himself. Goebbels attested in writing that he would follow his Fuhrer into death as would his wife, Magda, and his children. His wife Magda, presumably in order to save the lives of the children, had forced her way into Hitler's room where he was preparing for death and begged him to leave Berlin. This he refused to do and had her thrown out. After Hitler's death, Goebbels ordered Krebs, with a letter, to contact the supreme Russian commander and offer to negotiate a ceasefire. Krebs, amazingly, succeeded in doing this but a final reply came from Stalin himself saying that only unconditional surrender would bring about a ceasefire. Krebs had no authority to agree to

---

[61] The Goebbels archive on the Internet.

this and returned to the bunker. Magda arranged for the doctor to give the children shots of morphine and when they were asleep she crushed glass cylinders of cyanide in their mouths. His face blotchy with fear, Goebbels took his cyanide tablet and, possibly, shot himself. Magda did the same. Her belief in Hitler was religious in its intensity.[62] At no stage did any of them accept any responsibility for the disaster they had brought on Europe.

6b Heinrich Himmler and Josef Mengele

Heinrich Luitpold Himmler (1900-1945) was a serial killer of the same personality type as the Yorkshire Ripper. He could look benignly on prisoners he knew were going, under his auspices, to the gas chambers.[63] There was no appearance of malice or anger at any time and yet he was responsible for the murder of millions of unarmed civilians before and during the Second World War. He was born into an observant Catholic family in Munich. His father was a pompous headmaster of a high school, a vainglorious social climber and, according to one episode, a sadistic character himself. While headmaster he entered a class where a boy called Kien was doing badly at Greek:

'But Franz Kien had the impression that Himmler, despite managing to give an amiable appearance, was not harmless.

So it proved. Himmler took over the lesson, which became progressively more alarming. Kien was called to the blackboard

---

[62] Reuth, p.362.
[63] Photograph Wikipedia Heinrich Himmler Dachau Concentration Camp 1936.

and taken through a short translation word by word in a bullying belittling manner. Himmler bestowing no recognition for correct answers, only mocking, "Donnerwetter!" *An* achievement!

As he returned to his place afterwards had a feeling that his ordeal was not over. Himmler paced back and forth in silence, apparently pondering, then turned to the teacher, Kandlbinder, and asked him, in view of Kien's poor showing, what he proposed.

"Coaching", Kandlbinder replied.

"Coaching is expensive." Himmler made a dismissive gesture. "His father cannot pay. He cannot even meet the school fees. We have granted Kien an exemption of fees at his father's request."

Kien felt his cheeks flame. "The cur!" he thought, "the common cur! To announce publicly that my father cannot meet the 90 Marks a month school fees...the swine...to stand before the class and trumpet the fact that we have become poor..."

"We have granted Kien exemption from fees on his father's request, although the decision was not justified. Exemption from fees may only be granted to outstanding pupils. But I believed for the son of an officer with high decorations for bravery with high decorations for bravery, who probably through no fault of his own has fallen on hard times-I believed I could make an exception for such a boy. And how has he rewarded the school and his poor father?"

Himmler answered his own question with a recital of Franz Kien's low grades in maths and latin. "It would not do," he went on pacing, "to let him sit around for another year so that he could get a low grade in Greek." He stopped to look at Kien again. "Your brother Karl is another. How he reached the Untersekunda *is a mystery."*

Abruptly he changed his threatening tone. "How are things really with your father?"

"The sanctimonious Lump!" Kien thought. "Bad," he replied sullenly. "He has been ill for a long time."

"Oh, I'm sorry to hear that because it will not please him to learn that his sons are not suitable for education at a high school."[64]

It was in this way that Kien and his brother were dismissed from Himmler's school. The episode described above is an example of sadistic bullying as though Himmler, father, had to justify his dismissal of the boys in public so as to get public approval of what he was doing but also to cause maximum pain to the two sons of a sick man, thereby causing pain to the whole family. The fact that Himmler knew Kien's marks in maths and Latin demonstrates that this was a piece of theatre. If he treated his own son Heinrich in the same way he laid the foundation for the sadistic murderer he became. Professor Himmler was in the habit of presenting his essentially peasant forbears as though they were an ancient German family which went back to 1297.[65] Certainly one of the causes of bullying or sadism is to come from a dysfunctional family and Professor Himmler seems to satisfy that description.

This alone is not sufficient to explain the smiling psychopathic behaviour of Heinrich. In order to improve his sex life, Heinrich needed control and

---

[64] Quoted in Peter Padfield, Himmler Reichsfuhrer SS p16 from Alfred Andersch, *Der Vater eines Morders* – The father of a Murderer.
[65] Padfield, p.23.

sending people to their death fitted his psychological requirements.

When Heinrich Himmler entered the Royal Wilhelm Gymnasium he suffered from ill health, a puny physique, and was to some extent exposed as useless at gymnastics. He was clever in class but not the cleverest. After following his father to the gymnasium in Landshut he wanted to get a commission in the Navy but his short-sightedness ruled this out, but this was at a time when the death toll made vacancies available in the officer ranks which were formerly only available to those with noble blood. At the age of nineteen he wrote a patriotic poem which, in translation, went as follows:

Our bullets will whistle and whizz

And spread terror and dead among you

As we ravage so frightfully there.

For a young man educated in the classics and humanities and nineteen years old when he wrote the poem he appears remarkably immature. [66]

Thanks to the vigorous efforts of his father, Heinrich was accepted for officer training with the 11th Bavarian Infantry Regiment. It could well be that father made such efforts because he was frightened of the social opprobrium if his son had to serve in the ranks. Not the most courageous of recruits, Heinrich, aged nearly seventeen thought he was about to be sent to the front and begged his father to prevent this happening. It turned out to be a false alarm. In fact the German fleet mutinied and the front collapsed

---

[66] Padfield, p.28.

and Heinrich was discharged without a commission and with the status of officer cadet retired.[67]

Young Himmler, while finishing his education, joined the Freikorps and the Oberland, proto-military organisations with no legal standing, a move which his father did not support. Himmler, again with the help of his father, decided to study agronomy and found a position on a farm at Ingolstadt but his health was not equal to farm work and he was hospitalised. He drifted for several years, with the Freikorps his only constant interest, looking for a partner but, being physically unattractive and too shy to go to a prostitute, he did not find any. He assumed a high moral attitude to women to justify his failure in this respect.

'A woman was a trinity of dear child needing to be protected...faithful understanding comrade fighting life's battles with him, and godess of purity...she was also a dangerously carnal temptress.'[68] He imposed on himself a regime of sexual abstinence thus creating a virtue out of necessity. It was not until 1926 that Himmler met a woman who would have him. Margarethe Boden, a divorcee who seduced him and whom he married in 1928. The Himmler family refused to attend the wedding possibly because she was divorced and they were Roman Catholics. They had a child, Gudrun, in 1929. Margarethe was heavily built, manly looking and unattractive. The society columnist, Bella Fromm, in 1937, described her as dirty blonde, insipid and fat. She sold her clinic on marriage to supplement Himmler's Party salary.

[67] Padfield, p.31.
[68] Padfield, p.46.

His rise in the Party was inexorable and in 1929 he was appointed Reichsfuhrer SS expanding the organisation from 290 SS men to a million men and women. In 1936 his secretary and mistress to be, Hedwig Potthast, accompanied him to Buchenwald concentration camp but they probably did not start sleeping together until 1939. She bore him two children, a boy and a girl. In 1936 Himmler was probably sleeping with Nini Diehl, the ageing concert singer, later to become Frau Rascher.

No job was too foul for Himmler and he formed the Einsatzgruppen, middle-aged men not required for the services at that time, who followed the advancing German troops through Poland shooting Jewish Polish peasants after they had dug their own mass graves. There are pathetic photographs of men standing naked, covering their private parts with their hands and standing on the edge of the excavation waiting to be shot. This method of execution proved too slow and, apparently, somewhat upsetting for the volunteers who did it, and so the process was mechanised. The shooting period is fully covered by Daniel Jonah Goldhagen in his book, *Hitler's Willing Executioners*:

'Major Trapp assembled his battalion. The men formed three sides of a square around Trapp in order to hear his address.

"He announced that in the locality before us we were to carry out a mass killing by shooting and he brought out clearly that those we were supposed to shoot were Jews. During his address he bid us to think of our women and children in our homeland who had to endure aerial bombardments. In particular we were supposed to bear in mind that many women

and children lose their lives in these attacks. Thinking of these facts would make it easier for us to carry out the order during the upcoming [killing] action. Major Trapp remarked that the action was entirely not in his spirit, but that he has received this order from higher authority." [69]

Himmler also organised extermination camps at Kulmhof, Belzec, Sobibor, Treblinka, Auschwitz Majdenek and Trostenets where millions perished by gas. There were other methods of killing such as starvation, as practiced at Bergen Belsen. As late as 1944 there is a photograph of young women, stripped naked, walking to the gas chambers so that sexual sadism, like snuff movies, cannot be ruled out.

One of Himmler's supposed mistresses was a woman called Nini Rascher, the wife a Dr Rascher who carried out experiments at Dachau exploding living bodies under compressed air and carrying out dissection without anaesthetics, taking photographs of lungs as the human being, still alive, was expiring. [70] Frau Rascher took it upon herself to write to Himmler, because of her special relationship with him, for allocations of colour film. [71] She also wrote for more money, reduction of taxes, servant girls from the East and with all these requests he complied. [72] Himmler was kept in touch with all these so-called experiments. [73]

---

[69] Daniel Jonah Goldhagen, *Hitler's Willing Executioners. Ordinary Germans and the Holocaust*, p.212.

[70] Jonathan D Moreno, *Undue Risk Secret State Experiments on Humans*, p.61.

[71] Harvard Law School Library "Nini Rascher" Item 40.

[72] Padfield, p.377.

[73] Padfield, Chapter 12.

By 1945, Hitler was a walking corpse and Marshal Zhukov was storming towards Germany. Himmler was given command of Army Group Vistula and for a while stopped the rout on the Oder by giving orders to shoot deserters out of hand or carry out summary hangings. Bodies of German soldiers hung from the girders of broken bridges. It is difficult to understand why a man like Himmler continued to be loyal and continued to fight for Hitler while sending unknown numbers of Germans to their death. It has to be remembered that the only success Himmler had ever known was in the Nazi Party, and outside the Party he was as good as dead. Himmler had taken over the Vistula group in January 1944 and by March his army group had been caught in a pincer movement by Soviet forces and Himmler retired to his sickbed.[74]

When he recovered, Himmler tried to establish contact with the West through Count Bernadotte and a representative of the World Jewish Congress, Norbert Masur, who was brave enough to fly into Tempelhof Airport in the hope of saving Jewish prisoners, but to no avail. Himmler was ignored by Hitler and devoid of power. His mother and father took their own lives leaving instructions they were to be buried in unmarked graves and, possibly to cover what even he considered the most odious part of his life, he ordered the execution of Dr Rascher and Frau Rascher.

He started to travel south to reach a pocket of resistance in Bavaria but he was apprehended by British intelligence following information given by the Danes. When handed over to American interrogators

---

[74] Padfield, p.567.

he crushed the cyanide tablet he had had in his mouth for several days. Thus ended the life of a man who killed for control and to boost his sense of power, like any common serial killer.

Himmler also financed the career of another psychopathic personality, Josef Mengele. Mengele was the second son of devout Catholic parents who made money out of manufacturing machinery.[75] He read anthropology, obtained a PhD and published three learned papers on inherited racial characteristics and race being determined by, say, the measurement of the jaw bone. He married a rather austere-looking, young, fair-haired woman in 1939. He joined a nationalistic military organisation called Stahlhelm then served in the reserve medical corps and the Waffen-SS. He won several medals including the Iron Cross First Class. In 1943, he arrived in Auschwitz to perform a programme of research on genetically inherited racial characteristics. His grand plan was to open an institute which would restore the losses of the war by injecting the blood of selected twins so that the women would have multiple births of fair-haired, blue-eyed children. For this, he needed the blood and eyeballs of twins. He could be kind and murderously callous. One prison doctor said of him: *He was capable of being so kind to the children, to have them become fond of him, to bring them sugar, to think of small details in their daily lives, and to do all the things we would genuinely admire...And then, next to that...the crematorium smoke, and these children, tomorrow or in half an hour, he is going to send them there. Well, that is where the anomaly lay.*[76]

---

[75] Robert Jay Lifton, *The Nazi Doctors* p.338.
[76] Lifton, p.337 et seq.

He was also capable of killing directly. There are many examples of him giving lethal injections but one episode is particularly horrible. A pair of Gypsy, seven-year-old twins of great beauty and of whom he was particularly fond, were under examination. Against the radiological evidence, he maintained that they were suffering from tuberculosis. An argument arose and he disappeared for a time. When he returned, he agreed that the radiology was right and they had not been suffering from tuberculosis. It seems he had shot both of them in the back of the neck and performed a post-mortem examination.

Mengele himself was always immaculately dressed in his SS uniform. His shirts were gleaming white. The system at Auschwitz was that prisoners arrived by train and were divided into two; children and the old went one way, directly to the gas chambers and crematoria, while the rest were sent to barracks and slave labour. Mothers who thought that it was they who were going to die went stark staring mad when they realised what had happened to their children. Mengele was always on the ramp to select twin children and others for his clinic. He sometimes selected their mothers but, apparently, never the fathers. The actual process of selection and the control he had gave him a sense of power. A granter of life or death, almost godlike. It might be a coincidence but having married him in 1939, his wife gave birth to their only child, a boy, in 1944, a year after he arrived at Auschwitz. The children were always examined in the nude but there is no suggestion that anything improper ever took place. He had one or two rather handsome women working at the clinic but, again, there is no suggestion that anything improper was even proposed.

In 1945 Mengele was spirited away to Paraguay and then Brazil. He had considerable freedom of movement and in spite of the efforts of the Israeli and German governments he was never caught. He died while swimming at a Brazilian resort in 1979. Lifton maintains that Mengele, like some other high-ranking Nazis, was narcissistic[77] and he was certainly subject to narcissistic rages when his opinion was opposed. One of the defence mechanisms adopted by the narcissist is projection in which source of shame within the sufferer is projected on to the victim.

Since the purity of the German race was an obsession, the purity of Mengele's own race might be what troubled him because he thought it in doubt. It will now, never be known.

6c Mohammed Siddique Khan

Mohammed Siddique Khan was part of a new band of racists who were not psychotic, not even neurotic, but who became part of a band, increasing rather than declining, who justified the murder of civilians intellectually on the grounds that they were fighting for their own race in a just cause.[78]

Mohammed Siddique Khan, the leader of four young Muslims intent on a suicide mission, seemed to have no idea that what he was embarking on and what

---

[77] Lifton, p.420.

[78] The latest to come to prominence was Esteban Santiago who killed five people at random in Fort Lauderdale Airport, Florida, in January 2017. He was responding, he said, to a jihadist message from the government.

he succeeded in doing on July 7, 2005, was murder. The four exploded bombs, taking their own lives and the lives of 56 innocent people. Khan actually delayed the killing by one day because his wife was expecting a baby and needed to go to hospital and so he took her in. In a video, he can be seen playing with his two-year-old daughter and saying: "I am going to miss you," with a smile on his face. He had his own sense of integrity. In Beeston, Leeds, where he lived, he had been a member of the Muslim Boys, a vigilante group who kept order in the streets. He went to university where he got a second-class degree in business studies. In spite of a good degree he was only able to get a job as a teaching assistant for deprived children and though he was well thought of the job was beneath his capabilities. To be overqualified for a job is the fate of many members of minority groups, not only in Britain but around the world.

In 2004 he somehow went off the rails, stopped concentrating on his job and lost it. There is no obvious reason why this might have happened except that it seems fairly clear that he found a group of people who persuaded him that his duty lay in destroying Western society. This coincides with a visit to Pakistan in July 2003 when he is believed to have attended a Pakistani training camp. After he lost his job, he travelled through Pakistan again in 2004. With three associates he detonated bombs which murdered 52 people travelling to work on the morning of 7 July 2005.[79] He claimed to be a soldier of Islam and is still thought of as a hero among extreme members of the Muslim community.

---

[79] BBC News Channel 30 April 2007.

In Khan's suicide video he describes himself as a soldier of Islam and, more revealingly he says: *"Our words are dead until we give them life with our blood.... Our religion is Islam-and obedience to the one true God, Allah, and following the footsteps of the final prophet and messenger Muhammad..."* These words lead at once to the Arab intellectual Sayyid Qutb. They are a paraphrase of his words: *"Indeed our words will remain lifeless, barren, devoid of any passion, until we die as a result of these words, whereupon our words will suddenly spring to life and live amongst the hearts that are dead, bringing them to life as well."*

Sayyid Qutb was a gentle-faced academic who provided an intellectual basis to Jihad and resolved, by relying on the Hadith, any difficulties in interpreting the Koran. In 1949, Qutb spent some time working and teaching in the United States. He was born in 1906 and had a prolific literary career. He became one of the early members of the Muslim Brotherhood and had long philosophical associations with Gamel Abdel Nasser, who came to power in Egypt after deposing King Farouk, in 1956. Sayyid Qutb was eventually accused of plotting the downfall of the new government and was executed by hanging by the same Nasser, now president, in 1966. After his return from America he wrote, while he was in prison, a book called *Milestones*, the text of which had to be smuggled out. It contains an intellectual justification for jihad. The God-given way to govern a country was through Sharia law and anyone who set up a government to oversee and proclaim other laws was, by definition, godless. With regard to Jews Qutb said the following, which applies to any culture outside science and technology: *"explaining the purpose of man and his historical role in philosophical terms... Is one of the tricks played by world Jewry, whose purpose is to eliminate all limitations, especially the limitations imposed by faith and religion, so that Jews may penetrate into body politics of the whole world and then may be free to perpetuate their evil designs. At the top of the list of these activities is usury, the aim of which is that all the wealth of mankind end up in the hands of Jewish financial institutions which run on interest."*

It may be that Sayyid Qutb was set on his path of intellectualising Western hatred by the treatment he had in America or by some sexual inadequacy he sensed in himself. *'Unchecked, women's sexuality had the power to entice men. To follow the Western example ...was to open the door to social discord.'* [80]

In America he seems to have been subjected to an unknown amount of racist opprobrium.

'In America they talk about the white man as though he were a demi-god. On the other hand, they talk about coloured people like the Egyptians and Arabs generally as though they were half human." [81]

It will be noticed that he reserves his criticism of American racism to a defence of people like himself. Jews and Black people are left invisible or, worse still condemned more absolutely than Americans would dare to do.

With regard to Jews and Christians these are: People of the Book, i.e. people of the Abrahamic faith. In Sura 3.199 the Prophet says: *And among the People of the Book are those who believe in God, and in what He has sent down to you, and in what He has sent down to*

---

[80] John Calvert, *Sayyid Qutb and the Origins of Radical Islam Islamism*, p.108.
[81] Calvert, p.149.

them, humbling themselves before God. They barter not the signs of God for a mean price. These! Their recompense awaits them with their Lord: aye! God is swift to take account.

This is a demand for tolerance, i.e. even Christians and Jews, who are people of the book, can be God-fearing. Qutb deals with this by relying on the Hadith by Tirmidhi: *"they (the people of the book) have taken their rabbis and priests as Lords other than God. In the Haddith, one Adi retorts… "They do not worship their priests", God's messenger replied, "whatever their priests and rabbis call permissible, they accept as permissible; whatever they declare as forbidden, they consider as forbidden, and thus they worship them. The Prophet-peace be on him-clearly stated that, according to the Sharia, to obey is to worship. Taking this meaning of worship, when the Jews and Christians disobey God they become like those who associate others with God."* This means that Jews and Christians are polytheists and are accordingly condemned by the law. It may safely be assumed therefore that Sayyid Qutb is considered a respectable source when it comes to legalising indiscriminate murder of civilians.[82]

Thus armed mentally the four young men travelled to London, met in the car park, embraced each other and then proceeded to commit murder, including themselves.

In a paper by Manuel L. Saint Martin published in the Journal of Clinical Psychiatry, he discusses the personality of the Malaysian amok and gives several examples. *In 1901, in the province of Fang, Malaysia, a 23-year-old Muslim man who was formerly a member of the police*

---

[82] A much-used counter argument is that American drone attacks kill innocent civilians, as does any bombing including London, Dresden and Gaza.

force stole a Malay sword and attacked five individuals while they were sleeping or smoking opium. He killed three almost decapitating one victim, and he seriously wounded the others.

Saint Martin contrasts this with a modern case when, *in 1998 in Los Angeles, Ronald Taylor, aged 46, killed four of his family members and a friend, and then jumped to his death from a freeway overpass. The police discovered Taylor's victims when they went to his home to inform them of his death. Court records revealed that Taylor was experiencing financial problems, was filing for bankruptcy, and had debts of more than $64,000, including a $21,302 personal loan from his employer and a $5547 Sears credit card debt.*

The paper goes on to summarise the personality of the person who would commit mass murder as someone with a history of any or all of the following: violent behaviour, threats, prior suicide attempts combined with loss of a loved one, financial stress, employment problems and sudden job loss. These factors combined with any or all of the following: depressive symptoms, lack of social support, being a male of over 45 years of age, financial problems, alcoholism and drug abuse.

An example of this sort of personality was Andreas Lubitz who took control of a Germanwings plane and crashed it into a mountainside, killing all on board including himself. Lubitz was said to be polite and quiet and dependable. He took the Lufthansa course entrance test which has only a 3-7% pass rate. He was accepted in April 2008 but he found flight training school to be very difficult. He suffered from stress, similar to Combat Stress Reaction, and had to leave after two months[83]. This was not unusual because 3.5% of those on the course suffer such stress that they take their own lives. He was treated with drugs and by 2009 his drug use stopped and he applied again to go back on the course. In answer to the question: "have you ever been treated for depression?" he replied, "No."

He completed the programme with Goodyear on light aircraft and a further programme of jet training. He was assigned to Germanwings Airbus A320 jets. This did not have the prestige of Lufthansa and along with others he waited two years for a post, all the time being without pay. So desirable is the job that some postulants drive taxis and some become flight attendants. Lubitz became a steward. In September 2013 he got a paid post with Germanwings. Lufthansa, in competition with Ryanair and EasyJet, subsequently offered pilots a reduction in pay to keep their jobs. He suffered severe depression, paralysis, numbness, blurred vision and had he confessed to any of these it would have disqualified him from flying, but he did not and decided to take his own life. On 24 March 2015 Lubitz took the opportunity of locking everyone out of the cockpit and drove his Airbus A320 into the Alps and murdered the 149 people on board.[84] The similarity between Lubitz and Kahn was that they both took revenge on the very entity which had rejected them in spite of all their efforts.

Pilot suicide in this manner is not unknown and

---

[83] Jeff Wise, *Fatal Descent Andreas Lubitz and the Crash of Germanwings Flight 9525*.

[84] Jeff Wise, *Fatal Descent Andreas Lubitz and the Crash of Germanwings 9525*.

between 1997 and 2014 four previous crashes were thought to be caused by suicide. American regulations, for example, do not permit one person to be left alone on the flight deck.

6d Mary Tudor, Queen of England

The split with Rome and the arrival of Protestantism started very gradually with the absorbing of the Etruscan religion in the 4th century, with the adoption of multiplicity of godly figures called Confessors and, finally with the adoption of celibate priests. This alienated the people of Northern Europe who had grown up in a Nordic tradition with one god-like figure who was a great warrior, who attracted women and was a great fornicator.[85] This aversion to Roman Catholicism was finally rationalised by condemning it for the sale of indulgencies and carried on with various Popes taking an interest in the politics of Northern Europe. The schism between the two Christian faiths did not extend much further south than latitude 52 N, splitting what is now Germany, and finishing at the Polish border in the east. Generally Protestantism attracted those to the north of that line while the rest of Europe remained Catholic or Greek or Russian Orthodox.

The first wave of dissent and criticism of the Catholic Church was led by Jan Hus (1369-1415) in

---

[85] Odin or Wotan was father of the slain and only those who died in battle could enter Valhalla. Only they had life after death. Apart from his wife, Frigg, he had many liaisons which resulted in the birth inter alia of Thor, Balder, Hodr and Vali. Arthur Cotterell, *Norse Mythology* p.49.

Prague where religion has now almost disappeared, Peter Waldo (1140-1205) of Lyon, and John Wycliffe (1331-1384) of Yorkshire, England. They all failed to influence the Church possibly because the Popes at that time were French and held court in Avignon following the schism which divided Europe.

Edward VI (1537-1553) never reached his majority and, whilst he was crowned at the age of nine, the country was governed by a council. The council was led by his uncle, Edward Seymour, first Duke of Somerset, and then by John Dudley, first Earl of Warwick who, in 1551, became Duke of Northumberland. Edward was brought up a Protestant. War and riots marked his reign He ruled together with reforms such as the abolition of priestly celibacy and Catholic Mass together with compulsory services in English rather than Latin were brought in by Thomas Cranmer, Archbishop of Canterbury. Edward died in 1553, possibly of smallpox followed by tuberculosis but there were unsubstantiated rumours that he had been poisoned by Catholics. Anxious to keep England Protestant and further his own influence, John Dudley sought to put his daughter-in-law on the throne, Lady Jane Grey.

Edward nominated Lady Jane as his successor as he was dying, in a will witnessed by a hundred and two nobility including the whole of the Privy Council. Lady Jane had an excellent education, learned in Latin, Greek, Hebrew and Italian. She was the niece of Henry VIII but the Third Succession Act of 1544 made Mary and Elizabeth heirs to the throne even though they were illegitimate. Henry VIII in his last will and testament confirmed their succession unless they died without issue and in that case his younger sister's line should take the throne providing they were male. The gulf in these two propositions was bridged, not by the arguments of law, but by the use of brute force. Northumberland tried to capture Mary but she had been carried off very promptly by the Catholic Howards, Dukes of Norfolk. Jane, her husband, Guildford Dudley, together with two of Dudley's brothers and Thomas Cranmer, the Archbishop, were all found guilty of high treason. This followed a Protestant rebellion led by Sir Thomas Wyatt which probably influenced the matter. The Duke of Norfolk himself alongside Sir Thomas White, Lord Mayor of London and recipient of the revelations of the Nun of Kent, sat on the commission that condemned her to be beheaded in 1554. They all died bravely and with dignity.

Mary I (1516-1558), the daughter of Catherine of Aragon, deposed Lady Jane by means of an armed force in East Anglia. Mary was plain faced with a bass voice according to one biographer but others describe her as a pretty child when she was very young. When her mother's marriage to Henry VIII was declared void by Archbishop Cranmer, Mary was downgraded from "Princess" to "Lady". The same happened to Elizabeth upon the beheading of Anne Boleyn.

Several suitors were proposed for Mary but they all came to nothing. Mary's own goal in life was to preserve England for Catholicism and give birth to a son. Other suitors were proposed but it was a portrait by Titian of Prince Philip of Spain which won her over and, with the permission of Parliament, she married him at Winchester in 1554. Philip had no feelings for her at all according to one of his aides. In spite of one, possibly two pregnancies, Mary remained childless and when Philip left for Flanders to command his troops she fell into deep depression. By the age of 38, in 1554, a bronze coin showed Mary looking rather mannish. England's return to the Church of Rome and the Heresy Act of Richard II, which condemned Lollardy (people like John Wycliffe), was restored and the Marian persecutions of Protestants began.

Mary behaved in a damaged, depressed manner, causing pain to others in order to alleviate the pain in herself. During her depression she started burning Protestant heretics at the stake. She was by no means the first to do this. Henry had burned 63 human beings alive between 1530 and 1546 plus a further three who died in prison. Two Protestants were executed in the reign of Edward but Mary exceeded them by a long way and between 1555, after Philip departed for Flanders and 1558, when she died, in the depths of her depression, she martyred 288 by burning and a further 34 who died in prison. John Rogers, an eminent clergyman and a Protestant, thought that, for heretics, burning was quite mild. Mild, that is, until he was burned alive himself in 1555. Fox's book of martyrs contains an account of the suffering of Protestants in the reign of Queen Mary. Later additions included Henry and Edward but they leave out the six martyred by Elizabeth because the book was published during the reign of Elizabeth. It acted like the Bible on English consciousness and dammed Catholics in Protestants' eyes as unbelievably cruel. It would have been far better for Catholics everywhere and for Tudor

Protestants, for Mary to have lived out her life with another woman and forgotten about marriage as she would do today. The excesses of Mary's reign laid the foundations of anti-Catholicism which exists into the present time.

Elizabeth I (1533-1603) took the throne in 1559 and was an Anglican all her life. Her reign was marked by conflict with Catholicism or Catholic countries. There was a genuine fear in the population of returning to the Marian persecutions and the Act of Supremacy in 1559 established England's separation from Rome, and this was carried by the Puritans who emigrated to North America.

CHAPTER 7

THE PRINCIPAL PREJUDICES
APPROVED BY AUTHORITY

While it might be thought inaccurate to say that authority teaches racial discrimination, utterances by political and religious leaders certainly give authority to racial hatred. The oldest hatred known to man is found in the Christian tradition that the Jews were guilty of the death of Christ. To this day and for many days to come, the message that the Jews killed the Christian saviour is published at Easter in every Christian church in the world. The gospel of John, which is the favourite gospel at Easter to describe the suffering of Christ in both Catholic and Anglican churches in Britain says the following very specifically:

Then Pilate entered the headquarters again, summoned Jesus and asked him, "Are you the king of the Jews?" Jesus answered "Do you ask this on your own or did others tell you about me?" Pilate replied "I am not a Jew am I? Your own nation and the chief priests have handed you over to me. What have you done?" Jesus answered, "My kingdom is not of this world. If my kingdom were of this world, my followers would be fighting to keep me from being handed over to the Jews. But as it is, my kingdom is not from here. Pilate asked him, "So you are a king?" Jesus answered "You say that I am a king. For this I was born, and for this I came into the world to testify to the truth. Everyone who belongs to the truth listens to my voice." Pilate asked him "What is truth?"

After he had said this he went out to the Jews again and told them, "I find no case against him. But you have a custom that I release someone to you at Passover. Do you want me to release to you the King of the Jews?" They shouted in reply, "Not this man but Barabbas!" Now Barabbas was a bandit.

Then Pilate took Jesus and had him flogged. And the soldiers wove a crown of thorns and put it on his head, and dressed him in a purple robe. They kept coming up to him, saying, "Hail, King of the Jews!" and striking him in the face. Pilate went out to them again and said to them, "Look I am bringing him out to you to let you know that I find no case against him." So Jesus came out wearing the crown of thorns and purple robe. Pilate said to them "Here is the man!" When the chief priests and the police saw him they shouted "Crucify him! Crucify him!"[86]

Both the Jews and Jesus are thus condemned by and in the holiest book in the Christian library.

As if this were not clear enough, Acts 2.23 says: *this man handed over to you according to the plan and foreknowledge of God you crucified and killed...'*

Since this became part of the Holy Writ of Christianity in both the East and the West nearly 2,000 years ago, Jews have been labelled 'evil' and every disaster has been explained by saying and believing that it is the Jewish race causing it.

---

[86] John 18.33-19.6 from the Jewish Annotated New Testament.

The Black Death is a typical example. It struck Europe in 1348 and in a year, had killed an estimated 25 million people. It was said to have been started by an international conspiracy of Jews whose intention was to poison Christians. Amadeus VI, Count of Savoy, took a number of Jews from the shores of Lake Geneva and tortured them until they confessed to that very crime and implicated others. The murder of Jews spread down the Rhine until thousands of Jews had died. Needless to say, the killing of Jews had not the slightest effect on the spread and death from the plague. In October 1348 there is an account of a judicial enquiry in the castle of Chatel because the Jews were putting poison in the wells and springs, and there was an outcry demanding that they die. After and during torture, Agimet the Jew confessed that the poison was given to him by Rabbi Peyret, a Jew of Chambery, with instructions that he scatter it in the wells and springs of Venice when he went there to buy silks. He confessed, after a 'little' torture, that he did the same in Toulouse. He swore to the truth of what he said on the five books of Moses and the scrolls of the Jews.[87]

In spite of there being millions of poor Jews in the world, the fiction has grown that Jews manipulate the financial processes of the world. It must be accepted that this might appear to be true in the United States where the last three Presidents of the Federal Reserve System were Jews but the general acceptance of this fiction is there because it gives comfort to those suffering during a financial crisis. It is a downward

---

[87] Paul Halsaall, 1998, Fordham University, The Jesuit University of New York, posted on the internet.

social comparison which temporarily elevates the self-esteem of the sufferer. The Anti-Defamation League survey in Europe found that after the global financial crisis of 2008, 31% of European adults blamed the Jews in the financial world for the crisis. Of those, 58% admitted that their views were influenced by the Israeli treatment of the Palestinians. 40% of Europeans thought Jews had too much power. In Hungary, this percentage was 47% and in Poland 46%. Jews generally were blamed for Bernard Madoff who swindled people out of $50 billion. The Russian news agency, Pravda, reported that French, German and Italian leaders were bailing out the banks to help Jewish banker families.

The same process is being exhibited toward Muslims in Europe. After the attack on the Twin Towers in New York and the Pentagon in 2001 by Muslim suicide bombers, Tony Blair, the British Prime Minister, in a speech to his Sedgefield constituents spoke of a threat that is real and existential.[88] It would be futile to argue that, after the bombing of the Twin Towers in New York, additional security measures were not needed to keep means of transport safe but the response was, at best, disproportionate and, at worst, self-serving when the West invaded two Muslim countries, Afghanistan and Iraq.

Without in any way minimising the horror felt in Western countries at the destruction of the Twin Towers in New York, It must be remembered that the attack was carried out by men from a Sunni terrorist organisation financed and organised by

---

[88] Liz Fekete, *A Suitable Enemy, Racism, Migration, Islamaphobia in Europe*, p.43.

people from Saudi Arabia. To invade two countries outside Saudi Arabia seems illogical.

A wave of fear swept Europe and member states adopted the EU Common Positions and Framework Decision into their domestic laws. In the UK the Anti-Terrorism and Security Act (2001) permitted foreign nationals to be incarcerated without trial and without knowing the charges against them. Twelve people were incarcerated in this way. The whole Muslim community in Britain was looked upon as suspect to such an extent that, also in 2001, British lawyers started the Campaign against Criminalising Communities. More than 71,000 stop and searches were carried out between 2002 and 2003[89] with only 837 arrests made and, of those, only a minority connected to terrorism. Nevertheless, the invasion of two countries where the Muslim faith was practiced made everyone who practiced the Muslim faith into the enemy in the popular mind.

7a White Privilege

The economic preponderance of people with white faces is due to seafaring, aggression and gun powder.

Five thousand years ago, man invented agriculture in areas of the world where there was water and sunshine, notably in Mesopotamia where some of the great civilisations sprang from. The area was so rich that even at a primitive level there was a surplus capacity above the subsistence needs of the population.

---

[89] Fekete, p.53.

Kingdoms came into being with religions and priests who could regulate the planting of crops by understanding the seasons of the year and calculating, by astronomy, whether it was spring, summer, autumn or winter. Primitive religions regulated by priests sprang up all over the world where it was possible to gain a living by agriculture. Ruined temples still exist in Ireland, Stonehenge and on the Nile where the sun, at the equinox, shone directly into an inner sanctum. They had a need to understand the seasons and because any prolongation of winter threatened their very existence, even adopted human sacrifice as a means of ensuring, in the spring, the renewal of the cycle of nature. Other areas which did not lend themselves to agriculture remained pastoral, cultivating animals for slaughter such as sheep for meat, milk and, after 3000BCE, wool.

The areas of the world where water and agriculture and sunshine coincided were, relatively speaking, very rich. The surrounding tribes of more primitive people on less productive land were constantly invading and had to be repulsed. The little kingdoms which grew around rivers and in valleys created defended cities which grew into city states. In order to maintain the prosperity they had, armies of fighting men came into being where a man who could kill was regarded as a hero; some even became heroic generals. The ancient books are dotted with such people. From Mesopotamia, Gilgamesh comes to mind and from the Greeks, Achilles, Agamemnon and Menelaus. Among the Trojans, Aeneas and Hector, and from the Bible, David.

The constant fighting required to preserve abundant areas of land gave rise to various primitive but very necessary beliefs: that to fight for your country was the highest form of heroism; that the enemy of your country, i.e. those who wish to take it away from you, were repugnant both physically and morally.

Europe was just such an area but in addition to troops ready to give their lives to gain control of rich agricultural land, engaged in trade in ever-widening areas. The Mycenaean civilisation (1600-1100BCE), based on Athens, had strong central government, shipping and manufacturing. The Hittites were contemporaneous with the Mycenaean, based on Hattusa in Northern Turkey. They derived power from the control of trade routes, but, most importantly, they manufactured in iron. When they lost control of the trade routes at the Battle of Kadesh to the Egyptian Ramses II, their empire came to an end.

There then followed a succession of warring peoples whose success was based on armour and armies. The Babylonians, Persians and Macedonians come to mind who simply acquired gold. Alexander the Great was a prime example of a brilliant soldier who mistook gold for wealth, sent it back to Greece and demanded more and more troops to replace those killed in battle. The next great empire which took over the known world took root in the Italian peninsula based on Rome from about 500BCE which lasted, in the West, until 476 CE. It went through three phases of central government starting with king Romulus who founded the city in 759BCE, went on to become a Republic and ended as an empire. The Roman Empire ended by being infiltrated or invaded by Germanic tribes and Odoacer became the first

Germanic king of Rome. Odoacer was an Arian who believed that Jesus Christ was the son of God but they did not believe in the Trinity.

The Frankish Empire (481-843) was an agglomerate of separate kingdoms almost constantly at war. Under Charles Martel, they drove the Moors out of Europe. The Frankish kingdoms were not natural divisions, divided by mountains or rivers, they were artificially divided into equal fiscs. At the end of their wars, they gave birth to Belgium, the Netherlands, Luxemburg, Lorraine, Switzerland, Lombardy and certain of the Rhone districts of France.

The great change in world history was introduced by the Vikings who, for the first time, took small areas of land around the Baltic and the North Sea to establish trading posts and permanent settlements. The Vikings were pagans and the Christians refused to trade with them and formed cartels which the Vikings broke into by force of arms. They were active in this way from about 790 to 1066 and, during that period established settlements in the Faroe Islands, Wales, Greenland, around the Baltic Sea, Normandy, England and Scotland. They even reached North America and also established two settlements in Eastern Europe.

In contrast to the European and Mediterranean civilisations, there is only a transient reference to black people in Columbus's own writings. It was this spread of acquisitive Europeans which established the apparent supremacy of white skinned people together with, latterly, industrialisation.

Following the Vikings, several of the countries of Europe, with canon carrying shipping, established colonies across and around the Atlantic Ocean. The first colonials were the Spaniards who invaded the Americas looking for gold which they mistook for wealth. They first arrived at the end of the 15th century at a time when Europe was constantly at war. During the previous 100 years some 60 wars and rebellions are listed on Wikipedia. By the time they arrived they were armed with daggers, pikes, two-handed swords, halberds and pole axes (baldiches). More importantly they had the arquebus, which had to be mounted on a support to steady it before firing, muzzle loading canon and small bombs called petards for destroying fortified gateways. Against them were the native inhabitants who were armed with bows and arrows and slings for throwing stones. They were a Stone Age people. With this preponderance in armament waves of Spanish invaders, now armed with pistols, flintlock muskets and supported by cavalry, invaded North America. In the 17th century the English invaded the East Coast of North America while the French invaded the Southern Seaboard. The English speakers prevailed and reached a modus vivendi with the French but drove the Native Americans on to more and more confined reservations where they watched impotently while white-skinned English speakers ruled the USA.

The English arrived in 1607. The Jamestown settlement was founded and in a second wave of immigration, puritans from England set up a settlement in Massachusetts Bay in 1620. The impact on the native population was devastating. The childhood diseases of chickenpox and measles were fatal among the Native Americans. Smallpox epidemics followed every incursion of Europeans and disease wiped out some 30% of the native population who came into contact with Europeans between 1618 and 1619. Smallpox killed 90% of the Native Americans in the area of Massachusetts Bay and the children of Dutch traders in Albany in 1634 passed on the disease to the Mohawk tribe. On the other hand the most benevolent import was horses who had escaped from Spaniards in Mesoamerica and the Native Americans of the Great Plains became expert in riding both for warfare and for trade, using them to carry burdens.

The first large-scale Indian Rebellion called King Philip's war or Metacom's rebellion of the Wampanoag tribe, took place between 1675 and 1678. There was a great wave of immigrants into the Massachusetts area between 1628 and 1640 which put an end to peaceful immigration into Indian country. English puritans, wishing to practice their version of Christianity free of the taint of Catholicism, as they saw it, emigrated to Ireland, New England, the West Indies and the Netherlands at the rate of roughly 20,000 per destination. In New England they tried to create a nation of saints, a very narrow version of Christianity. So far as the Native Americans were concerned this influx of foreigners who had already brought disease and destruction to their country, was intolerable. The war involved the destruction of 12 of the colonial towns and King Philip, who had instigated this insurrection, was hunted down and killed in 1676. The war continued to 1678 financed by France, who used the Native Americans to carry on a proxy war with England. The Native Americans had armed themselves with flintlock muskets and Tomahawks but, even so, sustained approximately 3,000 casualties against the settlers' 600 casualties. The war was brought to an end by the Treaty of Casco in which it was agreed that captives on both sides should be released and English settlers should pay a peck of corn annually to every Indian family on their land except for a large landowner called Major Phillips who was to pay a bushel of wheat to every Indian family on his land. This was a recognition, effectively, that the English settlers were there on the basis that they paid rent. The British government sabotaged the entire agreement by placing a bounty on the head of every Native American of the Pokanoke tribe of the Wapanoag nation. The Native Americans were forced to flee without signing the treaty.

Fighting between the British and the settlers started in 1775 with both sides competing for the allegiance of Native American nations east of the Mississippi River. The tendency of Native Americans who were asked to join and side with the British was to agree in the hope that colonial expansion into Native American land would cease, but many were divided and for the Iroquois, for example, the American Revolution resulted in civil war. The British made peace with the Americans in the Treaty of Paris of 1783 through which they ceded vast Native American territories, to which they held no title, to the United States, as they became called, without consulting the Native Americans. The occupant Native Americans were clearly incensed by this piece of high-handed treatment as more and more settlers flooded into their lands.

The United States government tried to treat the Native Americans as though they were a conquered people who had lost their land but this sort of reasoning did not weigh very heavily and the Northwest Indian war started. The main fighting tribes were the Miami and the Shawnee. Both of them were supplied with modern armaments by the old colonial powers, notably the British in exchange for furs. The British were still present in the Lake Erie area. The leader of the rebellion was Little Turtle, a Miami, and, equipped with modern armaments he inflicted heavy losses on the United States troops but in the end the United States succeeded in quelling the rebellion and most of Ohio came under American rule. As has been noted the English left a huge area between the 13 states and the Mississippi River unallocated. They had given it to the United States government though they had no title to the land they were giving away. What became the state of Ohio was handled by the Ohio Land Company, an area that was still occupied by three tribes: the Eerie, the Kickapoo and the Shawnee. Some of these tribes were uprooted and moved into Indiana. Their land was bought by the Ohio Land Company for approximately $.67 per acre and sold to European settlers for approximately $1.25 per acre. There was nearly 1,000,000 acres in the first purchase. The gross profit available to the land company directors could have been huge. Some of the shares were owned by the Washington family.

In 1803 the United States purchased Louisiana, an area of 828,000 square miles, for $15 million or three cents per acre. The previous purported owners of the land had been the French and before them, Spain. What the purchase did was to remove the claims of both the French and the Spaniards and any grant of land by Spain to anyone was declared to be null and void whether in common law or in equity. At the time of the purchase there were 32 tribes listed and living in Louisiana and an act of 1804, purporting to be a limitation act, extinguished the title of any tribe that did not file a claim within one year. The Native Americans therefore, living in Louisiana were not conversant with English Law and lost all rights to their land. This was tested in 1982 by the Chitimacha tribe who went to court and lost. A Shawnee called Tecoma who had moved from Ohio to Indiana, having been driven out by the Iroquois, led a federation of Native Americans against the United States government, protested against the Treaty of Fort Wayne in which a delegation of Indians ceded 3,000,000 acres over the heads of the Indians living there. He argued that the land upon which Indians were living was communal land and that any land deal was null and void. In the 1812 war he allied himself with the British in the siege of Detroit which surrendered, though the United States recovered it a year later. His confederation fought in the war of 1812 against United States incursions into British-held Canada and he was killed at the Battle of the River Thames at Chatham, Kent, in Ontario.

The 19th century was labelled the age of Manifest Destiny. A statement by the white denizens of the USA which extinguished American Indian territorial claims and removed them to reservations as the United States population settled west of the Mississippi River. The Indian Removal Act of 1830 was a further encroachment on Native American land which authorised the President to conduct treaties to exchange Native American land east of the Mississippi River for the lands west of the Mississippi

River. This forcible removal was sometimes done in a brutal manner. For example, President Jackson used military force to gather and transport the Cherokee to the West and the lack of adequate supplies led to the deaths of an estimated 4,000 on what became known as the Trail of Tears. About 17,000 Cherokees, along with their black slaves numbering approximately 2,000, were taken by forced migration to Indian territories west of the river and located on reservations. Slowly Native Americans were forced to become and to accept attempted assimilation into European culture by accepting American citizenship and by wearing European clothing. In 1857 it was reasoned that Native Americans were a free and independent people and like any other independent nation they could be naturalised as United States citizens, always providing that they left their nation or tribe and took up abode among the white population.

When all resistance to the white man had been abandoned the beginning of a religious resurgence started. Looking at the Union Pacific Railroad crossing their land, a Piute holy man said that a train would appear and on it would be all the deceased of the Piute nation, and they would be resurrected. No such train ever appeared and the holy man, Wodziwob, was discredited. A further messianic figure named Wovoda, also a Piute, arose and assured his hearers that if they partook of a dance called the Ghost Dance the Great Spirit would come and bring back all the game. All dead Indians would be resurrected. They would be stronger and younger again and would be beyond the control of the whites. A flood will come and the white people will die by drowning and then there will be only Indians. All the

Indian has to do is dance and those who don't dance will be turned into wood and burned by fire. The Lakota Sioux had a version of the Ghost Dance which would render a sacred shirt immune to the white man's bullets.

The dreadful climax of the Ghost Dance occurred along Wounded Knee Creek in South Dakota. When the Indians assembled, they were being arrested. Somebody fired a shot and US soldiers fired repeatedly at unarmed men, women and children. A few minutes later 153 Indians lay dead and any belief in the Ghost Dance died with them. Many years later, Black Elk, a Sioux holy man, delivered a lament: *"When I look back now I can still see the butchered women and children lying heaped and scattered all along the crooked gulch as plain as when I saw them with eyes still young. And I can see that something else died there in the bloody mud, and was buried in the blizzard. A people's dream died there... There is no centre any longer, and the sacred tree is dead."*[90]

In order to force the assimilation of Native American populations the United States established Native American boarding schools where the children were forbidden to speak their native language, taught Christianity and denied the right to practice their native religions and, in numerous other ways, abandoned their Native American identities and adopted some sort of European American culture. However, investigations have shown that such schools harboured cases of sexual, physical and mental abuse and recognised tribes have taken over the operation of the schools and revived and

---

[90] Quoted in Don Nardo, *The Native Americans: The History of Weapons and Warfare.*

strengthened their cultures. In 1924 the Indian Citizenship Act came into being which made American citizens of all Native Americans who were not already citizens providing they were born in the United States and its territories. This act enfranchised about one third of Native Americans who were not at that time American citizens. During the Second World War Native Americans fought and died with American troops but this did not gain them equality with European Americans. In spite of Native American activism, Native Americans do not enjoy equality and whilst 70% of Native Americans live in urban areas, many live in poverty. Racism, unemployment, drugs and gangs are common problems, with Indian social service organisations attempting to redress them.

Hardly surprisingly the white Europeans had to invent a series of myths in order to justify the total destruction of an entire Native American social system which was carried out in order to enable them to take, with or without payment, with or without agreement, the land upon which thousands of people lived.

The Hollywood myth of the Native American slaughtering innocent settlers as they made their way west in covered wagons. This portrayal of the Indian so convinced the American public that it became part of American folklore and is taught in schools. The colonial period is mentioned, as is the Trail of Tears, but the real emphasis is on the Indian Wars and the defeat of the Indian in battle in the 1870s which gave the European the right to the land of a defeated people.

John Wayne, the American actor who appeared in many Western films, in a famous interview with

Playboy magazine, said that what happened a hundred years ago cannot be blamed on the people living today and that the reservations, upon which many Indians live, would have an ill effect on anyone, but they were the creation of the Socialists. What happened between their forefathers and our forefathers was a matter of indifference to him and could not be undone. In olden times things were much harder than they are today and Indians should not bellyache because they didn't get a good break.

Sierra S Adare in her book *Indian Stereotypes*, upon which much of this information is based, writing in 2005, sets out the extent to which casual discrimination still exists in America today. She and her husband, who is also a Native American, have both been denied jobs that they were over qualified to do. In addition to this Native Americans are accused, by way of excusing white European behaviour, of refusing to integrate. This sort of accusation is frequently levelled at minority racial groups who are discriminated against. In contrast with the Irish, the Native Americans are still living under the American yoke with unemployment, poverty, poor housing much of it without sewerage, below average healthcare and below average life expectancy. Like all depressed peoples, they suffer from alcoholism and drug abuse.

Adding to the completely accidental nature of white skin is the fact that, in the Northern hemisphere, white skin is a survival advantage because, in poor sunlight and less UVR it manufactures more Vitamin D which prevents rickets (the softening of the bones would prevent child birth). *Homo sapiens'* predecessor *Homo erectus* never entered Europe[91] and is shown with black skin. Indeed, UVR tails off rapidly above 30 degrees N. An additional random factor is the presence in human beings of a mutant gene, MC1R, which produces light-skinned children.[92]

White supremacy in the USA seems to be based on nothing more than aggression, trade, gunpowder and weaponry. It seems to contain no inherent superiority either moral or social, indeed, after extensive reading around the subject, none can be found.

7b Christian Anti-Semitism

The story which rationalised Jew hatred throughout the ages has been that the Jews have committed deicide and what they did condemned the son of God to death for 30 pieces of silver. The bare outline of this account is given in the preamble to this chapter. So many have died because of this calumny that it is worth spending a few pages examining whether it has any historical basis. In this section there is a description of how authoritative figures in Christianity persuaded others to share their Jew hatred and in Section 10a, the lack of historical basis for this claim will be examined.

Commenting on the Holocaust, the murder of six million Jews in gas chambers by the Germans, the Archbishop of Canterbury (1980-1991), Robert Runcie, said:

'Without centuries of Christian anti-Semitism, Hitler's

---

[91] Smithsonian. *Homo erectus* on the Internet.
[92] Nina G Jablonski, *Skin*, Chapter 6.

*passionate hatred would never have been so fervently echoed...
Because for centuries Christians have held Jews collectively
responsible for the death of Jesus. On Good Friday Jews have,
in times past, cowered behind locked doors with fear of
Christian mobs seeking revenge for deicide. Without the
poisoning of Christian minds through the centuries, the
Holocaust is unthinkable."*

Archbishop Welby, commenting on the Holocaust
after a visit to Auschwitz, in 2017 said that what
surprised him was the normal way in which people
involved in the slaughter thought they were doing a
normal job without looking at the true nature of what
they were doing.[93]

In the preceding chapters it may be taken as read
that Jews occupy a low position in every racial
hierarchy quoted with the exception of China which
has never been Christian. The main reason for this is
the Christian doctrine that the Jews were guilty of the
death of the Christian saviour. Indeed, the New
Testament leaves the reader in no doubt on that score.
Paul's letter to the Thessalonians says very baldly as
follows:

*For you, brothers and sisters, became imitators of the
churches of God in Christ Jesus that are in Judaea, for you
suffered the same things from your own compatriots as they did
from the Jews, who killed both the Lord Jesus and the prophets,
and drove us out, they displease God and oppose everyone by
hindering us from speaking to the Gentiles so that they may be
saved.[94]*

The accusation against the Jews is twofold. One,

---

[93] Interview on Channel 4 News, January 26 2017.
[94] 1 Thessalonians 2.14-16.

that they killed both Jesus and the prophets and two, that they are hindering the spread of Christianity. The facts themselves are more fully examined in Chapter 8a.

These twin ideas that the Jews are guilty of deicide and were standing in the way of the expansion of Christianity have given rise to the most vitriolic tirades from Christians against Jews. Even the most senior Christians have given vent to their unhappiness with Jews in the most forthright way. Dean Farrar, 1831-1903, Canon of Westminster and Chaplain in Ordinary to the Queen, in his book *The Life of Christ* begins by saying the following:

"... In the writings of many Jews, a clear conviction that Jesus, to whom they have quite ceased to apply the terms of hatred found in the Talmud, was at any rate the greatest religious teacher, the highest and noblest Prophet whom their race produced. They, therefore, would be the last to defend that greatest crime in history-the crucifixion of the son of God. And while no Christian ever dreams of visiting upon them the horror due to the sin of their ancestors, so no Jew will charge Christians of today with the looking with any feeling but that of simple abhorrence on the long cruel, and infamous persecutions to which the ignorance and brutalities of past ages have subjected their great and noble race."[95]

But, having made this statesmanlike declaration, he goes on to make the following statement describing the Jews' verdict at the trial of Jesus:

...deliberately putting the question to them, Pilate heard with scornful indignation their deliberate choice; and then, venting his bitter disdain and anger in taunts, which did but

---

[95] Preface, pxii.

irritate them more, without serving any good purpose, "what then," he scornfully asked them, "do you wish me to do with the King of the Jews?" Then first broke out the mad scream, "crucify! Crucify him!" In vain, again and again, in the pauses of the tumult, Pilate insisted, obstinately indeed but with more and more feebleness of purpose-for none but a man more innocent than Pilate, even if he were a Roman Governor, could have listened without quailing to the frantic ravings of an Oriental mob...

Apart from the cry from the multitude calling for crucifixion, the paragraph and indeed most of Dean Farrar's book is pure fiction and designed to exonerate Rome from any guilt and place the death of Jesus entirely at the feet of the Jews. The Jews are accused of avarice, bloodlust, and it reiterates time and again the accusation of bloodlust and the crucifixion of the innocent. Yet the book was well respected in its day and translated into many European languages.

Nineteenth-century Popes were, at times, as anti-Jewish as the estimable Dean Farrar. Pope Pius VI (1775-1800) issued edicts which censored certain books, forbade Jews from enlarging their synagogues, and forced them to wear a yellow badge and live in the ghetto. They were not allowed to engage Christian wet nurses for their infants, or to drive through the city of Rome, but they had to attend conversionist sermons in an attempt to convert them to Christianity. The same policy was pursued under Leo XII in 1826.

Pius IX (1846-1878) condemned any policy which gave political freedom to the Jews and maintained the ghetto in Rome until it was abolished by the Italian occupation of Rome in 1870.[96]

The 19th century was a particularly virulent time for Jews. In Germany a journalist called Wilhelm Marr claimed that Jews were a threat to the Aryan race and would take over the world. He coined the term anti-Semitism in 1879 to avoid using the term anti-Judaism because the old Testament forms part of the Christian holy canon. Racism became complete with the conviction that conversion to Christianity could not alter the identity of a Jew.[97] This was particularly true of the Germans in the 1930s who developed a dictum "once a Jew, always a Jew".

Following the French Revolution Jews all over Europe were emancipated and given full civil rights but a right-wing Christian organisation called the Holy Alliance fought bitterly against this and after 1815, in Germany, Austria and Italy, emancipation collapsed. In Russia where the Tsarist government held the rule of law by only a tenuous margin the Jew hatred propagated by the Church was used for social engineering to divert the minds of the peasant population away from the rising cost of grain and in the direction of killing Jews. Mark Twain leaves his readers in no doubt that the massacre of Jews in Bialystok in 1906 was provoked by Christian dogma and carried out on the orders of the government and their soldiery. He gives the following account:

Horrible details have been sent out by the correspondent of the Bourse Gazette who arrived in Bialystok in company with deputy Shepkin on Saturday, and who managed to send his

---

[96] Papal Laws Against the Jews.
[97] Gabriel Wilensky, *Six Million Crucifixions,* James Carroll, Constantine's Sword, pp.446-447.

story by a messenger Sunday afternoon. The correspondent, who accompanied Shepkin directly to the hospital escorted by a corporal's guard, says he was utterly unnerved by the sights he witnessed there.

"Merely saying that the bodies were mutilated," the correspondent writes, "fails to describe the awful facts. The faces of the dead have lost all human resemblance. The body of teacher Apstein lay on the grass with the hands tied. In the face and eyes had been hammered 3 inch nails. Rioters entered his home, killing him thus, and then murdered the rest of his family of seven. When the body arrived at the hospital it was also marked with bayonet thrusts.

"Beside the body of Apstein lay that of a child of 10 years, whose leg had been chopped off with an axe. Here also lie the dead from the Schlachter home, where according to witnesses, soldiers came and plundered the house and killed the wife, son, and neighbour's daughter and seriously wounded Schlachter and his two daughters.

"I am told that soldiers entered the apartments of the Lapidus brothers which were crowded with people who had fled from the streets for safety, and ordered the Christians to separate themselves from the Jews. A Christian student named Dikar protested and was killed on the spot. Then all the Jews were shot."

Here is the account of a badly wounded merchant named Nevyazhiky:

"I live in the suburbs. Learning of the pogroms I tried to reach the town through the fields but was intercepted by roughs. My brother was killed, my arm and leg were broken, my skull was fractured, and I was stabbed twice in the side. I fainted from loss of blood, and revived to find a soldier standing over me, who asked: What, are you still alive! Shall I bayonet you?

I begged him to spare my life. The roughs came again but spared me saying: He will die; let him suffer longer."

The correspondent, who adopts the bitterest tone towards the government, holds that the pogrom undoubtedly was provoked and attributed the responsibility to Police Lieutenant Shermetieff. He declares that not only the soldiers but their officers participated and that he himself was a witness as late as Saturday to the shooting down of a Jewish girl from the window of a hotel by Lieutenant Miller of the Vladimir Regiment. The governor of the province of Grodno, who happened to be passing at the moment, ordered an investigation.[98]

The murder of Jews in Odessa began in 1881 prompted, it is thought, by the assassination of Tsar Alexander II in Saint Petersburg. He was, by Romanov standards, a reformer. He emancipated the serfs but his reforms were not fast enough for an organisation called Norodnaya Volya who believed that there could be no progress whilst autocratic control remained in place. For this reason they killed the Tsar. Jews were blamed for the assassination. The murder of Jews in Odessa took place at Easter time when, it is preached in the churches, the Jews killed Christ. It is suspected that the real incentive for the murder of Jews was economic. Money was owed to certain Jews and, clearly, if the Jews were dead then the money would not need to be repaid.

Grain prices in Europe, including Russia, became more and more uniform so that following the Franco-Prussian War of 1870, prices tended to rise. Odessa

---

[98] Mark Twain, *Reflections on Religion Part 3*, published in 1906.

was a major outlet for grain and the grain merchants were largely Jews and Greeks. They would have profited from the increase in the European grain price.[99] As will be seen, there is a relationship between poverty, food prices and racial hatred and, certainly in the days of the Romanovs, there was a Christian input in targeting Jews for any misfortune. Even today the catechism of St Philoret of Moscow contains the following explanation:

109. What means the name devil?

It means slander or deceiver.

110. Why are the evil angels called Devils that is, slanderers or deceivers?

Because they are ever laying snares for men, seeking to deceive them, and inspire them with false notions and evil wishes.

Of this Jesus Christ, speaking to the unbelieving Jews, says: ye are of your father the devil, and the lusts of your father ye will do. He was a murderer from the beginning, and abode not in the truth, because there is no truth in him. When he speaketh a lie he speaketh of his own, for he is a liar and the father of it. John 8.44

The impetus given by the church in Russia and by the Tsarist government was evident in an article which appeared in the New York Times in 1903 which described the first Kishinev pogrom which took place that Easter:

"The anti-Jewish riots in Kishinev, Bessarabia are worse than the sensor will permit to publish. There was a well laid out plan for the general massacre of the Jews on the day

---

[99] David Hackett Fischer, *The Great Wave*, p.155, 159.

following the Orthodox Easter. The mob was led by priests, and the general cry "kill the Jews", was taken up all over the city. The Jews were taken wholly unaware and were slaughtered like sheep. The number of dead 120 (the actual number of dead was 47 or 48) and the injured about 500. The scenes of horror attending this massacre are beyond description. Babies were literally torn to pieces by the frenzied and bloodthirsty mob. The local police made no attempt to check the reign of terror. At sunset the streets were piled with corpses and wounded. Those who could make their escape fled in terror, and the city is now practically deserted of Jews."[100]

The pogroms, in all, affected 64 towns and 626 small towns and villages in the Ukraine and Bessarabia. Aided by the Church, the Russian government found the murder of Jews to be convenient in that it diverted the minds of the peasants from their own poverty to the hatred of a culprit which both the Church and the government put in front of them. It gave the population, short of food which it could afford, the illusion that the government was in control and it was in pursuance of this aim that the Tsarist Russian secret police (the Okhrana) vilified Jews as the enemy in accordance with what may be thought of as the Ponsonby rules[101]. They composed a document which purported to be the Zionist aims when the Jews took over the world. It was called the Protocols of the Elders of Zion and was a well-written work discussed elsewhere.

All these lies led nowhere. The maladministration of the Tsarist government gave rise to the bread riots of 1915 and the Revolution of 1917. Two million

---

[100] Wikipedia, Anti-Jewish Pogroms in the Russian Empire.
[101] Reification N22, Arthur Ponsonby.

Jews left Russia to take refuge in the United States and in Palestine where they helped to create the state of Israel.

The 18th century in Europe was the age of Enlightenment. The power of the Church waned and with it anti-Semitism waned. Nevertheless, in some parts of Europe Jews were still subject to discriminatory laws and regulations. The Prussian king, Frederick the second, passed laws restricting the number of Jews and banning them from marrying. In Austria, Jewish families were only permitted to have one son. In other places Jews had to pay additional taxes or face expulsion and were banned from holding public office. Napoleon Bonaparte however, ordered the emancipation of the Jews in all French territories but it seems that anti-Semitism was only pushed beneath the surface and hatred of Jews was given a new twist. Judaism and the Jews with it, were attacked as holders of an outdated belief that hampered human progress. Even Voltaire adopted this new form of anti-Jewish hatred and he saw Jews as a fanatical, religious people opposed to his declared goal of liberating mankind from the grip of a irrational, violent religion. He based his hatred of Jews not on the allegation that they killed the Christian saviour but on their innate character as opponents of liberalism and Enlightenment. In France, emancipation succeeded only in transforming anti-Jewish behaviour but did not end it and with the loss of the Franco-Prussian war it burst the into the public consciousness with the allegation in *La France Juive* that the Rothschilds had made a fortune out of financing the war and blaming their love of money over their love of France for the loss of the war. The Dreyfuss affair started shortly later.

In 1095 the Byzantine Emperor Alexios I Komnenos applied to the court of Pope Urban II in Piacenza, Italy, to ask for help in waging war against the Seljuk Turks. In Jerusalem Jews and Christians lived quietly and were tolerated by the Islamic rulers. The Normans were, at that time, conquering and occupying Sicily and southern Italy. This they continued to do over a period of 70 years between 1060 and 1130. Pope Urban II saw an opportunity for diverting the Normans onto a holy crusade to capture Jerusalem and to drive out the Turks. Pope Urban's position was made stronger when a rumour arrived in Europe that the Turks had desecrated the shrine of the holy sepulchre in Jerusalem and a wave of religious zeal swept Europe coupled with a wave of anti-Jewish hysteria in Germany. The growth of cities along the Rhine indicates a large increase in population in both France and Germany. As a result of this growth the price of raw materials increased steadily throughout the second half of the first millennium. Large numbers of the population moved northward from France into Germany along the Rhine River. It may have been this level of immigration which caused the discontent which gave rise to the anti-Jewish sentiment promoted by the Crusades. The European nations only started trying to control migration late in the 19th century at the height of relative prosperity.

Peter the Hermit who preached in Amiens, raised a rabble in Germany and led them towards the holy land. In Germany, in 1096, he had little control over his men and they went on the rampage providing themselves with the provisions for such a long journey. Prominent among those they killed were

Jews. Peter started his crusade in Cologne with 40,000 men and women. By the time he reached Constantinople he was down to 30,000 and there can be no doubt that they were left to themselves in order to survive. When they reached Constantinople they were a growing nuisance. They were starving and pilfering from the Imperial stores. They wandered off in large numbers into Turkish territory and were slaughtered or enslaved.

The Jewish communities living along the Rhine were prosperous. In the main they pursued certain standard trades, namely: baking, cheese making, vineyards and wine production. As trade became more sophisticated there was a need for funds to be transferred from one end of France and Germany to the other and because, being of the same race, Jews trusted each other. They issued travellers with letters of credit, taking funds in one place and, upon production of the letter of credit, a fellow Jew would pay the requisite sum to the traveller. This was a system which was widely used by merchants, both Jew and Gentile, and obviated the need for carrying large sums of coin.[102]

The Pope's declaration of a holy war to avenge the destruction, as it was thought, of the holy sepulchre in Jerusalem and to clear the way to for pilgrims to pray at the Church of the holy sepulchre produced, from Germany, numbers of marauding gangs who preyed on Jewish homes in order to raise funds for their journey. Jews, in the main, paid large sums in order to protect themselves and their families. It is not clear

---

[102] See Robert Chazen, *European Jewry and the First Crusade*, Kindle Ed, Location 143.

whether the leaders of the mobs ever really intended to go to the Holy Land at all or whether they were merely using the crusade and the religious fervour it engendered to enrich themselves at the expense of those who had "murdered the Christian Saviour". Prominent amongst these people was Count Emicho who, after plundering several cities, notably Mainz and Cologne, headed for the Jewish houses in spite of the fact that the Christian inhabitants did all they reasonably could to protect the Jews. Having plundered enough funds, Emicho and his band of thousands of men and women set off east for Jerusalem. They were met by the King of Hungary, totally defeated and returned to Germany in disgrace. When attacked, the Bishop of Speyer managed to protect his Jews by sheltering them in his palace and resisting all attempts to drive them out.

The Jewish Chronicles of that time record that the main justification for the murder of Jews and taking their money was the revenge Christians were entitled to take for the Jewish killing of Jesus. It is interesting to take a few examples:

In Worms: "They, the Gentiles, took a trampled corpse of theirs that had been buried 30 days previously and carried it through the city saying: *Behold what the Jews have done to our comrades. They took a Gentile and boiled him in water. They then poured the water into our wells in order to kill us.*" This was a precursor to the justification for the murder of Jews during the Black Death, late in the 14th century, that the Jews were poisoning the wells and causing the death of Christians. Pope Clement was able to put a stop to this over an area where his jurisdiction held sway around Avignon.

Robert Chazen says in his book *European Jewry and the First Crusade*, the following: *The two Christian historians who accord attention to the popular crusading bands and to the anti-Jewish assaults-Albert of Aix and Ekkhard of Aura-assert that these attacks arose out of anti Jewish principles. According to Albert, these Crusaders "arose in a spirit of cruelty against the Jewish people scattered throughout all the cities and slaughtered them cruelly especially in the Kingdom of Lorraine, asserting it to be the beginning of their expedition and of their duty against the enemies of the Christian faith"…. He claims that the destruction of the Jews was seen by those crusading bands as an integral part of their sacred task. The same view is reflected in the brief comments of Ekkehard of Aura. He indicates that the German Crusaders "likewise in this matter zealously devoted to the Christian faith, took pains to destroy utterly the execrable Jewish people wherever they found them or to force them into the bosom of the church"… The Jewish chroniclers share this perception of doctrinally grounded hatreds…. It came to pass in the year 1028 after the destruction of the Temple that this evil befell Israel…. The Princes and the nobles and common folk in France, who took counsel and set plans to ascend and to rise up like eagles and to do battle and to clear the way for journeying to Jerusalem, the holy city, and for reaching the sepulchre of the crucified,… They said to one another: Behold we travel to a distant land to do battle with the Kings of that land. We take our souls in our hands in order to kill and to subjugate all those kingdoms which do not believe in the Crucified.*[103] *How much more so should we kill and subjugate the Jews who killed and crucified him."*

The justification for the killing of Jews was thus

---

[103] Kindle Edition, Location 749.

quite clearly, in the minds of those who provided contemporary records, the fact that the Jews had crucified Christ.

It will be noticed that the role of Pontius Pilate was omitted. The common people who did the killing could not read and were relying entirely on what their priests were telling them. Even had they been able to read, the first bible in Low German was not available until 1614.

The Jewish Chronicles also quote the Crusaders (unspecified) as saying: "*Behold, we journey a long way to seek the idolatrous shrine and to take vengeance upon the Muslims. But here are the Jews dwelling among us, whose ancestors killed Him and crucified Him groundlessly. Let us take vengeance first upon them. Let us wipe them out as a nation; Israel's name will be mentioned no more. Or else let them be like us and acknowledge the son born of menstruation*"[104]

The need for funds to make the Crusade possible was never far from the Crusaders' minds. Duke Godfrey of Bouillon, after the German bands had terrorised the Jewish communities, announced that he would not begin his crusade "without avenging the blood of the crucified with the blood of Israel". He then travelled up the Rhine to Cologne where the Jews handed over 500 silver marks, as did the Jews of Mainz. It has to be said that Godfrey then led a fairly orderly Crusade, funded by Jewish money, to the holy land where he occupied Jerusalem with great loss of Muslim and Jewish lives. On the other hand, the Jewish Chronicles recorded many examples of the

---

[104] Kindle Edition, Location 767.

Crusader mobs preferring that the Jews convert to Christianity rather than face death. Many Jews did this in order to save their lives but continued, in secret, to read the Torah and pursue the Jewish religion.

This long history of persecuting and denigrating Jews for the death of Jesus has had a lasting effect on the Christian psyche. Even those who no longer go to any church service, even those whose parents were agnostics still denigrate the Jews and they rationalise it by looking at the behaviour of the Israelis bombing Gaza and their natural moral indignation spills over into a general anti-Semitism which gives them a feeling of righteousness. They forget that the behaviour of their Christian forebears all over the Christian world actually created the state of Israel and that they themselves are not free of blame. The same syndrome is exhibited against people with black skin and against people whose sexuality is not heterosexual. They too have been subjected to generations of discrimination which is resistant to rational argument.

7c Homophobia

Any group which society has been taught to look down on, will themselves exhibit racism directed at some other group. Jews or blacks are obvious examples, simply because it brings order and control into their lives and makes them feel better. Happily the prejudice against homosexuals, both male and female, is disappearing and the substitute racism which they, from time to time exhibit, will also disappear. Homosexuals, in particular, have been subjected to prejudice for thousands of years. Its roots lie in the Bible, in the book of Leviticus where it says: *"if a man also lie with mankind, as he lies with a woman, both of them have committed an abomination: they shall surely be put to death, their blood shall be upon them (20.13)"*. This edict applies generally because Leviticus 18.26 says: *"any stranger that that lives among you and commits this crime shall also be put to death"*. In spite of the liberal attitude of Greek civilisation to homosexuality, when they adopted Christianity, the Greeks also adopted the homophobia expressed in Leviticus.

The Catholic Church has never varied since the 5th century on what it calls moral issues such as abortion, sex, the role of women and the family. Certainly on any question of homosexuality the Church's position never varied and all these moral issues were sinful. In their eyes the Church was persecuted by what it called "the gay lobby" and the highest echelons of the Church regard homosexuality as a debilitating illness which goes against the natural order and closes off the sexual act from the gift of life. Pope Benedict asserted in a paper entitled *"Some Considerations on the response to Private Bills on the Non-discrimination of the Homosexual People"* in which he asserted: *"In certain areas, taking sexual orientation into account is not just discrimination, for it is in the adoption of children or placing in foster care, in the hiring of teachers and sports coaches and in military recruiting"*.

John Paul II was against decriminalising homosexuality in his homeland of Poland without considering the homophobic outbursts of violence that he was encouraging. The question of same-sex marriage was condemned in 2000 when the Vatican demanded that same-sex marriage should not be officially recognised as it would have grave consequences on the family and on the common good of society in general. In Spain civil unions were condemned as an assault against the family and marriage and the views of the Church must be preserved. In Canada the Catholic Church led a crusade against any law that would recognise same-sex unions and give gay couples the right to adopt. In the case of Canada these efforts were ignored[105]. In Europe, gay couples were using IVF and donated sperm to become pregnant or using surrogate mothers to have a child using the father's sperm. In 2015 an Italian gay couple with a worldwide reputation decided, for no apparent reason, to say: "*We oppose gay adoptions. The only family is the traditional one. No chemical offsprings and rented uterus: life has a natural flow, there are things that should not be changed*". This was an example of very successful homosexuals who had internalised the Church's teaching and were restricting their own and other people's lives. It is interesting to note that the Jews who started this phobia over 3,000 years ago have now quietly let it lapse and there are gay synagogues in America at the present day.

The aversion to homosexuality seems to be confined to the Abrahamic faiths. The Greeks, before they were converted to Christianity had a homosexual phase in their emotional and intellectual lives as they were growing up, when young men formed a liaison with an older man which involved nudity but might not have involved penetration:

It was in classical Greece male love carried associations very

---

[105] Wikipedia, Homosexuality and the Catholic Church (Before Pope Francis).

much at odds with those in republican Rome. Among the Greeks it was associated with courage in battle, philosophical mentorship, and the defence of democracy; among the Romans, with handsome slave boys and the disgraceful loss of manhood...in Japan, nanshuko (male love) was associated with Buddhist saints, samurai warriors and the Kabuki theatre.[106]

When the Greeks adopted Christianity, all such practices disappeared or were hidden because they were decreed to be shameful. Among the Japanese, who did not adopt Christianity, male love was never considered shameful. There is a description of Saint Francis Xavier's first contact with Japan c1549:

The people, he reported enthusiastically "are the best who have yet been discovered, and it seems to me that we shall never find among heathens another race to equal the Japanese"...

One custom, however, marred the picture. When Xavier visited the monks of the Zen monastery at Hakata, he found-to his horror-that "the abominable vice against nature is so popular that they practice it without any feeling of shame..." He was shocked again to find that male love was also common among the Samurai warriors who ruled the district.[107]

There were similar reports from the Jesuit Alessandro Valignano who visited Japan between 1579 and 1603 because the priests (bonzes) teach that it is not a sin and is quite natural. The Japanese priests are not allowed women and this might promote another sexual outlet.[108] There could also be a certain amount of unconscious selection because Shinto

---

[106] Louis Crompton, *Homosexuality and Civilisation*, Loc 272 Kindle Ed.

[107] Louis Crompton, Loc 8455 Kindle Ed.

[108] Louis Crompton, Loc 8473 Kindle Ed.

ritual involves a good deal of ceremonial dancing by both male and female dancers. The ritual dancers in the temples and the court were male while those in the shrines were female.[109] A study of the sexuality of 136 male dancers provided in a report in the 1990s gave, as an opinion, that over 50% were openly gay. This is not the case with women dancers of whom only 5-7% are lesbian.[110] This compares with the highest estimate of 10% in the general population given by Kinsey in his report published in 1945. He also put the percentage of those who attained orgasm by same-sex contact, even if only once in their lives, at 37%. Even so, it seems that gays are more attracted to dance and are better at it, than heterosexuals. It is for this reason that the Japanese people, not brought up in an Abrahamic faith, might seem more liberal than they really are but they certainly have a more relaxed attitude to homosexuality than the Western nations. If so, it means that the West's phobias are cultural and are taught and can, as a matter of pure logic, be untaught.

7d Islamophobia

The fear of Islam in the West began in the 19th century with the British moves to contain Russian expansion in the Middle East. It was called at the time 'The Great Game' and the battle ground was Afghanistan which resulted in three Anglo-Afghan wars while Britain and Russia manoeuvred for power

---

[109] *Cambridge History of Japan* Vol 3, p.526.
[110] JM Bailey and M Oberschneider, *Sexual Orientation and Professional Dance*.

between 1827 and 1907 when the greater threat of the German Empire caused Britain and Russia to enter into a treaty.

The Soviets were pushed out of Afghanistan in 1989 after an estimated 1.5 million civilians were killed in the fighting.[111] This victory by ordinary Muslims without special training or sophisticated armaments over a major world power had a marked effect on the Muslim population in other countries in the rest of the world. The lack of social integration in both Britain and France was quite marked and remains so to this day. For a variety of reasons the British and the French remain racist. The USA is becoming more Islamophobic as a result of their armed entry in Afghanistan and Iraq followed by the lesser European powers. The fear of Islam has been heightened by the arrival of Sunni Muslim trying to establish Caliphates in Shia Muslim countries by armed intervention. This group, currently calling themselves 'Islamic State' or 'IS' are currently using non-integrated Muslims, which they themselves have helped to create, to commit mass murder of civilians on a random basis from time to time.[112]

In Britain, the media inform the population that murderous attempts by Muslims have been foiled at intervals but, thankfully, only one such attempt has succeeded. This was when more than 50 Londoners were murdered on their way to work on 7 July 2005. On a casual level Muslims are discriminated against all over the British Isles. In a report called: "Experiences

---

[111] Wikipedia, Soviet Afghan War.

[112] What are called terrorist acts are listed on Wikipedia on a monthly basis. They happen all over the world.

of Muslims Living in Scotland" written by Sara Kidd and Lynn Jamieson, more than 100 pages long, the following extracts are sufficient to give the flavour of anti-Muslim remarks made in Scotland.

One man described how he was challenged on a bus by a passenger for speaking to a friend in his native tongue. The man demanded to know if he could speak English. "Because," he said, "you are in Scotland and you need to speak English." The interfering man was reprimanded by another passenger who told him that it was not his problem.

The media were also highlighted for portraying Muslims in a negative light. One participant said: *"How many times do you see a story in the paper saying something about some successful Muslim. There are successful Muslims, obviously there are. And why do they all write about Muslims that are doing this in doing that? Why do they not write about how Muslims are successful, who helped the country, or who helped the economy or whatever. They never have anything like that."*

In a school group, one boy said: *"...But you do, get to be called, like, black bastard a lot. That is written on the walls, said to you in your face, so yeah that's been said. But obviously it... They used to be a lot of kind of, I don't know, Europeans came, and you used to get a lot of abuse then."*

In Scotland the perpetrators are more accurately described as 'Neds' which stands for Non-Educated Delinquents.

Discrimination against a minority group can be measured by the unemployment rate within that group. Unemployment in Britain was 5.4% in 2008 but thereafter, as austerity measures were brought in, unemployment peaked at 7.8% and then started a very slow decline to 5.5% of the economically active population in 2015. This compares with 10.4% in France where, apparently because of the German economic success the euro has remained high and France has been hampered in expanding her economy. In 2011 the Muslim Council of Britain reported that amongst Muslims of 50 years of age and above the unemployment rate was double the average unemployment rate for the country as a whole. In 2008 when Muslims were 3% of the total population of Britain, 24% of Muslim graduates were not in work whilst the number of graduates not in work for the country as a whole was 13%. In 2011 the unemployment rate among ethnic minority women was 14.3% but among Muslim women it was 20.5% whilst among white women the unemployment rate was 6.8%. These numbers seem to indicate a degree of discrimination.

Stemming from the same source, i.e. belonging to a group of people who are looked down upon, there are regular violent episodes which take place in France prompted by the low status of Muslims in that country. Their low status is imposed upon them because they are not treated equally. There might be as many as five million Muslims living in France in 2015 of Algerian, Moroccan or Tunisian origin and their low status stems only partly from the lack of growth in the French economy, with first choice being given to non-Muslims. This in turn gives rise to a general lowering of their sense of well-being among the French people. That being the case, they gain comfort from looking down on another social group. The French GDP has been more or less static since

2009. Long-term unemployment has increased since 2012 and unemployment generally has gone from 9.7% in 2012 to 10.4% in January 2015. By European standards this is somewhat high and static. More seriously, youth unemployment has remained at about 24% which means that young people at the time of writing (2015) are faced with the real possibility that they will never find a job. As a result, the general public, looking for a reason for their continuing lack of improvement in their standard of living, support right-wing parties who are opposed to immigration and to anyone with a foreign heritage generally.

The Front National got 11.3% of the vote in 2002 rising to 24.86% of the vote for the European Parliamentary Elections in 2014. In 2013, 39% of the French people were of the opinion that Islam was an intolerant religion and only a minority, 26%, thought that Islam was compatible with French society. In contrast, Germany, which is also in the Eurozone with France, had an economy which grew by 35% between 2006 and 2014. Their right-wing party got 1.6% of the vote in 2005 and has never had a representative in the Bundestag. Angela Merkel, the Chancellor of Germany, herself described economic recession as the 'serpent's egg' thinking of the state of affairs which gave rise to the dictatorship of Adolf Hitler. As a result of the despondency caused by debt, lack of liquid assets and continuing economic recession, French society does not deal with Muslims in an even-handed way. There is a bias against them. Before the recession in 2008 unemployment in France generally was 9.2% whilst amongst Muslims it was 14%. Such numbers are no longer compiled in France because all Frenchmen, theoretically, are treated equally, but typically amongst graduates, those of French origin suffer 5% unemployment whilst those of North African origin suffer 26.5% unemployment.

The media coverage in 2012 and 2013 in France contains articles such as: "Is Islamism going to win?" and "Islamism the domestic threat". Relying on Andrew Hussey's book *The French Intifada*, those who have the means live in the centre of Paris and those who cannot afford to do this, live in what can be translated as "the suburbs" outside Paris and fringe the city mostly in the north. The transport systems there are limited and haphazard, the maps make no sense and nobody goes there unless he has to and when one does, it is terrifying. This is where the Muslims live. It is a concrete jungle. In order to keep the peace the police use brutal methods and fire on unarmed civilians on occasion[113]. The French become used to violence, to mini riots and clashes between the police and youths. Not surprisingly, French Muslims themselves look down on the French establishment and, somewhat more surprisingly, the Jews. This latter is an emotional to gain control by projecting the pain they suffer on to another race. It is rationalised by the Israelis' treatment of Palestinians in which Jews are depicted as identical to the Nazi Party. Very few Muslims have even met a Jew let alone an Israeli. It is common, in order to reinforce this image, to deny the existence of the Holocaust. Such a person is called Kemi Seba, who is the representative of the Black Panther movement in

---

[113] Amnesty International: France: The Search for Justice; The effective impunity of law enforcement Officers in case of shootings deaths in custody or torture and ill-treatment, 2005.

France. He has a website critical of Jews which is notorious in France. In a revealing interview with a young black woman who has a degree, a good job in publishing and a white boyfriend who is a lawyer, when she spoke to Hussey she said:

"Only if you are black or Arab in France can you understand the contempt people feel for you, and the hate and desire for revenge that this inspires in you. Kemi is nasty but I understand his appeal. He is about war and violence. What angry young man in the banlieues doesn't feel the same at some point? It's the same for the Taliban as for the youth in the banlieues: they are fighting to let us know that they exist and that they hate society as it is. They feel that the Jews rule the world, and from one point of view it can look that way. They see Iraq and Gaza and Rwanda and Kenya and the Jews of Paris or New York who have profited from their pain. To them, it all makes sense."

What this intelligent young woman was demonstrating was that when people are discriminated against, they gain control by themselves, discriminating against someone else of another race, or even class.

In support of this, it seems that the young woman had no evidence for what she was saying and, indeed, it appears that she did not even know any Jews. She needed someone to hate to alleviate the pain she felt because of the contempt that people meted out to her but it is based on this sort of hatred that Ilan Halimi, a Jew, was murdered after his body had been tortured and mutilated in 2006. In 2012 a little Jewish girl called Miriam was murdered in a spate of killings in Toulouse. The killer said he attacked the French army because of France's involvement in Afghanistan and Jews because the Jews kill our brothers and sisters in

Gaza. (Neither the little girl nor her family had killed anyone.)

In 1989, after the eviction of the Soviet army from Afghanistan by Afghan tribesmen the fight for what was thought of as Muslim dignity was led by Osama bin Laden, a Saudi Arabian businessman, and his terrorist organisation, Al Qaida. Unfortunately the American establishment underestimated Al Qaida as *'an organisation of thugs led by a sociopath; the 9/11 attacks were atrocities; bin Laden's pronouncements are rants unworthy of attention and analysis; the Islamists are either nihilists or freedom haters...'* [114] Bin Laden himself told Muslims they had remained inactive for too long in the face of the superpowers and the time for action was now. [115]

Osama bin Laden was the seventeenth son born of one of his father's wives, Allia Ghanem, a Syrian. He grew up in awe of his father, Shaikh Mohammed bin Laden, and a desire to integrate into the Bin Laden clan. Mohammed was a giant among men, pious, honest and a shrewd businessman according to his daughter-in-law Carmen bin Laden, who, with his own money had rebuilt the Al Aqsa mosque in Jerusalem. Mohammed had a deep-rooted hatred of the State of Israel. Osama in an interview with the Pakistani journalist Hamid Mir put this down to Israel's victory in the 1967 war. [116] The Six-Day War was a decisive victory for Israel against three Muslim states, Egypt, Syria and Jordan. As a result, Osama himself focussed on Israel and thought that one of

---

[114] Michael Scheuer, *Osama bin Laden*, Kindle Loc 69.

[115] Statement by Osama bin Laden in Al Qal'ah (internet), 14 October 2002.

[116] Scheuer, p.25, Loc 550.

the aims of Islam should be to reclaim Palestine from the Jews, and his thinking on that score deteriorated into racism. He condemned Shaikh bin Baz for his fatwa permitting peace with the Jews. He described those working for peace as treacherous, cowardly Arab tyrants[117] and Saudi Arabia allowing US forces to be stationed on what he regarded as sacred land in 1990 at the start of the First Gulf War, though he never openly criticised his family or country. He contented himself with condemning 'Jews and Crusaders'. According to the Advice and Reform Committee, set up in London, in part by Bin Laden himself, he made clear that he would continue jihad until the Arabian Peninsula was clear of US military presence. In 1996 he declared war on the United States which declaration was published in the London-based *Al-Quds al Arabi* on the 23 August together with an announcement on the website *Al-Islah*. [118] He had, by then, formed al Qaida in both Sudan and Afghanistan and they bombed the Gold Mihor Hotel in Aden in 1992 which killed two civilians and missed the US soldiers thought to be staying there.

In 1998 he himself declared jihad against Jews and Crusaders.

In 1998 he organised truck bombings of US embassies in Dar es Salaam and Nairobi which killed over 200 people while the Nairobi driver ran away. The same year, an attack on the USS Cole was foiled.

In 2001 he launched his most devastating attack

---

[117] Scheuer, p.98, Loc 1928.
[118] Scheuer, p.110, Loc 2154.

on the Twin Towers in New York and on the Pentagon in which 3,000 civilians lost their lives.

In 2011 a US assassination squad found him in Abottabad, Pakistan, and killed him though he had by then handed over his authority to others.

Being the 17th son, it is possible that Bin Laden was homosexual, see below under homosexuality, and the pornography found by American forces at Abottabad has not been disclosed. Nevertheless, Pink News is convinced that he was gay. Homosexuality is condemned by Islam and Bin Laden was forthright in his condemnation of it. *They are the ones who vote in favour of human alien satanic practices such as homosexual marriages and infant butchery in the wombs of their selfish heartless prostitute mothers.*[119] This would be in accordance with the practice of projection and splitting in which the 'sinner' projects his sin onto his enemy and condemns the very thing he practises himself.

The Mujahadeen victory over Soviet forces in 1989 and Bin Laden's terrorist organisation left a lasting burden on Western governments which has steadily worsened as right-wing Arab dictatorships have collapsed, leaving behind millions who believe a return to the fundamentals of Islam and Sharia Law is the way to a golden future while millions of others are trekking westward in the hope of sanctuary in Europe.

The lead given by the Mujahadeen has been taken up by Muslim individuals all over Europe in completely random way. In 2015 four Jewish shoppers were shot down in a kosher supermarket in

---

[119] Quoted in Pink News.

Paris. This latter followed the murder of 12 members of the staff of the magazine Charlie Hebdo because they published cartoons of the Prophet. Interestingly, there were 54 messages of support for the killers and a number of churches in France were burned.

The mother and her two children who took themselves off to Syria in June 2015 said she did not want her daughters to grow up in Britain, was simply distancing herself from the prejudice she encountered on a day-to-day basis. The mother had not been radicalised, she had simply been made to feel an alien in her own country. Muslim children, when interviewed usually say that they were not made to feel welcome in Britain.

Not only Muslims project, quite unconsciously, their own unhappiness onto people of another race providing they are weak enough. They give voice to their dark thoughts in the presence of others and even in the presence of completely blameless people of the target race. Pejorative references to banks with what might be Jewish names, pejorative references to Israel and pejorative references to Jewish politicians. Finally there are references urging other Muslims to kill Jews. Osama bin Laden was a rich source of such references: 'Kill all Christians and Jews and re-establish a Caliphate'. 'A World Front against Crusaders and Jews [would be] a great step forward'. '...totally in the control of American Jews whose first priority is Israel not the United States...'

Abu Hamza, an extremist, when living in Britain said:

You must have a stand with your heart, with your tongue, with your money, with your hand, with your sword, with your

Kalashnikov. Don't ask shall I do this, just do it.[120]

In saying this, Abu Hamza, born in Egypt and Imam of the Finsbury Park Mosque at the time (he has since been dismissed and deported) was outlining the ways in which Jihad could be waged. He was urging others who had been alienated by society to use violence. He told his followers not to be afraid of death:

'*It is not called suicide-this is called* shahadah, *martyring, because if the only way to hurt the enemies of Islam except by taking your own life for that, then it is allowed...The person who hinders Allah's rule, this man must be eliminated.*'[121]

The intention of such statements, and there were many of them were made before The Serious Crime Act 2007, which came into force in 2008, was to incite others to violence. Members of alienated minorities in London, Paris and Boston were moved to commit murderous acts by these statements and completely innocent, unarmed civilians paid with their lives.

The killing sprees which disaffected Muslims engage in is indulged in by alienated, depressed people of any nationality or race and is known throughout the world but has been studied in the Malay sociopathic custom of running amok.

In a paper by Manuel L. Saint Martin published in the Journal of Clinical Psychiatry he discusses the personality of the amok and gives several examples. *In 1901, in the province of Fang, Malaysia, a 23-year-old Muslim man who was formerly a member of the police force*

---

[120] Abu Abdullah Al-Atharee, *The Rise of Jihadist Extremism in the West*, Loc 681 Kindle Ed.

[121] Abu Abdullah Al-Atharee, Loc 693.

stole a Malay's sword and attacked five individuals while they were sleeping or smoking opium. He killed three, almost decapitating one victim, and he seriously wounded the others.

He contrasts this with the modern case when, *in 1998 in Los Angeles, Ronald Taylor, aged 46, killed four of his family members and a friend, and then jumped to his death from a freeway overpass. The police discovered Taylor's victims when they went to his home to inform them of his death. Court records revealed that Taylor was experiencing financial problems, was filing for bankruptcy, and had debts of more than $64,000, including a $21,302 personal loan from his employer and a $5547 Sears credit card debt.*

The paper goes on to summarise the personality of the person who would commit mass murder as someone with a history of any or all of the following: violent behaviour, threats, prior suicide attempts combined with loss of a loved one, financial stress, employment problems and sudden job loss. These factors combined with any or all of the following: depressive symptoms, lack of social support, being a male of over 45 years of age, financial problems alcoholism and drug abuse.

All these factors point to someone whom will run amok. Frequently, there are no previous signs of anger and the person who is planning to kill is frequently, apparently, a steady, well-placed member of society. But there is a syndrome which travellers in Asia described as a military amok in which a sudden frenzy comes over a man facing defeat from an enemy and in the sudden display of death-defying courage he chooses either victory or an honourable death. This syndrome has been displayed in battle and given a name: Berserker by the Norse, amongst the

Zulu it was known as Battle Trance.

Another, but in some ways, similar symptom was displayed by Andreas Lubitz, a Germanwings pilot who was said to be polite and quiet and dependable. He took the Lufthansa test which has a 3-7% pass rate and he passed in April 2008, but he found flight training school to be very difficult and suffered from troops stress and had to leave after two months. The course was so difficult and demanding that 3.5% of those on the course took their own lives. He was treated with drugs and by 2009 his drug use stopped and he applied again to go back on the course. In answer to the question "have you ever been treated for depression?" he answered, "No." He completed the programme with Goodyear on light aircraft and a further programme of jet training. He was assigned to Germanwings Airbus A320 jets. This did not have the prestige of Lufthansa and along with others he waited two years for a post, all the time being without pay. So desirable is the job that some postulants drive taxis and some become flight attendants. Lubitz became a steward. In September 2013 he got a paid post with German wings. Lufthansa in competition with Ryanair and EasyJet offered pilots a reduction in pay to keep their jobs. He suffered severe depression, paralysis, numbness, blurred vision and had he confessed to any of these it would have disqualified him from flying but he did not and decided to take his own life. On 24 March 2015 Lubitz took the opportunity of locking everyone out of the cockpit and drove his Airbus A320 into the Alps and murdered the 149 people on board.

Pilot suicide in this manner is not unknown and

between 1997 and 2014 four previous crashes were thought to be caused by suicide. American regulations do not permit one person to be left alone on the flight deck.

The tragic phenomenon of the suicide bomber, murder born of the failure of a person to integrate or be allowed to integrate, is not confined to Muslims living in the West, it is a characteristic of mankind. Pope Francis, returning from a visit to Mexico, made a general remark which applies to everyone: 'A person who thinks only about building walls, wherever they may be, and not building bridges is not a Christian.'[122] It is a statement which applies to non-Christians and Christians alike. It is of general application and echoes Matthew 5.9: 'Blessed are the peacemakers for they will be called children of God'. Not as easy as it sounds.

7e Misogyny

This, the male hatred and belittling of women, is not, strictly speaking, racist, since both men and women could be members of the same race and male antipathy could still exist. However, in many cases, misogyny occurs as part of a male defence mechanism used to preserve a man's self-esteem. The difference is merely that some men, on occasion, use racism, homophobia, anti-Semitism, anti-black or class, to preserve their self-esteem. Misogyny simply provides someone, particularly when they feel failures, to look down on. As a general rule the racist and the misogynist is someone struggling with depression. In a modern society some men who suffer humiliation

---

[122] Emily Flitter reporting for Reuters, 19 Feb 2016.

will turn on a woman who is, of course, physically weaker and use violence against her. This can be verbal, physical or sexual but while it is meted out the failed male is in control. In many societies, the woman's weakness was economic so that she could not defend herself and needed to remain under the defence of a man. With the arrival of abundant, though expensive, sources of energy and universal education, economic parity is more of a reality.

In very broad terms, over thousands of years, human society changed from Hunter-Gatherers/Tribal to Agrarian and then to Industrialised during and after the 19th century in Europe, which gave Europeans a massive advantage over the rest of the world at that time.

The most primitive form of society is **tribal** which, until the year 2000, still existed, at least, in India. *The tribe is a group of persons having a common definite territory, common dialect, common name, common religion and common culture. They are united by blood relationship and have a peculiar political organisation*[123]. I.e. the political organisation is peculiar to the tribe, a chief who exercises authority over the whole tribe. The principal binding forces are territory, which has to be defended, and the worship of a common ancestor. The main economic activity is hunting and food gathering. The division of labour, apart from giving birth, is almost non-existent. Women take care of domestic affairs while men, with their superior physical strength, take care of hunting and preserve the territory upon which the life of the tribe depends. When European settlers

---

[123] Definition by the Shelly Shah Society, Tribal Agrarian and Industrial Society, p.2, Internet.

arrived in Virginia and started putting up fences as they did at home, they must have been seen as threatening the very existence of the native tribal people. Because both genders in a tribe can be seen as being of importance, misogyny is non-existent. This is supported by an Indian survey published in 2000 in India. The author, Samita Manna, makes an important observation:

'It is observed that if the socio-economic condition of women is high in a particular culture her status will be high automatically. For example, in the case of the Toda, South Indian Tribe, the status of women is not high because they do not take upon themselves the direct economic burden as men do. The women are not allowed to do all economic activities like the men, whereas among hunting-gathering tribes, like the Andamanese, Birhor, Lodha, women enjoy parallel status with the men because they also take part in their daily economic activities. Gond women enjoy better status and greater freedom, specially in the choice of a husband, premarital sex licence, seeking of divorce and so forth. But women form a depressed lot in other areas[124]

Tribal life is simple and integrated, devoid of private property. People in Tribes possess hunting weapons and war regalia but this falls short of the institution of private property. Members of the Aquascogoc tribe took a silver cup from English settlers in 1585 and Sir Richard Grenville had their village burned to the ground by way of teaching them a lesson. He left fifteen soldiers to keep the peace but when he returned in 1587, he found only their

---

[124] Samita Manna, *The Fair Sex in Tribal Culturers(sic) Problems and Development* pp.14-15.

bones.[125] In the light of what is now known about human beings living in tribal communities there must be some doubt that the Aquascogoc tribe thought that taking a cup was dishonest by their standards.

In a tribe order is maintained by common accord rather than official censure. It is group censure that counts and the most extreme punishment which can be exacted is banishment.

The Agrarian Society came into existence about 10,000 years ago and it was in this kind of society that the human male, because of his superior strength, became economically dominant. The agrarian society depended upon the domestication of plants and animals. As importantly, land ownership was invented with tenant farmers and share-croppers, the latter too poor to handle money, evolved. Both categories were in thrall to the landlord who could throw them off his land and leave them to starve. On the brighter side, the relative abundance of food produced an increase in population so that there was an abundant supply of labour.[126] Settlements became static and the rich river valleys which produced the food had to be defended by standing armies against hungry outside wandering tribes. Religion was invented to ensure the renewal of the harvest while the priests became expert astronomers to record the seasons of the year. The ploughs were pulled by oxen and as ploughs became

---

[125] Wikipedia.

[126] It is estimated that world human population in 70,000 BCE might have gone through a bottleneck and have been between 1,000 and 10,000. At 10,000BCE it might have been between 1 million and 15 million whereas by the 4th C there were between 50 million and 60 million alive in the whole of the Roman Empire alone.

heavier they required teams of oxen to pull them. Both the cultivator and the soldier required physical strength which put men as economically preeminent. This one fact put women in an inferior position with respect to men. In India in 2002 it was recorded:

...women in general and rural women in particular do not enjoy the status as the male do. It has also been stated that among the rural female, Scheduled Castes and Scheduled Tribes women have been able to make little progress though they also engaged in different occupations along with their male counterpart. [127]

Women in an agrarian society are deemed to be incapable of managing independently and are in the care of a father, a husband or a son in their old age.[128] Women in India perform back-breaking tasks like grinding grain, gathering fuel and feeding children and the elderly. The point is made that the great ladies of India like Indira Gandhi are not Indian women but the daughters of India. At the farm level women are defenceless, marginalised and subjugated.[129]Nor are women paid the same wages as men for the same, or even harder, labour. If this was the situation in India in the last decade, it may safely be assumed that in even more ancient times the situation for women was even harsher. The Bible treats a woman as one of the chattels owned by your neighbour in one famous paragraph:

You shall not covet your neighbour's house: you shall not covet your neighbour's wife, or his male or female slave, or his

---

[127] Dr Ramesh Chaube, Dr Kalpana Saini, *Status of Women in Rural Societies,* p. 51.
[128] Dr Ramesh et al, p.71.
[129] Dr Ramesh et al, p.80.

ox or his ass, or anything that is your neighbour's.[130]

The difficulty which a man finds himself in an agrarian community is that whilst he is superior to a woman he still desires her for many years of his life and if she does not give herself willingly it is a blow to his self-esteem. Worse, if she gives herself to another man and even worse if she goes to school and becomes superior to him.

Dealing first with woman the temptress and, almost by definition, such a woman is evil.

The first woman disseminator of evil to be recorded in writing was by the poet Hesiod in the 8th century BCE: Pandora who opened the box and released all the evils of the world. Pandora herself is known in Greek as *kalon kakon*, the beautiful evil.

Using the translation given by Jack Holland in *A Brief History of Misogyny*: *From her comes all the race of womankind The deadly female race and tribe of wives Who live with mortal man and bring them harm.*

The greater the beauty then the greater the irresistibility of the woman and, therefore, the greater the evil in her nature. The corrupting influence of women was embedded in the puritan mentality. John Milton (1608-74): "He for God only, she for God in him". The necessary subservience of women was one of the characteristics that underpinned a moral society. Lawrence Stone, the social historian, says: *"The ideal woman in the 16th and 17th century was weak, submissive, charitable, virtuous and modest, like the wife of the Massachusetts Minister in the 1630s, whom he publicly praised*

---

[130] Hebrew Study Bible Exodus 20.1, 'covet' in Hebrew means some active preparation to take possession of.

for her incomparable meekness of spirit towards myself especially". I.e. the sort of woman who did her husband's bidding and remained constant only to him.

In the same mould as Pandora came this utterance of Tertullian (160-220CE), one of the early Christians who identified the doctrine of the Trinity:

You are the devil's gateway; you are the unsealer of the forbidden tree; you are the first deserter of Divine law. You are she who persuaded him whom the devil was not valiant enough to attack. You destroyed so easily God's image, man.[131]

The reference to the 'forbidden tree' might be a veiled reference to Eve who, in Greek, persuaded Adam to eat the forbidden fruit. This is not quite as straightforward in Hebrew because Eve (Havva in Hebrew) has a connection with 'giver of life' and, as such, is the equal of Adam ('Man' in Hebrew). Helen of Troy is another staggeringly beautiful seducer though, in her case, she makes no effort but is so beautiful she cannot be resisted. In Euripides' *The Trojan Women*, Hecuba, the widow of Priam, cries out to Menelaus, the victorious Spartan, warning him that Helen has such magic, she is a cup of death. In vain, Helen's beauty is such that Menelaus cannot set her aside and continues their married life.[132]

At the present time in communities which are still largely agricultural, women are not only looked down upon but, at times, do not even get rudimentary justice.

On 22 June 2002, in a remote area of the Punjab, a Pakistani woman named Mukhtaran Bibi was sentenced on

[131] Jack Holland, *A Brief History of Misogyny: The World's Oldest Prejudice*, Loc 217 Kindle Ed.
[132] Jack Holland, Loc 457.

the orders of the tribal council to be gang raped because,
allegedly, her brother had been seen in the company of a higher
caste woman.[133]

In fact her young brother, Shakur of the Tatla agricultural tribe, had allegedly had sex with Salma, a young girl of the Mastoi tribe, also owners of land for agriculture. It was the insult to their tribe which was considered by the tribal council. The sentence was carried out by four men, raping her for an hour in spite of her pleas for mercy. This was after her family had offered compensation of marriage and land. Her brother had been raped (sodomised) by three Mastoi men but Mukhtaran Bibi was publicly humiliated and her life should have been ruined. That was the intention. However, Mukhtaran became a human rights activist, was declared woman of the year 2005 by Glamour Magazine, married a police constable in 2009 and had a child in 2011. It seems that the tribe which Mukhtaran belonged to, the Tatla, were considered 'lower' than the Matloi and atonement could only be made by illicit sex being avenged by illicit sex. This is the code of retaliation which the Quran (Sura 2.178) explicitly qualifies and the Tatla family's offer of compensation should have been accepted. This episode illustrates that certain aspects of primitive custom date from a time well before the divine revelation which gave birth to the Quran. The rape and humiliation of both Mukhtaran and her brother is related more to some ancient code of compensation and restoring the honour of the tribe who still abided by a law of retaliation. It is often very ancient codes of honour which govern the behaviour

---

[133] Jack Holland, Loc 179.

of present-day people. Retaliation was found in Babylonian law and in Judaism (Exodus 21.24) which, like Shia Islam has its roots in Mesopotamia.

The sexual mutilation of women involves several degrees of severity depending on the degree of 'purity' sought by the parents of the child. In increasing order of severity it begins with the removal of the clitoral hood and clitoral glans, removal of the inner labia, in the most severe form the removal of the inner and outer labia and closure of the vulva. In this most severe form, a small hole is left for the passage of urine and menstrual fluid, the vagina is opened for intercourse and opened further for child birth. These procedures are performed with or without anaesthesia[134] and sometime before the age of fifteen. This incredibly savage procedure is sincerely believed to have some religious significance which gives it legitimacy and the World Health Organisation in 2013 estimated that, at that time 125 million women and girls had been genitally cut.

Muslim scholars have differed on whether any form of genital cutting is required, recommended or optional in Islam. There is evidence in the hadith from Sunan Abu Dawood:

A woman used to perform circumcision in Medina. The Prophet said to her: Do not cut severely as that is better for a woman and more desirable for a husband.[135]

In Egypt, though the practice has been banned since 2007, in 2013 27.2 million women had undergone some sort of FGM. FGM in Egypt is not

---

[134] Wikipedia, Female Genital Mutilation.
[135] Wikipedia, Religious Views on Female Genital Mutilation

confined to Muslims but is also practiced among the Copts, but is carried out mostly in Upper Egypt and in 2007 nearly all Coptic women were cut.[136] In Ethiopia 92% of Muslims, 72% of Protestants, 67% of Catholics and 67% of traditional religions were all cut in spite of the fact that it had been illegal since 2004. As in Europe where the incidence is much lower, it is not enforced. It is futile to blame religion for this brutal procedure.

The result of FGM is well documented:

Excision of the clitoris and/or other sensitive parts of female genitalia reduces the female sexual response, may lead anorgasmia and even frigidity, cases of tight infibulations, where the husbands are unable to penetrate the vagina, resort to anal intercourse or even use the urethral meatus as an opening and consummation of the marriage may take several weeks. The process of infibulations is painful and may take a long time, up to two years, to complete the consummation during which women seek medical help for infertility.

The psychological and social impact of being sterile is profound because a woman's worth is usually measured by her fertility.

On the other hand, some circumcised women report having satisfying sexual relations including sexual desire, pleasure and orgasm.[137]

---

[136] Assyrian News Agency, 26 Jan 2007, published on the Internet.
[137] Baasher T, Psychological Aspects of female circumcision in traditional practice affecting health of woman, 1979. Report of a seminar WHO/EMRO Publication No 2.

It has to be accepted that in most cases the women become frigid and are in intense pain during intercourse. Anecdotal evidence obtained by the author, described above, suggests, but is by no means conclusive, that the pain will ensure that the woman does not seek sexual enjoyment and therefore is unlikely to be unfaithful to her husband. The shame to the man of being cuckolded is more probably avoided so that, if the poor child has been 'purified' it makes her more desirable and her bride price might go up.

FGM appears to have no basis in faith but is tied to the locality in which it takes place. The author suggests that it is related to the agrarian economy where women are treated as chattels. Egypt where FGM is prevalent has exports of which 80% are oil which is handled by foreigners, and 20% cotton and other agrarian products which are produced by the rest of the population who are employed. The amount of industrialisation is minimal.

Another primitive practice directed at women is 'honour killing', the murder of a young girl to preserve the honour of a family in families which are so poor that honour is all they have. This is similar to FGM in that it preserves the honour of the family and it is better that the child should die than that the father or the brothers have no control over her. If you have no control over a mere girl what sort of a

Dorkeno E, Elworthy S, Proposals for change Minority Rights Group International 1992 379/381 Brixton Road London SW97 DE UK.

El Dareer, Female circumcision and its consequences for mother and child Yaounde 1979.

CR Horowitz, JC Jackson, Female Circumcision. Journal of General Internal Medicine Aug 1999.

man are you? The girl might have done no more than wear Western clothes or even date a young man without the permission of the father. If the girl is pretty there is the possibility of a bride price and she might even bring with her the chance of a Western passport. All these are factors which may or may not have some bearing on the girl's death.

With the increase of migration after the Second World War (1939-1945) and the flood of oil money which entered the Middle East, this made some of these men very rich indeed. Nevertheless, the tribal customs they were born with remained with them and amongst these customs was the murder of the daughters who failed to obey their fathers. The actual task of killing the girl was given to the youngest son who was still unmarried and still a minor so that, in most jurisdictions, he would be given a lighter sentence. Even if not a minor it was still the duty of one of the male relatives, even the father, to do the killing.

Though not poor, the Shafia family decided to murder three daughters and a first wife in an episode which took place in Canada in 2009[138]. Mohammed Shafia came from Afghanistan and seems to have been quite an astute man of business making money out of electronics in Kabul where he married Rona Amin Mohammed. Mohammed travelled to Dubai and settled there making a small fortune in real estate. Unfortunately Mona was unable to have children. In 1989 Shafia married Tooba Yahya and she gave birth to seven children. When in Canada the older three

---

[138] Michae Friscolati, *The Shafia Honour Killing Trial* and Wikipedia.

girls wore tight jeans and painted their nails. They had boyfriends, fell in love and behaved like other young Canadian girls so that Shafia not only considered them 'too Westernised' but he lost control of them in spite of warnings and beatings.[139] The first wife, Rona, was kept as a servant by retaining her travel documents and refusing her a divorce. Hamed Shafia, acting on behalf of his father and mother beat his four sisters over the head, put them in a car, three in the backseat, one in the front, and pushed them with a second car into the Rideau Canal. The three suspects gave contradictory evidence and while they were being questioned the police put a microphone in their camper van. The evidence gained was not admissible in court but many admissions of guilt were overheard:

Even if they hoist me up onto the gallows, nothing is more dear to me than my honour. Let's leave our destiny to God and may God never make me, you or your mother honourless.

There is no value of life without honour

All three defendants were found guilty of first-degree murder and are serving life sentences without the possibility of parole.

In the primary agrarian societies of the world where a living is scratched from the land, the man owns the women in his family like chattels and their honourable behaviour is not only his responsibility but reflects on him and on the whole family. The honour of the family is vested in the women and once lost, can never be restored except by death. Even

---

[139] Michael Friscolati, Loc 245, Loc 270, Loc 1862. Rona too was subjected to beatings Loc 216, Loc 1340, Loc 2913.

when the family have moved away from the land into the towns to become market stall holders and, sometimes, shop keepers, the same sense of honour has travelled with them. A woman, like a piece of white silk, once stained can never be cleaned again.[140] Honour killing is primarily a crime against young women and, worldwide, the average age of the victims is 23 years. Again two thirds of these young victims are killed by their families, sometimes by multiple members of their family and nearly half were tortured before death and died in agony. Like the Shafia killings described above, more than half are murdered for being 'too Western' which means being too independent, not being subservient or refusing to wear Islamic clothing. Friends from another ethnic group is also considered 'too Western'. Outside Europe nearly half the young women are murdered because they have committed a sexual impropriety like being raped, having an alleged extra marital affair or even being considered 'promiscuous'. All without evidence, mere gossip is sufficient to take a woman's life.[141]

The most cogent explanation for this behaviour is given by a young man called Murat who killed his mother. Ayse Onal in her book *Honour Killing: Stories of Men Who Killed* gives the facts of her interviews with ten honour killers which she used in her television programme in Turkey. Murat's mother, Hanim, was subjected to an arranged marriage when she was still under the age of sixteen. Her husband was a night watchman. She must have been beautiful because an

---

[140] Hero in Much Ado About Nothing
[141] Phyllis Chesler, Middle East Quarterly, Spring 2010 pp.3-11.

earlier proposal involved gifts of gold but she, herself, resisted this because it involved leaving her home town of Urfa. Her husband's job of night watchman soon allowed her to start an affair with her cousin and Murat, while still a child, remembered hearing them together when his mother used the same terms of endearment to him as she used to Murat: *'My lion, my hero, my ram'.* Even as a child Murat began to hear rumours about a man his mother let into the house at night when she was alone. He attended the mosque and learned from the Imam. His uncle gave him a stall in the market and he began an affair with a married woman who was a regular customer. He slowly discovered that his affair was fairly common knowledge and he went through torment and guilt. To the fury of his mistress, he fell in love with a girl and went to see his mother who gave him her life's savings she had hidden in a mattress. He then went to the girl's family who told him that his family were unworthy of their daughter and the girl, herself was threatened with death from her brother if she went on seeing him. His uncle told him to clean the stain on his family's honour and gave him a fistful of notes. At the next meeting, the girl he loved had been severely beaten and could only see through one eye. With difficulty, the girl said:

'My mother says your mother is a bad woman and that you are a bastard. They will never give me to you. I told you to take me away and now it is too late. They have taken me out of school and my older brother beat me up. They are forcing me to get married. Your mother has deprived me of my education. What kind of mother is that?'

Everything Murat hoped to live for was in ruins.

Murat went home, took his father's gun and held it to his head. His mother came in and they exchanged a few words. 'His mother bowed her head: *"I know what I did, my son, may God forgive me."* She fell silent again, took a deep breath, then whispered: *"Shoot my son. It is my destiny".* He remembered firing three shots'. His mother had bowed her head to make it easier for him.

Everyone deserted him and he gave himself up to the police. He was not a minor when he fired the shots and he got the full sentence. No one came to visit him. At the end of the interview with Ayse Onal he made the following statement:

'The conclusion is a mother cannot be bad. I don't need to explain how sacred the person who brought me into the world is. But people also think this: when a father does the same thing...you forgive him, you don't take it as a personal offence, you say, "He's a man, he's my father, it's completely nature." Bur when your mother does it, you can't accept it. And when people get to hear of it you can't accept it at all. You lose all respect in the eyes of society and feel oppressed. You feel very lowly among them as though you're something inferior, insignificant.

I was involved with someone too, even though she was married. I asked her why she was unfaithful to her husband..." *Because he does not take any notice of me, or pay any attention to me."* When I asked another woman I knew who was unfaithful to her husband she said *"Because the brute beats me. I do it for revenge..."'*

'...The person you have killed has the same blood as you. Your mother, your wife, your daughter, your sister. When you consider it logically there is always an alternative. If you have not lost the use of your reason you can always consult someone and find some solution. People's mentality has to change, and

the only solution to that is economic and cultural.'

As a complete after thought Onal asked him: '*Are you religious?*' and immediately regretted it.

'*Don't worry, If what you are asking is why my religious beliefs didn't stop me committing murder, I'll tell you. For someone who is oppressed, public censure carries more weight than religious commandments...'*

'*You'll ask, has your honour been cleansed? No, it's much worse now. I've become a murderer. I've murdered my own mother. I've lost my entire family and all of my friends. I don't know where I'm headed in the next life. Allah knows it, but the most likely place for me in the next life is hell.*[142]

Murat's soliloquy is well worth reading in full. It might be the most profound statement on the importance of human 'self-worth' ever written. It points to the heart of the matter for the primitive mind. The honour of the family is carried by the women of the family. If a man cannot control his woman, what sort of man is he? He is a laughing stock among his fellow men and therefore the woman must die. It is the same with stalking. This beautiful girl is my girl and when she dumps him, she must die to save him from looking a fool. Love does not enter into it. The only sentiment such a man felt was lust and then humiliation.

In Britain the lot of women began to improve in the 18th century with the start of the industrial revolution which centred on the wool trade and women began working at home in cottage industries. Women commonly carried out carding, combing out

---

[142] Ayse Onal, Chapter 2 Headed Hanim.

the wool for spinning, and spinning itself on a large spinning wheel. Men sheared the sheep by hand and without power and more commonly did the weaving. Women were thus making a considerable contribution to household income as well as caring for the children which was accepted then, as it is today, as part of the natural order of things. The English peasant had started to be forced off the land by the Inclosure Acts which began in 1614 and went on until 1914 so that there was ample labour for the cottage industries and the industrial factory revolution which followed it.

However, all the money brought in by the wife in wages or the sale of cloth belonged to her husband under the principle of coverture described by Blackstone as follows:

By marriage, the husband and wife are one person in law: that is, the very being or legal existence of the woman is suspended during the marriage, or at least is incorporated and consolidated into that of the husband: under whose wing, protection, and cover, she performs every thing; and is therefore called in our law-French a feme-covert; is said to be covert-baron, or under the protection and influence of her husband, her baron, or lord; and her condition during her marriage is called her coverture. Upon this principle, of a union of person in husband and wife, depend almost all the legal rights, duties, and disabilities, that either of them acquire by the marriage. I speak not at present of the rights of property, but of such as are merely personal. For this reason, a man cannot grant any thing to his wife, or enter into covenant with her: for the grant would be to suppose her separate existence; and to covenant with her, would be only to covenant with himself: and therefore it is also generally true, that all compacts made between husband and wife, when single, are voided by the intermarriage.[143]

The use of power, either steam or water mill, gobbled up men for the factories and left women in the home or taking in piecework such as washing, ironing or sewing. Outside the home there was domestic service. The more educated, usually single, women could get work as teachers or nannies. Any money earned by a married woman belonged automatically to her husband.

After the industrial revolution, the labour market was looking for men. Women were abused both verbally and physically by men who looked upon them as inferior chattels who could not manage without a man. Jack London (1876-1916) made a study of the East End of London, then occupied by one million people living in one of the worst slums in the world, and said: *"... The men are economically dependent on their masters and the women are economically dependent on the men. The result is the women get the beating the man should give the master and she can do nothing..."* She was an ideal object of abuse being both physically weaker and economically dependent on the man who was beating her. Happily, this is no longer the case and though abuse still takes place, it is much reduced.

This was remedied by the Married Woman's Property Act, 1870, when a woman was allowed to own money in her own right. Women had been campaigning for such legislation since the 1850s and had to campaign much longer for the right to own land until a further Married Woman's Property Act

---

[143] Blackstone Commentaries on the Laws of England in the 18th century.

was passed in 1882. Out of sheer necessity, women were recruited for the factories and became wage earners, during the two world wars. The right to vote in Europe was granted first in the Isle of Man in 1881 and last in Liechtenstein in 1984. Full rights were not given in the United Kingdom (which includes Northern Ireland) until 1928 and it had to be fought for. Blacks in the Southern States of the United States had their votes effectively negated by shifting the electoral boundaries until 1965 when this kind of gerrymandering was stopped.[144] The right to vote shows that even the most basic democratic right has to be insisted on or it will be overlooked. British GDP in real terms has grown from 86million to 382million between 1955 and 2013 i.e. 4.4 times.[145] In the US growth from 1955 to 2013 has been from 2.5trillion dollars to 15trillion i.e. 6 times. [146] To achieve this kind of growth, it is impossible to ignore half the population and more and more women have been employed in executive jobs.

Until about 1990 there was still a prejudice against employing women in the most senior jobs in Britain. There is an observed fact of sociodynamics that any minority in any organisation will make itself felt when its proportion in the organisation reaches a tipping point or critical mass after which its presence in the organisation continues to grow. One American writer puts that tipping point for women at between 20%

---

[144] Wikipedia, 'Women's Suffrage' and 'Racial Segregation in the US'.

[145] Office of National Statistics quoted in Guardian Data.

[146] Standard and Poor.

and 30%.[147] In both Congress and Senate, women represent about 20% of the total membership and 35% of Federal judges are women. In Britain, women were allowed by the Representation of the People Act to become members of Parliament in 1918. One of the members for Plymouth was the first woman elected in 1919 and at the time of writing 29.6% of the total membership of the House of Commons are women. 55% of the judges under the age of 40 are women[148] 50% of law students are women[149]. It would very much appear that the influence of women is here to stay.

---

[147] Jay Newton-Small, *Broad Influence: How Women Are Changing the Way America Works.*

[148] The Guardian Newspaper, July 2015.

[149] National Women's Law Centre, 1992.

CHAPTER 8

THE DELUSION OF
RATIONALISING PREJUDICE

At the present time, those with high self-esteem but suffering from what they imagine is some sort of defect, usually sexual but not always, and need someone to look down on, usually choose Jews because of the bombing of Gaza and the lack of equality accorded Palestinians. Those who are subjected to discrimination themselves also gain comfort from being very critical of Israel and by some sort of inference, Jews in general. They might not even know any Jews. Others, less intelligent usually, choose to gain comfort by looking down on foreigners. The most common reason they give themselves is that immigrants are taking 'our jobs' even though they have no evidence of this and can become abusive and even violent towards people arguing against this proposition and, as it were, standing between them and happiness. Some, see Muslims as the 'nation's enemy' after a murderous atrocity carried out in the name of Islam. They might even see Israel as their ally because Israelis are seen as the enemies of Islam. Presidential candidate Donald Trump was quoted as saying: '*Overseas ISIS has carried out one unthinkable atrocity after another. Children slaughtered, girls sold into slavery, men and women burned alive. Crucifixions, beheadings and drowning. Ethnic minorities targeted for execution. Holy sites desecrated' Christians driven from their homes and hunted for extermination. ISIS rounding up what it calls "nations of the cross" in a campaign of genocide. We cannot let this evil continue'.*[150] Examples of this can found in Syria but it cannot justify banning the flight of Muslims fleeing the very terror he describes, from entering the USA because these people are, beyond reasonable doubt, innocent.[151] Many people suffering relative economic hardship believe vehemently that they could regain control of their lives if barriers were put up to exclude foreign nationals.

Everyone who loses their locus of control needs some form of prejudice to give them their sense of control back and disguise and dignify it by purporting to give it some sort of rational basis. Some of the reasons given to rationalise contemptible treatment are fantastic. In the era of slavery in the United States, the rape of black women was justified by saying that black women were avid for sex and welcomed the brutal attentions of their white owners. The owners of slaves, at least some of them, would rape the women even when they themselves were married to a white woman. Rape is clearly, in any modern culture, wrong, but it was rationalised by saying that black women were closer to animals and loved sex at any time. In such a case the rapist need never use force and was exonerated of all blame.

Going back to Chapter 4, the psychology students

---

[150] Dr Susan Berry, article in Breitbart 16 August 2016.
[151] Lizzie Deardene, Independent Saturday 28 January 2017.

who were told they were below average intelligence regained some of their self-worth and control by doing a disservice to and marking down, what they thought was a Jewish applicant for a job. It is in this way that racism continues and is maintained. They were showing that no matter how low their intelligence rating, they were superior to a Jewish woman when they were allowed to express an opinion which injured her and they felt better for it.[152]

Sir Gerald Kaufman, a British MP, alleged in letters to the Guardian Newspaper (posted 10.9.14) that, inter alia, Sir Charles Taylor had told him to go back to Tel Aviv. Sir Gerald Kaufman was born in Leeds, went to Leeds Grammar School and then Oxford. He became MP for Manchester Ardwick in 1970. So far as one can tell, he had never lived in Tel Aviv and had possibly only been there as a casual visitor. It might be relevant that Sir Charles was a member of the Order of St John of Jerusalem, whose members are protestant but other Christians are admitted by invitation. They are all chosen by invitation.

To a person with something in their character which they are ashamed of, anyone with a foreign name will always be an immigrant and it is considered by many, normal to tell them to go back where they came from. In the mind of the staunch Christian with a 'defect' in their past which they are ashamed of, the rationalisation is, as has been shown, that the Jews killed the Christian saviour or, more to the point, that the Jews behave brutally towards the Palestinians. Therefore all Jews are evil and should go back to where they came from. The latest piece of

---

[152] See Racial Hierarchy, Chapter 2.

rationalisation is that East Europeans are taking British jobs and should be evicted from the country. At a recent referendum in 2016 the majority of the British population voted to stop the arrival of East European immigrants. One man interviewed thought he was voting for the removal of Muslims and reinforced what Socrates thought of the 'common man'. British productivity is one of the lowest in Europe, 70% that of Germany,[153] and until that is remedied, Britain can only remain competitive by using cheap immigrant labour and making up a skill shortage which ranges from plumbers to surgeons. This can only be changed by training British born people with a will to succeed.

What follows is a logical examination of the main reasons damaged people give themselves for prejudice.

8a An Examination of the Historical Basis of the Gospels

The Christian conviction that the Jews caused the death of Christ has been the cornerstone of rationalising the abuse of Jews. It is worth examining whether this claim is true. This examination places emphasis on the works of Flavius Josephus (37-c100CE) and on the Aramaic gospels still used by the Christian communities of Syria, the Peshitta, because these sources are closer to the events to be examined and Aramaic, it may be inferred, was the original language of the gospels. Where the gospels portray Jesus fulfilling a biblical prophecy, the reader should regard that with a critical eye.

---

[153] The Guardian, 24 November 2016.

The original Jesus, depicted in the Gospels, was the originator of a social movement to distance Jews from rabbinic Judaism which latter was, almost by definition, very legalistic, onerous and burdensome on poor people who had to work seven days per week to survive. The Talmud records many strictures on not doing work on the Sabbath. An example of Jesus's interpretation of the law is contained in Matthew 12: 'At that time Jesus went through the grainfields on the Sabbath; his disciples were hungry and they began to pluck heads of grain and to eat.' Jesus was accosted by the Pharisees who always took a narrow legalistic view that work on the Sabbath was forbidden. The work was that plucking ears of corn was reaping forbidden by the law (Exodus 34.21). Jesus simply replied: 'They are hungry.' This should be the principal of humane social treatment of those in need but is lacking even to the present time.

Clearly Jesus is postulating that there is a greater law than is found in the Talmud and, since it is doubtful whether a Galilean or any Jew believed that the whole of the Bible was the word of God he is quoting the First Book of Samuel 21 as evidence of former practice. No Jew could 'work' on the Sabbath but the definition of work was legalistic in the extreme. For example, Mishna 1 of the Babylonian Talmud stipulated the maximum amount of food which could be carried around on the Sabbath before it amounted to 'work': a goblet of wine and water, a mouthful of milk, honey sufficient to cover a wound and so forth. Very small quantities, and very burdensome to people who did not have non-Jewish servants or slaves, who could be ordered to carry as much food as was required. Jesus rebelled against all these strictures and became a champion of the poor.

It will be demonstrated that the name 'Jesus' was taken over by a later generation of Jews who rebelled against Rome then taken over again and added to by the Hellenic population of Israel by adding episodes from the pagan Greek religion, presumably to make it familiar and acceptable to a Hellenic population. Judaism also offered resurrection at the end of the world and so they too offered a resurrecting god who was renewed every year. Such gods are familiar in agrarian economies to bring about renewal in the spring. It was this amalgam of Judaism, the rebellion against Rome, and Hellenistic cults which became Christianity. The early words of Jesus have been largely submerged under the later additions but are still discernible in Quakerism and in the behaviour of what are thought of as good people. The author recalls hearing the story of a Benedictine priest who abandoned his headmastership of a big school to give comfort to an elderly widow whose son had just died with the words 'people count'.

The longer ending of Mark does not appear in the Sinaiatic Codex written in about 380CE and so must have been added later. The gospels were written and added to over a period of hundreds of years.

The gospels are dotted with the social rebellion on behalf of the poor which might be taken as coming from the time of Jesus. The requirement of ritual purity to be found by a reading of Leviticus in relation leaving a woman alone when she is having her menstrual period (Leviticus 18.19) was designed to protect women and given the general term *Niddah* included inter alia, adultery, in which both parties became unclean. By the time of Jesus, this simple requirement had been subdivided into *tumah* and *tahareh* with non-mandatory clarification *Vestos, Bedikah, Ben niddah and bat niddah* and subdivided into *Onah benonit, veset hachodesh and veset haflagah.*[154] The interpretation of these strictures require more space than this book is capable of and a far greater intellect than the present author possesses. Jesus deals with the matter by means of a miracle when a woman with an issue of blood touches his cloak and is immediately cured (e.g. Matthew 9.20). One can only suppose that that was wishful thinking. Jesus himself would have been subject to the requirements of ritual purity having come into contact with a woman who was *Niddah*.

An outstanding example of ignoring the rules, in this case the impurity contracted by possibly touching a dead body, made the observant Judean pass by on the other side of the road. The Samaritan, lower in the social hierarchy than a Judean, cared for the injured man (Luke 10.25). The ritual purity requirements for touching a dead body were particularly onerous and Jesus provides this story as an example of common humanity taking precedence over regulations. The meaning of the story is still being discussed and the interpretation given here would not be universally accepted.

It must be clear from what has gone before that the main argument to justify the hatred of Jews has been that Jews were the killers of Jesus. It is always true that those who need to hate somebody, are doing so to alleviate some sense of failure in themselves and raise their own feeling of self-respect. In Christian

---

[154] Wikipedia, Niddah.

countries the people to hate are the Jews because they are guilty of deicide, in other parts of the world it is women who are kept down and even their education is resented. Any man in a lowly state could say: 'If a schoolgirl knows more than I do then what am I?' In the meantime, because the culpability of the Jews is taught in every church at every Easter, it is worth considering the historicity of the gospel account of the death of Jesus and to look at it in a completely dispassionate way.

It will be demonstrated that the Gospels, when read with care, divide themselves into three parts: The original Jewish Jesus; a later Jewish addition to the story of Jesus and, finally, a Greek addition based upon the Greek religion and sects. There was a final addition in the 4th century when Christianity reached Rome.

From the tone of the Gospels but without any historical justification, it seems logical to say that they were first listened to by the very poor who could not read or write, and therefore were probably an oral tradition.[155] This is not an unreasonable assumption because the Mishnah, the earliest part of the Talmud, was also an oral tradition and was not written down until after the destruction of the Temple in Jerusalem in the year 70 CE.[156] In a second stage the gospel oral tradition would have been written down in various places in the Levant whether story of Jesus was popular. There were a great many of these collections which might account for the 50-odd versions,

---

[155] Poverty in the whole of Israel is an accepted fact in some quarters. See for example Richard Horsley, *Bandits Prophets and Messiahs*, p.52 et seq.

[156] Jewish Annotated New Testament, p.1.

including the Gnostic Gospels, which have survived to the present day. In a third stage these collections got bigger and became more consolidated. The choice was made on the basis of popularity and could therefore be said to have been chosen by divine providence: for example: the Greek Church base their choice on a letter from Athanasius in 367 CE; the Latin Church base their decision on the Synod of Rome in 382 CE; the African Church made its decision on the synods at Hippo in 393 CE and Carthage in 397 CE (they followed Rome); the Syrian Church, who spoke Aramaic, are closest to the oldest version of the Gospels, the Peshitta, which they retain to the present day. The Ethiopian Church also followed Rome.

Jesus is said to be the Messiah which simply means one who is anointed king. The expectation of an anointed one appears in several parts of the Old Testament but, quoting 1 Chronicles 17.11-12 as the most explicit: "*And I declare to you: the Lord will build a house for you. When your days are done and you follow your fathers, I will raise up your offspring after you, one of your own sons, and I will establish his kingship. He shall build a house for Me, and I will establish his throne forever.*"

This is the word of God and it can be seen that in the Jewish version, the derivation of the Messiah was a mortal man. There was no question of creating a deity.

"I know that my Redeemer liveth", apart from being an exquisite aria from Handel's Messiah is a line taken out of Job 19.25. Reverting to the Hebrew, the word for 'lives' is 'Haiy' meaning 'living' in the sense of being a living entity (BDB 312). Following this, another translation might be: "The one who redeems me is alive". This biblical edict was developed in the book of Daniel 2.4 for-45 in which the arrival of the Messiah heralds the establishment of the kingdom of God.

The original Jesus begins with his home town. In Mark, translated from the Greek into English he is said to be Jesus of Nazareth, but the Aramaic version of Chapter 9 says quite clearly that he is one of the Nazerot of Galilee and this is much more likely than his derivation from Nazareth, a town which, in all probability, did not exist until the beginning of the 3rd century. Nazareth is possibly a bad translation of Nazerot when going from the original Aramaic into Greek and Jesus being a Nazarite fulfils the prophecy in Judges 13.3:

And the Angel of the Lord appeared unto the woman, and said unto her, Behold now, thou art barren, and bearest not: but thou shalt conceive, and bear a son. Now therefore beware, I pray thee, and drink not wine nor strong drink, eat not any unclean thing: For, lo, thou shalt conceive, and bear a son; and no razor shall come on his head: for the child shall be a Nazarite unto God from the womb: and he shall begin to deliver Israel out of the hand of the Philistines. Then the woman came and told her husband, saying, a man of God came unto me, and his countenance was like the countenance of an angel of God, very terrible: but I asked him not whence he was neither told he me his name: But he said unto me, behold thou shalt conceive and bear a son; and now drink no wine nor strong drink neither eat any unclean thing: for the child shall be a Nazarite to God from the womb to the day of his death.

A Nazarite was somebody who took a vow for as little as a month and for as much as his whole life to:

Abstain from the vine. All the days of his Nazariteship

shall he eat nothing that is made of the Grapevine from the pressed grapes even to the grape stone (Numbers 6.4).

He shall refrain from cutting his hair-all the days of his vow of Nazariteship there shall be no razor come upon his head (Numbers 6.5).

Avoid death-All the days he consecrateth himself unto the Lord he shall not come near to a dead body. This part of the Nazirite vow extends even to the Nazirite's own family (numbers 6.7)

The argument that Jesus was a Nazirite and avoided of the fruit of the vine is supported by the Gospels saying: *'And he took the cup, and gave thanks, and said, take this, and divide it among yourselves: For I say unto you, I will not drink of the fruit of the vine until the kingdom of God shall come.'* (Luke 22.17). While Jesus being a Nazirite is the fulfilment of a biblical prophecy, it is perfectly possible, that, in real life Jesus *was* a Nazirite.

The virgin birth of Jesus's mother Mary has a long and complicated history. It started with the prevalence of rape by an occupying army of Romans which stretched through the whole of the Levant. In Rome itself the use of rape was a crime but the use of violence to achieve its ends was not an aggravating circumstance until the days of Augustus and only rape where penetration occurred was punishable. Attempted rape was not a crime and this was the state of affairs against Roman citizens[157]. Against non-Romans in the provinces, it can well be imagined that rape was widely tolerated. The rape of Jewish women was as equally common an event as the rape of any other woman. In Alexandria in particular it appears

---

[157] Natalie Schwarz, *Corruption in Ancient Rome*, Kindle Edition.

that young women were raped before marriage to such an extent that Rabbi Hillel was called in to give guidance. The obvious problem was that the husband, when he discovered that his wife had known another man, albeit unwillingly, was ready to set her and the unborn child aside. The equally obvious problem was that the wife and child had to be provided for. Rabbi Hillel gave his judgement on the problem in a very legalistic sort of way. He said that the marriage contract was made to create a marriage as soon as the couple stepped under the Chupha (canopy). It made no special provision for children and therefore the husband had to care for all his wife's property and therefore he had to care for both the wife and the unborn child.[158] Moreover, if a woman was with child at the time she married, that child was not a bastard. It seems to be the case that if the woman gave herself willingly to another man then she was committing fraud on her husband, the child would be a bastard and the husband had no obligation to care for it. The judgement of Rabbi Hillel can be discerned in Chapter 1.19 of the book of Matthew. When Joseph discovers that Mary is with child it says:

"Then Joseph her husband, being a just man, and not willing to make her a public example, was minded to put her away privily."

Without the judgement of Hillel the Talmud was very harsh on bastardy but the fact that Jesus was not to be treated as a bastard enabled him to be a descendant of David or Solomon, depending on the terms of the gospel which was followed, and therefore, in Jewish eyes at that time, Jesus could be a

---

[158] Babylonian Talmud, p.276.

great social reformer freeing the poor from the bonds of the Talmud. It is worth noting that Jesus himself never claimed to be the Messiah and the Gospel of Matthew describes him, as he dies, as an apocalyptic prophet. The idea that a lowly born man who might have even been of doubtful parentage could still convey the word of God was an overturning of conventional thinking. The story of the immaculate conception obscured all that for the established Church leaving only the Quakers to carry the torch.[159] The immaculate conception is so alien to Jewish thinking at the time that it must be a subsequent addition to the birth story. In support of this are the words of Celsus, a 2nd-century Greek philosopher, as relayed by Origen, an early Christian father. In his book, *The True Word*, Celsus claims that the natural father of Jesus was a Roman soldier named Pantera. Whether this is true or false, probably the latter, the name Pantera is not Roman, but the Panther is the Greek symbol for the God, Dionysus,[160] and when the Greeks took over the story of Jesus, which will be demonstrated later, they introduced his divine birth with the following words:

…Behold, the Angel of the Lord appeared unto them in a dream, saying Joseph, thou son of David, fear not to take unto thee Mary thy wife: for that which is conceived in her is of the Holy Ghost.

There is a curious parallel in the Palestinian Talmud that Jesus was Ben Pandera, whose nickname was Ben Stada, who was accused of bringing magic

---

[159] Advices and Queries No. 35: 'Respect the laws of the state but let your first loyalty be to God's purposes…'.

[160] Dr Susanna Roxman, List of Emblems of Classical Deities.

out of Egypt. According to Rabbi Eliezer ben Hyrcanus (c45-117) the magic was smuggled out in an incision in his body. Dionysus, the god with a mortal mother, Semele, was born from an incision in the thigh of Zeus. Ben Stada was stoned and hanged on the day before Passover, the same day Jesus died according to John. John is the most Hellenistic of the four gospels and according to Clement of Alexandria (c 150-211/216) was written to supplement the pre-existing gospels.

With the failing health ending with the death of Herod the Great in 4 BCE, a number of Messianic figures appeared in the power vacuum that prevailed. Horsley describes two of them: Judas the son of a bandit c4BCE, and a shepherd called Athronges c4-2BCE. There were also a number of social bandits, rather on the style of Robin Hood, who robbed the rich and occasionally benefited the poor. Such people arise in poverty-stricken agrarian economies and Horsley suggests the Galilean Cave Brigands and Eleazar ben Dinai, both appeared early in the 1st century. Jesus was neither a Messianic figure nor a Bandit as will be demonstrated by his dying words and the account in Matthew.

Josephus tells us that Judaea was out of control and full of robberies and so it was up to the procurator, Gratus, to restore Roman rule. This goes some way to explaining his energetic behaviour calling in the Roman legions from Damascus and the crucifixion of thousands of Jews. He cast about to find a high priest who could help him with pinpointing the troublemakers among the locals. At that time the high priest was a Roman appointee.

Gratus's story is as follows:

In 15 CE the Emperor Tiberius sent Valerius Gratus as Procurator of Judaea. Gratus removed Eleazar ben Ananus from the high priesthood and appointed Simon ben Camithus. He then removed him and after only a year he appointed Joseph Caiaphas. Gratus had then been in Judea 11 years and went back to Rome to be replaced by Pontius Pilate in 26 CE. It might well be supposed that these changes in the high priesthood were not motivated by the spiritual welfare of the Jewish people. Procurators took these posts on the fringes of the Roman Empire in order to become rich and to maintain an iron discipline over the local population. The job of the high priest, so far as the procurator was concerned, was to pay regular sums of money for the privilege of being high priest and to provide information in order to apprehend any disorderly element in the countryside. In 15 CE the situation was almost out of control and General Varus had to come south from Damascus with at least two legions to restore Roman rule after which he crucified some 2,000 Jewish prisoners. The power to appoint a high priest must have been a perk because there is a note about Agrippa II, when only 17 and recently arrived from Rome and owning no land around the temple was given the right to appoint the priest by the Emperor Claudius.[161]

There is an example of Joseph Caiaphas earning his salt in Matthew 26.47:

While he was still speaking, Judas, one of the twelve, arrived; with him was a large crowd with swords and clubs,

---

[161] Josephus, Antiquities Book XX.8.11.

from the chief priests and the elders of the people.

This is the only example of an actual arrest, this time of Jesus, by the irregular vigilantes summoned up by a High Priest.

The Gospels portray Pontius Pilate as being a rather weak, decent man manipulated by the Jewish high priest but the historical Pontius Pilate, depicted by Josephus in Antiquities Book 17, is nothing but an energetic, ruthless Roman leader. As an example there is an account of a charlatan holy man who was going to show the Samaritans where the treasures of Moses were buried on Mount Gerazzim. At a time when a great throng of people were gathered together to go up the mountain, Pilate arrived in person with a large number of armed men and prevented them going up by closing the side roads. The armed men and horsemen fell upon those who were gathered together in the nearby village of Tirathaba and killed them. Those that put up a fight or fled were, on Pilate's direct orders, pursued and killed. There is no record of anyone being captured and put on trial. They were slaughtered for no other reason but that they were there in the hope of seeing the treasures of Moses. Jesus was treated with slightly more consideration. Jesus is what Horsley describes as an apocalyptic prophet. Three occasions when he predicts his own death are given in Wikipedia but the description in Matthew 28.45 et seq describe the end of the world with the veil of the Temple being rent in two and mankind coming face-to-face with God, the very earth splitting and the bodies of the Saints rising from their graves. This is an image of the resurrection. It never happened, of course, and subsequent followers of the faith have quietly forgotten that it was the most momentous event hoped for by the suffering poor of Israel. They had taken as much as they could bear.

The high priest who apprehended Jesus on the Mount of Olives merely had to ascertain whether he had got the right man. In Matthew 27.63 the high priest says to Jesus: "...Tell us if you are the Messiah, the son of God." To which Jesus gives a reply which is out of character with the rest of the gospel. He says: "You have said so." The high priest takes him to Pontius Pilate who treats him as a common criminal and sends him for crucifixion, his crime being sedition. Pilate fixes a *tabla* over his head which says: King of the Jews. It is unheard of for a common criminal to get a trial or even a hearing of any kind. Trials were reserved for Roman citizens with appeal to the Emperor in Rome.

Matthew 27.38 describes the crucifixion itself as follows: *"Then two bandits were crucified with him, one on his right and one on his left. Those who passed by derided him, shaking their heads and saying, You who would destroy the Temple and build it in the three days, save yourself! If you are the Son of God, come down from the cross. In the same way the chief priests also, along with the scribes and elders, were mocking him, saying, He's saved others, he cannot save himself. He is the King of Israel; let him come down from the cross now, and we will believe in him. He trusts in God, let God deliver him now, if he wants to; for he said I am God's Son. The bandits who were crucified with him also taunted him in the same way."*

Isaiah 53.3 et seq:

"He was despised, shunned by men, A man of suffering, familiar with disease. As one who hid his face from us, He was despised, we held him of no account. Yet it was our sickness

that he was bearing, Our suffering that he endured. We accounted him plagued, Smitten and afflicted by God; But he was wounded because of our sins, Crushed because of our iniquities. He bore the chastisement that made us whole, And by his bruises we were healed."

"Assuredly, I will give him the many as his portion, he shall receive the multitude as his spoil For he exposed himself to death And was numbered among the sinners, Whereas he bore the guilt of the many And made intercession for sinners."

The words used in Matthew 27 and quoted above, are a pointed reference to the words used by Joash in Judges 6.31 when he was taunting the townspeople who were followers of the god, Baal: *"If he is a God, let him fight his own battles, since it is his altar that has been torn down!"* In other words, Jesus is being treated like a follower of a false god. The final paragraph of Isaiah, as quoted, refers to his being among the sinners and explains the presence of the two thieves. This is fulfilling a prediction in the Hebrew bible and might therefore be a Jewish addition.

On his way to the place of execution, the place of the skulls, Jesus dragged his cross piece through the streets of Jerusalem to the place where the posts were erected for crucifixion. The Romans put a superscript on the cross piece saying: "King of the Jews" the crime for which he was being made to sacrifice his life. It seems to mean that the Romans found him guilty of sedition i.e. setting himself up as an alternative power to the Roman administration.

When he was nailed to the cross he uttered the words, taken from Matthew 27.46 which have considerable significance. In the Gospel version Jesus's final words are 'Eli Eli lema sabachtahani' which, whilst it is a mixture of Hebrew and Aramaic with the word 'lema' whose origin cannot be found in any language but has finally been taken to mean Li-Mah in Hebrew or 'To Why' in English by most concordances.[162] 'Eli' means 'My God' in Hebrew, 'lema' sabachthani, which has been translated as 'My God, My God, Why have you forsaken me' to correspond, it is said, with Psalm 22. In the Aramaic version the translation could be rendered *'Help, Help, Why have You spared me'*. More literally: Help, Help You have restrained me (BDB p583) in a net or trap (BDB p959} ie God has spared his life but trapped him in his mortal coil.

This has a certain parallel in Judaism:

1 Kings 19.4, speaking of Elijah, says: *"...he himself went a day's journey into the wilderness. He came to a broom bush and sat down under it, and prayed that he might die. Enough! He cried. Now, O Lord, take my life, for I am no better than my fathers."*

The similarity between them, the last words of Jesus on the cross and the cry of Elijah lying in the wilderness was not lost on the onlookers. In Matthew 27.47: *"When some of the bystanders heard it, they said, This man is calling for Elijah."* The Jewish Encyclopaedia states, under the heading Eschatology: *'the expectation of the Messiah from the house of David was kept in the background and the prophet Elijah, as the forerunner of the Great Day of the Lord who would reassemble all the tribes of Israel was placed in the foreground.'* It seems therefore well within the realm of conjecture that the translation given above suggested the coming of Elijah and the

---

[162] Brown Driver and Briggs, p.521.

apocalypse to the onlookers.

At the end of the world Jewish eschatology predicts the dead will rise again in accordance with Isaiah 25.7:

And he will destroy in this Mountain the face of the covering cast over all people, and the veil that is spread over all nations. He will swallow up death in victory; and the Lord God will wipe away tears from all faces; and the rebuke of his people shall he take away from off all the Earth: for the Lord hath spoken it.

Matthew 27.50 describes the end of the world with the death of an apocalyptic prophet: *Then Jesus cried again with a loud voice and breathed his last. At that moment the veil of the Temple was rent in two from the top to the bottom and the Earth did quake and the rocks rent; and the graves were opened and many bodies of the saints who had fallen asleep were raised and came out of the graves. After his resurrection they came out of their tombs and went into the holy city and appeared unto many.*

Only Jews could have redacted these verses because they are close to the essence of Jewish faith. The reference to the veil of the Temple is the scarlet curtain which was renewed every year and was very thick. It shielded the holy of holies from the common gaze. It is therefore highly probable that these verses were Jewish and described the original Jewish Jesus as an apocalyptic prophet. It also indicates that the Aramaic is the original language of the Gospels because a translation from Aramaic corresponds more exactly with what follows in Matthew.

The story of Jesus became very popular amongst the deprived classes in the whole of the Levant, from

Byblos in the North to Alexandria in the South, and with Jesus himself a folk hero. Until the Temple was destroyed in the year 70, the reverence for him seems largely to have been confined to Jews. He injected a new social idea into human thinking, namely that no matter what the law says or whether a person is deserving or undeserving, if they need help then there is a social obligation to help them if one can and, if necessary, to disobey the law in order to do it.

After the destruction of the Temple in the year 70CE the heroes of the fight against the Romans were attached, by popular myth, to the story of Jesus. The great outside observer of what was really happening in Israel was the Jewish historian, Josephus, who recorded the entire history of the Jews and, in more detail, the destruction of the Temple. The insertions made by later, anonymous Jewish hands were sometimes satirical and sometimes lauded the heroes of the revolt like Simon bar Giora and John of Gischala, and reviled traitors like Judas ben Judas who tried to betray Simon to the Romans. All the apostles are to be found in the pages of Josephus but, in reading them, it has to be remembered that Flavius Josephus regarded these characters not as heroes but as people who, against all rational advice, had opposed Rome and brought about the destruction of the Temple in Jerusalem. The Hellenics, who came after them, took the story of Jesus as it came down to them at face value and added their own Greek myths to turn it into a world religion.

The names Judas, John and Simon Peter were all added to the gospel considerably later than the crucifixion of Jesus which is believed to have happened in the year CE 33, though this date has never been ascertained with any certainty. The name Judas appears several times in the gospel story as the man who betrayed Jesus to the Romans for 30 pieces of silver. He is, in reality, a much later addition and he attempted to betray, not Jesus but Simon bar Giora, the young, ruthless Idumean who led the rebellion against Rome and defended Jerusalem during the siege which ended in disaster for the Jews in 70 CE. Judas, as the betrayer of Christ, has been advertised by Christians as the archetypal Jew. All the Gospels mention him but Matthew is typical:

26.14: *"Then one of the twelve, who was called Judas Iscariot, went to the chief priests and said, What will you give me if I betray him to you? They paid him 30 pieces of silver and from that moment he began to look for an opportunity to betray him."*

26.20: *"When it was evening, he[Jesus] took his place with the twelve; and while they were eating, he said, Truly, I tell you, One of you will betray me. And they became greatly distressed and began to say to him one after another Surely not I Lord? He answered: The one who has dipped his hand into the bowl with me will betray me. The Son of Man goes as it is written of him but woe to that one by whom the Son of Man is betrayed! It would be better for that one not to have been born. Judas, who betrayed him said Surely not I, Rabbi? He replied, You have said so."*

27.1: *"When morning came, all the chief priests and the elders of the people conferred together against Jesus in order to bring about his death. They bound him, led him away, and handed him over to Pilate the Governor. When Judas his betrayer, saw that Jesus was condemned, he repented and brought back the 30 pieces of silver to the chief priests and the elders. He said, I have sinned by betraying innocent blood. But they said, what is that to us? See to it yourself. Throwing down the pieces of silver in the Temple, he departed; and he went and hanged himself. But the chief priests taking the pieces of silver said, It is not lawful to put them into the Treasury, since they are blood money. After conferring together they used them to buy the Potters field as a place to bury foreigners. For this reason that field has been called the field of blood to this day. Then was fulfilled what had been spoken through the prophet Jeremiah, And they took the 30 pieces of silver, the price of the one on whom price had been set, on whom some of the people of Israel had set a price, and they gave them for the Potters field, as the Lord commanded me."*

These episodes, even though they allegedly took place centuries ago, have provided the Jewish race as a focus for unhappy Christians. They have proved absolutely damning for Jews but fortunately they are completely without historical foundation. The true account of Judas is to be found in the writings of Josephus:

As a demonstration of the bloody ruthlessness of Simon bar Giora, we have Josephus's description of him. His treatment of a man who had once been of great service to him and High Priest:

Chapter 13. The Wars of the Jews: *Simon would not suffer Matthias, by whose means he got possession of the city, to go off without torment. This Matthias was the son of Boethus, and was one of the high priests, one that had been very faithful to the people, and in great esteem with them; he, when the multitude were distressed by the zealots, among whom John was numbered, persuaded the people to admit this Simon to come in to assist them, while he had made no terms with him, nor expected anything that was even from him. But when Simon was come in, and had got the city under his power, he esteemed him that had advised them to admitting him as his enemy equally with the rest, as looking upon that advice as a piece of his simplicity only; so he had him then brought before him and condemned to die for being on the side of the Romans, without giving him leave to make his defence. He condemned also his three sons to die with him; for as to the fourth, he prevented him by running away to Titus before. And when he begged for this, that he might be slain before his sons, and that as a favour, on account that he had procured the gates of the city to be open to him, he gave order that he should be slain the last of them all; so he was not slain till he had seen his sons slain before his eyes, and that by being produced over against the Romans; for such a charge had Simon given to Artanus, the son of Bamadus, who was the most barbarous of all his gods. He also jested upon him, and told him that he might now see whether those to whom he intended to go over would send him any succour or not; but still he forbade their dead bodies should be buried. After the slaughter of these, a certain priest, Ananias, the son of Masambalus, a person of them in eminency, as also Aristens, the scribe of the Sanhedrin, and born at Emmaus, and with them 15 men of figure among the people, were slain. They also kept Josephus's father in prison, and made public proclamation that no citizen whatsoever should either speak to him himself, or go into his company among others, for fear he would betray them. They also slew such as joined in lament to these men, without further examination."*

This terrifying slaughter was described by Josephus to be the work of Simon bar Giora who controlled the upper part of Jerusalem together with John who controlled the lower part. Simon bar Giora was an Idumean who prosecuted the rebellion utterly without pity and Judas was, finally, repelled by him according to Josephus who witnessed many of the events surrounding the destruction of Jerusalem with his own eyes. This pitiless slaughter explains Judas's attempted betrayal of Simon. Josephus despaired of Simon, who he could see was going to bring about the destruction of Jerusalem but to the poor, Simon promised salvation and he could do no wrong.

With regard to Judas he says the following:

"Now when Judas, the son of Judas, who was one of Simon's under officers and a person entrusted by him to keep one of the towers, saw this procedure of Simon, he called together 10 of those under him, that were most faithful to him, (perhaps this was done partly out of pity to those that had so barbarously been put to death, but principally in order to provide for his own safety) and spoke thus to them: How long shall we bear these miseries? Or what hopes have we of deliverance by thus continuing faithful to such wicked wretches? Is not the famine already come against is? Are not the Romans in a manner got within the city? Is not Simon become unfaithful to his benefactors? And is there not reason to fear that he will very soon bring us to the like punishment, while the security the Romans offer us is sure? Come on, let us surrender up this wall, and save ourselves and the city. Nor will Simon be very much hurt, if, now he despairs of deliverance, he be brought to justice a little sooner then he thinks on. Now these ten were prevailed upon by those arguments; so he sent the rest of those that were under him, some one way, and some another, that no discovery might be made of what they had resolved upon. Accordingly, he called to the Romans from the tower about the third hour; but they, some of them out of pride, despised what he said, and others of them did not believe him to be in earnest, though the greatest number as believing they should get possession of the city in a little time, without any hazard. But when Titus was just coming thither with his armed men, Simon

was acquainted with the matter before he came, and presently took the tower into his own custody, before it was surrendered, and seized upon these men and put them to death in the sight of the Romans themselves and when he had mangled their dead bodies he threw them down before the wall of the city."

It seems, therefore, according to this account, that Judas and his fellow conspirators were thrown over the walls of the city and fell to their death on the ground below where their dead bodies lay. This is supported by the book of Acts Chapter 1.16 where Simon speaks as follows:

"Friends, the Scripture had to be fulfilled, which the holy spirit through David foretold concerning Judas, who became a guide for those who arrested Jesus-for he was numbered among us and was allotted his share in this ministry. Now this man acquired a field with the reward of his wickedness; and falling headlong, he burst open in the middle and all his bowels gushed out."

It was, in all probability, the field where the bowels and blood of Judas gushed out, outside the walls of Jerusalem, that became known as 'the field of blood'. Bearing in mind that Judas was defending one of the towers on the walls of Jerusalem he is likely to have been a sicarii, one of the dagger men whose loyalty to the death would have been taken for granted. Indeed the name by which he has come down to us at the present time is Judas Iscariot, Judas of the sicarii.[163] The ending 'ot' is the plural in Aramaic.

The common people who embellished the story of

---

[163] These were men who, with a short dagger concealed in their clothing, walked up to anyone known to be friendly to Rome, either Jew or Gentile, and killed them.

Jesus were looking at the utter desolation of Jerusalem and would have included Judas as one of the worthless shepherds depicted in Zechariah 11.1:

Throw open your gates, O Lebanon, And let fire consume your Cedars! Howl, cypresses, for cedars have fallen! How the mighty are ravaged! Howl you oaks of Bashan, For the stately forest is laid low! Hark, the wailing of the shepherds, for their rich pastures are ravaged; Hark: the roaring of the great beasts, For the jungle of the Jordan is ravaged... So I attended the sheep meant for slaughter, for those poor men of the sheep. I got two staffs, one of which I named Favour and the other Unity, and I proceeded to tend the sheep. But I lost the three shepherds in one month; then my patience with them was at an end:, and they in turn were disgusted with me. So I declared, I am not going to tend you; let the one that is to die and the one that is to get lost get lost; and let the rest devour each other's flesh!

Taking my staff Favour, I cleft in two, so as to annul the covenant I had made with all the people; and when it was annulled that day, the same poor men of the sheep or watched me realised that it was a message from the Lord. Then I said to them, if you are satisfied, pay me my wages, if not, don't. So they weighed out my wages, 30 shekels of silver-the noble sum that I was worth in their estimation.

Once it is realised that the author who introduced into the story the 30 pieces of silver was looking at the devastated vista of Jerusalem razed to the ground by the Roman 10th Legion, it can be understood why he introduced this cry of desolation from Zechariah.

Simon bar Giora, who commanded the upper part of the city, came from Idumea and is thought, by the Jewish Encyclopaedia, to have been born in approximately the year 50 CE. At the time Jerusalem was destroyed in the year 70 CE he would have been in his 20s. A very young man but extremely strong and violent according to Josephus. In Aramaic the name Simon Peter is Shimoun Capa, which means Simon Rock. Simon bar Giora can be translated from Aramaic as Simon, son of Rock Chalk and, taking into account that he was a contemporary of Judas it is almost certain that Simon Peter and Simon bar Giora were one and the same person. The leaders of the rebellion emerge as 'Jesus' and helping Jesus. They emerge without blemish. Fortunately there is Josephus taking an opposite view and lending some balance to the story.

When the Romans overran Jerusalem, Simon and some of his closest henchmen went underground and tried to escape in tunnels to a safe place but they failed. Simon put on the clothes of royalty, a white girth and a purple cloak, and then emerged from the sewers to face his Roman captors. This scene is repeated in the Gospels. In Luke 23.11: "*Even Herod* [Antipas Tetrarch of Galilee] *with his soldiers treated him with contempt and mocked him; then he put an elegant robe on him, and sent him back to Pilate.*"

Simon and John were placed in bondage and then taken to Rome and placed in the triumphal procession together with 700 Jews who represented the tallest and strongest looking of the enemy. Simon was led as the enemy general into the forum with a rope around his neck and he was then thrown from the Tarpeian Rock which was near the Temple of Jupiter. The Mamertine prison in Rome still has an inscription which says: "Simon of Giora, defender of Jerusalem against Titus and Vespasian. Decapitated in 70 CE." Josephus's description of him being thrown from the top of the Tarpeian Rock is probably the more accurate since there is a convention that Simon Peter, when taken to Rome, was crucified upside down and this corresponds to a greater extent with Simon bar Giora being thrown headlong from the top of a rock. John of Gischala who commanded the lower city was also taken prisoner and was imprisoned for life in Rome.

Seven more of the apostles had the same first names as Jews who died on the walls of Jerusalem. The word 'apostle' in Greek merely means: "sent out" and they were sent out by John and Simon to defend the walls and towers of Jerusalem. In Aramaic, 'apostle' has the root ShLCh which means 'to send' or 'send and do something', or 'send a weapon' in the sense of throwing a spear or shooting an arrow. The possible meanings are given in pages 1018, 1019 of Brown, Driver and Briggs, and are too numerous to set out here but they are aggressive as though 'sent out to fight'.

A complex figure who found her way into the Gospels as a heroine of the Jews was Princess Berenice of the house of Herod. Born in 28 CE, she was the younger sister of Agrippa II, also born in 28 CE, and she had two younger sisters, Marianne born in 34 CE and Drusilla born in 38 CE. It is not absolutely clear whether these dates are accurate or whether Berenice was younger or older than Agrippa.

Berenice herself was married off three times: in 41 or 43 to Marcus Julius Alexander who died in 44 CE; then, in 44, she was married off to her uncle, Herod of Chalcis, who died in 48. She had two sons, Berenicianus and Hyrcanus, but when Herod of

Chalcis died she was married off to Ptolemy II of Cilicia. She was therefore Queen of Cilicia but she deserted him soon after the marriage. She spent most of her life with her brother Agrippa II and there were strong rumours from Josepus and Tacitus that they had a long-standing, incestuous relationship.[164]

She became a heroine for the desperate lower class of Jews in Judaea because of her brave attempts to defend them from the rapacious cruelty of the Procurator Gessius Florus, 64-66 CE. Josephus tells us that she was sorely affected by the wicked practices of the soldiers and she sent her guards to Florus and begged him to leave off these slaughters, but he would not comply with her request. Nor would he have any regard either to the numbers already slain or to the nobility of her character that interceded but only to the advantage to him he should make by this plundering. The violence of the soldiers rose to a degree of madness that it was expended on the Queen herself and they would have killed her also had she not been able to escape to the palace and been protected by her guards which she had to keep about her for fear of assault. She took a mighty vow, the Nazarite Vow, that for 30 days before offering her sacrifice she would abstain from wine and shave the hair of her head which things Berenice did and stood barefoot, with shaven head, before Florus's tribunal and besought him to spare the Jews. She managed to escape without being killed herself. This happened on the 16th day of the month of the Jyar and on the next day those Jews who were suffering most ran as a demonstration to the upper marketplace and

---

[164] War of the Jews, Books I and II.

lamented the death of so many in the recent past.

The men of power and the high priest rent their garments and fell down before the multitude and besought them to leave off and not to provoke the procurator to some incurable procedure in addition to what they had already suffered. The multitude complied immediately. Florus called for the high priests and other eminent people to tell them that he wished the people to go out and meet the soldiers that were coming up from Caesarea. There were two cohorts en route for Jerusalem as reinforcements. The multitude therefore were divided, some of them welcoming the cohorts and others looking for action. It was to these latter that Berenice became a monument of heroism.

Some five to ten years earlier Berenice's sister Drusilla had left her husband and married the procurator Antonius Felix. The story of Berenice and Drusilla became conflated with the heroism of Berenice, being endowed on the wife of the Procurator and recorded in the Gospels as Matthew 27.19: *"While he was sitting on the judgement seat, his wife sent word to him, Have nothing to do with that innocent man, for today I have suffered a great deal because of a dream about him."* So far as we know Pontius Pilate had no known wife and so the suffering classes of the Jews added their own heroine into this part of the story.

Berenice formed a long-standing liaison with the Roman general, Titus, 11 years her junior, who laid waste Jerusalem. She went back to Rome with him and, whilst it would not have been proper for him to marry a foreign Queen, she became quite powerful and Quintilian records that in one case in which he was pleading her cause she was both litigant and judge. When he became Emperor, Titus had to put her to one side and died two years later. Those of a suspicious mind might comment on the number of husbands and lovers who had died within a reasonably short time of abandoning, or being abandoned by, Berenice. Her name in Greek was Berenike which, when Latinised became Veronica and tradition has it that a woman called Veronica wiped Jesus' face with her veil.

Berenice became an important observer to another part of the gospel stories. Agrippa II tried to avert the coming rebellion by addressing the multitude who were desperately trying to rid themselves of the reign of terror that Florus, the Procurator, was subjecting them to. He therefore called the multitude together into a large gallery and, because she was so popular, placed his sister Berenice in the house of the Hasmoneans nearby, so that she might be seen by all. He then gave one of the most inept speeches ever designed to bring peace. During the course of it he is reported as saying: *"...Nor has Caesar against whom you are going to make war, injured you: it is not by their command that any wicked Governor is sent to you, for they who are in the West cannot see those that are in the East; nor indeed is it easy for them there even to hear what is done in these parts.* **Now it is absurd to make war with the great many for the sake of one, to do so with such mighty people for a small cause;** *and this when these people are not able to know of what you complain; such crimes as we complain of may soon be corrected, for the same procurator will not continue forever and probable it is that that the successors will come with more moderate inclinations."* He then went on to say that because they had been in thrall to Rome for so long, the time for rebellion was past and they had lost the will to attain freedom.

Agrippa II is thus recorded as saying that it is better for the nation to survive rather than for it to go to war for the sake of one man. John 11.49 imputes similar words to Caiaphas: *"But one of them, Caiaphas, who was high priest that year, said to them, You know nothing at all! You do not understand that it is better for you to have one man die for the people than to have the whole nation destroyed."*

The most damning insertion into the story of Jesus, presumably by Jews themselves, is to be found in Matthew 27.24: *So when Pilate saw that he could do nothing, but rather that a riot was beginning, he took some water and washed his hands before the crowd saying, I am innocent of this man's blood, see to it yourselves. Then the people as a whole answered, "His blood be on us and on our children!" So he released Barabbas for them, and after flogging Jesus, he handed him over to be crucified.*

It must always be retained that the Gospels were written over a considerable period of time, possibly as much as 300 years, and portions were added to the basic Jewish story both by Jews and Greeks to reflect the current state of affairs and, in the case of the Greeks, to win over new converts to the new religion that they had appropriated from a Jewish sect. After the year 70 CE, which is pivotal in Jewish history, the Jews were looking at the devastation perpetrated by the Romans and their own guilt in starting and prosecuting a rebellion against Rome in the first place, a rebellion which they had been told by Josephus and Agrippa II, would end in failure. The word used in Aramaic is DAMHA which means "his blood" and has always been taken to refer to the blood of Jesus. However, it could also be translated as "its blood" and could refer to the blood of Jerusalem which had been shed over four months of siege in the year 70 CE. It is clearly remorse at a dreadful mistake made by Simon bar Giora and his followers but it refers to the destruction of Jerusalem and not to the death of Jesus which happened one generation earlier.

More poetically, the words from Matthew echo the words of Jeremiah who was looking out at the devastation caused by the Persians and the destruction of the first Temple. In the words of the Jewish Study Bible, "*Jeremiah lived during one of the most crucial and terrifying periods in the history of the Jewish people in biblical times: the destruction of Jerusalem and the Temple of Solomon, followed by the beginning of the Babylonian exile. Because he is one of the key witnesses to the last years of the kingdom of Judah, Jeremiah emerges as one of the major figures who grappled with the theological problems posed by the destruction of the nation, and who laid the foundations for the restoration of Jerusalem and the Temple in the years following the end of the exile.*"

In particular Jeremiah 26.7 is a model for this part of the story of Jesus: "*The priests and prophets and all the people heard Jeremiah speaking these words in the house of the Lord. And when Jeremiah finished speaking all that the Lord had commanded him to speak to all the people, the priests and the prophets and all the people seized him, shouting, "you shall die! How dare you prophesy in the name of the Lord that this house shall become like Shiloh and this city made desolate, without inhabitants?" And all the people crowded about Jeremiah in the house of the Lord. When the officials of Judah heard about this, they went up from the Kings Palace to the house of the Lord and held a session at the entrance of the New Gate of the house of the Lord. The priests and prophets said to the officials and to all the people, "this man deserves the death penalty, for he has prophesied against this city, as you yourselves have heard." Jeremiah said to the officials and to all the people, "It was the Lord who sent me to prophesy against this house and this city all the words you have heard. Therefore mend your ways and your acts and heed the Lord your God, that the Lord may renounce the punishment he has decreed for you. As for me, I am in your hands: do to me what seems good and right to you. But know that if you put me to death, you and this city and its inhabitants will be guilty of shedding the blood of an innocent man. For in truth the Lord has sent me to you to speak all these words to you."*

It has to be remembered that it is in this context, not as a result of the death of Jesus but as a result of the destruction of Jerusalem, that the words: "His blood be on us and on our children," which have been used to condemn the Jews as a race to 2,000 years of prejudice. It is ironic that words taken out of context have been used to down the very people who uttered them, though it must always be remembered that the motive that drives people to racism is social rejection rather than mere words alone.

All these items of information which have been used against Jews were actually preserved by Jewish folklore many years ago. When the sect was taken over by a more Hellenic population these words were translated into Greek and formed the basis of a new religion – Christianity.

8b *Greek insertions into the story of Jesus*

Sometime after the bar Kokhba rebellion in 135 CE, the Jewish story of Jesus which had been enhanced by the insertion of Jewish heroes and traitors, notably Judas, had become extremely popular amongst the lower social categories in Israel. The landless, jobless and ruined people took comfort from the story of Jesus. For them, Jesus was a hero. His encounter with the Scribes and the Pharisees set him apart as a man of integrity and champion of the poor. At this stage a second wave of followers to the story appeared, namely, those with a Hellenic background who lived in the coastal cities of the Levant from Alexandria to Byblos in what is now the Lebanon. They inserted their own religious ritual. This was convenient because it made the new religion more widely understood and therefore more popular.

The Greek addition to the story at this stage is largely the one that is celebrated in Christian churches all over the world every Easter and is the one, apart from the role played by Judas, which has been used to justify the greatest amount of anti-Jewish feeling.

Like any other religion, Judaism generated huge sums of money just as Christianity did in the 17th century. Enough funds by the sale of indulgencies were raised to build St Peter's Basilica in Rome. Two thousand years ago there might have been between 700,000 and two million Jews living in Palestine with a further two to five million living in the Diaspora. With the tithes alone standing at half a shekel of silver (a week's industrial wage) per family per annum this might have generated an income for the Temple, at today's prices, of between 200 million and 1,000 million per annum of any Western currency. In addition to this, the Temple acted as a bank to safeguard private wealth. The rich Jew was always related to the high priesthood. Josephus in his "Life" makes this clear when he says: "I am of the Royal Blood for the children of the Hasmoneans, from whom that family was derived, had both the office of the high priesthood and the dignity of the King..."

The Hasmoneans were high priests and led the rebellion of the Maccabees as were the Onids before them both in Palestine and in Egypt. The cult of Jesus became very numerous and was slowly taken over by followers of Hellenism in Israel after the destruction of the Temple left a theocratic power vacuum. In the main, Greeks took over the beliefs of other cults and attached them to the Jesus story. Religion was big business.

The gospel of John begins resoundingly: *"In the beginning was the Word, and the Word was with God, and the Word was God."* The Word is translated as the Greek concept "Logos". In Aramaic there is a direct link between 'word' and 'logos'. Aristotle made a distinction between logos, persuasion by reason, and pathos, persuasion by appealing to the emotions. By the time the expression reached the Hellenic thinking of the Levant, Philo of Alexandria, a Jew, had adopted the Platonic distinction between imperfect matter and perfect Form and therefore intermediary beings were necessary to bridge the enormous gap between a perfect God and the imperfect material world. The role of the intermediary beings was Logos. In theory, to a Jew, this would introduce the established idea that some prophets were inspired by the word of God and this would have been acceptable. The Gospel of John, however, goes on to make a more striking statement at 1.14: "and the Word became flesh and lived among us, and we have seen his glory..." This introduces some sort of second deity which would have been unacceptable to the monotheists who believed in Judaism. The idea of a demigod was familiar to the Greeks but alien to the Jews. The opening sentence might even have been redacted by a Jewish hand but verse 1.14 is more probably a Greek addition.

As another illustration of an insertion we have Jesus's prowess as a fisherman in John 21.11:

When they had gone ashore, they saw a charcoal fire, with fish in it, and bread. Jesus said to them, Bring some of the fish that you have just caught. So Simon Peter went aboard and hauled the net ashore, full of large fish, 153 of them; and though there were so many, the net was not torn.

The number 153 is precise and leaves the reader wondering why such a number was chosen. To the modern eye it has no significance at all but to those with a slight mathematical bent it puts them in mind of the teachings of Pythagoras and the Tetrakys, the Golden Triangle in which the number of balls making up a triangle four layers high comes to exactly 10. In this case the sum of the balls in a Triangle 17 layers high comes to exactly 153, or, to put it another way, the sum of the numerals from 1 to 17 comes to 153. Pythagoras is famous for his expression defining the hypotenuse of a right-angled triangle i.e. $a^2+b^2=c^2$ and every three integers, a, b and c, which comply with the formula are known as Pythagorean triples. The basic triple which ends with 17 is 8-15-17 and 17×9 is equal to 153 and forms another triple. The expression and the number 153 has a certain symmetry which the Pythagorean cult might have considered significant since, in their belief the number itself was part of the perfect order of things.

The cult had a wide following particularly among women who, for possibly the first time, were admitted to the mysteries. Members were required to maintain strict loyalty and secrecy and probably, like Orphics they obtained an insight into the divine by intoxication. More importantly, they believed in the transmigration of the soul and that upon death the soul migrated to another living being either an animal, a human being, or a bird or, apparently, a butterfly. The end of transmigration was the Cosmos at the upper end and the Tytara at the bottom. The members of the cult also believed that an ascetic life except, possibly for the drinking of wine as a sacrament, would assist in the flight of the soul upon death. The point of including the fishing story would be to demonstrate that the greatest Pythagorean of them all was Jesus himself so that followers of the cult could safely abandon it and become Christians. Even more speculative, the extensive use of the image of Jesus catching fish might have been intended to wean the population away from the cult of Dagon.[165]

An aspect of Judaism which would have been abhorrent to the Pythagoreans was the necessity to sacrifice birds and animals which, as far as they were concerned, contained the souls of human beings, as offerings at the Temple. For a sin committed

---

[165] The priests of Dagon wore mitres.

unintentionally a sin offering of a beast or a fowl was necessary except that for the very poor a turtle dove or a small pigeon would be sufficient. For giving a false oath or giving evidence knowing it to be untrue the offering could be a bullock, a he-goat, a she-goat, a ewe lamb, a turtle dove, a young pigeon or a small quantity of fine flour. These depended on the wealth of the sinner but depending only on that, the offering would expiate the sin. In Matthew 21.12, Jesus shows his disgust at these procedures and cleanses the Temple: *"Then Jesus entered the Temple and drove out all who were selling and buying in the Temple, and he overturned the tables of the moneychangers and the seats of those who sold doves."* John is more detailed. John is generally the most Greek of the gospel writers. At 2.14 he says: *"in the Temple he found people selling cattle, sheep, and doves, and the moneychangers seated at their tables. Making a whip of cords, he drove all of them out of the Temple, both the sheep and the cattle. He also poured out the coins of the moneychangers and overturned their tables."* It may well be imagined that this verse made it easier for Pythagoreans to become Christians.

The reference to the moneychangers is harder to understand. The moneychangers were there to stop foreign currency with the head of Caesar from entering the Temple. The presence of such coinage and representations of human beings would have been blasphemy. The moneychangers started work in the provinces a month before the month of Nissan and for every silver half shekel paid by the head of the family, they exchanged it for a token called "a shekel of the sanctuary". By the time Passover came, any remaining Jews who had not obtained a shekel of the sanctuary would have arrived with exactly half a silver shekel in order to purchase one as a token to enter the Temple. This served for them, their wife and their children who were included in the family until they could walk to the Temple under their own steam. When they could walk to the Temple on their own they would have to pay their own half shekel in silver. This might explain the reference to Jesus being 12 years old in Luke 41-52 and the inference that he was still a child. It is difficult therefore to understand what the redactor was referring to with regard to the money changers or, could it simply be, that he was not a Jew and did not understand the system? He had seen the money changers in the provinces but none of his family had ever visited the Temple before it was destroyed in 70CE.

One of the most alien descriptions of the Passover supper is given in Matthew Verse 26.26:

And as they were eating Jesus, took bread and blessed it and brake it, and gave it to the disciples and said take, eat; this is my body and he took the cup and gave thanks and gave it to them saying 'Drink ye all of it; for this is my blood of the new testament, which is shed for many for the remission of sins.

This is the most extraordinary way of celebrating Passover. Rabban Gamaliel, a near contemporary of Jesus and the man who taught Paul about Judaism, used to say: 'whoever has not spoken of these three things at Passover has not fulfilled his obligations: Pesach, Matzah, and Marror'. By this was meant that Jews should remember their deliverance out of Egypt, Matzah, the unleavened bread they carried with them, and Marror, the bitter herbs that reminded them of this. At the time of Jesus, lettuce dipped in salt was considered sufficient to represent the bitter herbs.

Gammaliel continued: 'Therefore we are required to give thanks, to praise, to glorify, to honour, to exalt, to extol and to bless Him who performed all these wonders for our fathers and for us. He brought us from bondage to freedom from sorrow to gladness from mourning to Festival, from darkness to great light, and from slavery to redemption. Let us say before him: alleluia.' After this the Hallel may be recited. This is six Psalms, numbers 113-118.

At Passover, after the meal the great Hallel is recited, Psalm 136.[166] None of this appears in verse 26 because the author of verse 26, it has to be assumed, was unaware of the procedure at Passover; neither the food nor the prayers were known to him and it must be assumed that he was not a Jew, nor was he connected with Jews.

When Jesus says of the bread: "take, eat; this is my body. And he took the cup and gave thanks and gave it to them saying, drink ye all of it; for this is my blood." He is laying down the foundation for what is known in Christianity as the Eucharist. This is a very primitive rite that was commented on by Sir James Frazer in the Golden Bough with the following words:

"it is now easy to understand why a savage should desire to partake of the flesh of an animal or man whom he regards as divine. By eating the body of the god he shares in the god's attributes and powers. And when the god is a corn-god, the corn is his proper body; when he is a vine-god the juice of the grape is his blood; and so by eating the bread and drinking the wine the worshipper partakes of the real body and blood of his god. Thus the drinking of wine in the rites of a vine- god like Dionysus is

---

[166] Mishnah Pesahim 10.5.

not an act of revelry, it is a solemn sacrament. Yet time comes when reasonable men find it hard to understand how anyone in his senses can suppose that by eating bread or drinking wine he consumes the body or blood of a deity. "When we call corn Ceres and wine Bacchus," says Cicero, "we use a common figure of speech; but do you imagine that anybody is so insane as to believe that the thing he feeds upon is a god?"[167]

Such beliefs have absolutely no connection with Judaism. The point of indulging in them was that in eating the body of the god and drinking the blood of the god the celebrant was going to acquire the characteristics of the god and hence acquire resurrection and eternal life. These beliefs are a direct reference to the cult of Dionysus which was popular among Greeks.

Verse 26.30: *And when they had sung a hymn, they went out into the Mount of Olives.*

This is Jesus and his disciples leaving the Passover supper and going out to pray on the Mount of Olives an action which is strictly forbidden by Judaism. Exodus 12.22 says: *And ye shall take a bunch of hyssop, and dip it in the blood that is in the basin, and strike the lintel and the two sides those with the blood that is in the basin; and* **none of you shall go out at the door of his house until the morning.** Exodus 12.22: *And ye shall observe this thing for an ordinance to thee and to thy sons forever.* To this day observant Jews remain in the house until the morning. It is clear that the author of this part of Matthew was not aware of the elements of Jewish practice.

---

[167] Sir James George Frazer, *The Golden Bough*, p.578.

8c The Trial of Jesus

The trial of Jesus which has been used to rationalise the murder of Jews through the centuries, is one of the great conundrums of history. It corresponds to no historically recognised social or legal procedure known to Jews or Romans. This is strange, because Jesus, being a Jew and not a Roman citizen, was not entitled to a trial at all.[168] The Greek trial, on the other hand, took place in three episodes: A preliminary hearing called the 'Anakrisis', a second episode was a jury decision as to whether the accused was guilty or innocent of the charge and, in a final stage, what the sentence should be. The most famous Greek trial, then, as now, was the trial of Socrates recorded by both Plato and Xenophon. It is suggested here that the version of the trial of Jesus given in the gospels is, indeed, Greek, then it can safely be assumed that, like other Greek portions of the Gospels, it is fiction. The other omission in the Gospels is the absence of any mention in the Gospels of a translator and praetor which even so lowly a functionary as Pontius Pilate could not manage without. Jesus, judging by his last, moving words on the cross, spoke Aramaic. Are we to assume that Pilate had some command of that language?

A good version of the trial in the Gospels is given in Matthew 26.63 and in Matthew 27.11.

26.63: Then the high priest said to him, I put you under

---

[168] Acts 22 alludes to the right of a Roman Citizen to a trial in Rome before a Praetor. Each Praetor could set out his own rules but in practice they were mostly the same and included 'A paterfamilias could put to death his children or hi slaves for any act of disobedience or disloyalty.'.

oath before the living God, tell us if you are the Messiah, the son of God. Jesus said to him, You have said so. But I tell you, from now on you will see the son of man seated at the right hand of power and come in on the clouds of heaven. Then the high priest tore his clothes and said, He has blasphemed! Why do we still need witnesses? You have now heard his blasphemy. What is your verdict? They answered, He deserves death.

This is the depiction of a preliminary hearing before the high priest before what seems to be a kangaroo court. It correspond with the Greek preliminary hearing, the Anakrisis. The high priest insists on condemning Jesus for blasphemy when he should know full well that blasphemy involves the use of the Tetragram (yud hay vav hay) which it is forbidden for Jews to utter.[169] There is no evidence adduced and there is no attempt to adduce such evidence, that Jesus used the tetragram.

When Jesus goes before Pontius Pilate, the Governor, he is accused and found guilty of sedition as evidence of which a superscript "King of the Jews" is nailed on his cross above his head. The question of blasphemy is never raised again. The proof of blasphemy and penalty applied by the high priest who had no power to judge because at that time the Sanhedrin, required to judge a capital offence, was controlled by the Pharisees, none other than the great rabbi Gamaliel himself. The accusation of blasphemy is intended to involve a Greek audience. There is an almost exact parallel in of the trial of Socrates who was accused in the following terms, quoted by Robert Garland in *Introducing New Gods*:

---

[169] MishnahI Chapter VII.

"Meletos, son of Meletos, of the deme of Pitthos, has brought this charge and lodged this affidavit against Socrates, son of Sophroniskos of the deme of Alopeke. Socrates has broken the law by not acknowledging the gods whom the state acknowledges and introducing other new daimonic things. He has also broken the law by subverting the young. The penalty should be death."

It appears that the accusation of blasphemy has been put in merely to strengthen the parallel between the fate of Jesus and the fate of Socrates and emphasise that there was a parity in the trial of Socrates and the trial of Jesus. Educated Hellenes would have read Plato and known that Socrates was unjustly accused and condemned and were invited to think the same of Jesus.

Verse 27.11: *"Now Jesus stood before the Governor; and the governor asked him, Are you the King of the Jews? Jesus said, You say so. But when he was accused by the chief priests and the elders, he did not answer. Then Pilate said to him, Do you not hear how many accusations they make against you? But he gave no answer, not even to a single charge, so that the Governor was greatly amazed.*

Now at the festival the governor was accustomed to release a prisoner for the crowd, anyone whom they wanted. At that time they had a notorious prisoner, called Jesus Barabbas. So after they had gathered, Pilate said to them, Whom do you want me to release for you, Jesus Barabbas or Jesus who is called the Messiah? For he realised that it was out of jealousy that they handed him over. While he was sitting on the judgement seat, his wife sent word to him, Have nothing to do with that innocent man, for today I have suffered a great deal because of a dream about him. Now the chief priests and the elders persuaded the crowds to ask for Barabbas and to have Jesus killed. The Governor again said to them, Which of the two do you want me to release for you? And they said, Barabbas. Pilate then said to them, then what should I do with Jesus who is called the Messiah? All of them said, Let him be crucified! Then he asked, Why, what evil has he done? But they shouted all the more Let him be crucified!"

Apart from blasphemy the question posed by Pilate: "Do you not hear how many accusations they make against you?" is mirrored in Plato's apologia by a rhetorical question posed by Socrates himself: *'Perhaps then one of you might retort, "Well, Socrates, what is your affair? Where have these slanderers against you come from? For surely, if you were, in fact, practising nothing more uncommon than others, such a report and accounts would not then have arisen, unless you were doing something different from the many."* Socrates is, of course, reducing the argument against him to an absurdity but Pilate is taking the question seriously. In short he is saying, in modern idiom, 'Where there is smoke there must be fire.' But taken at face value, it provides another parallel between the two trials, Socrates and Jesus.

The entry of Barabbas into the story creates a difficulty for any theologian. Most eloquently, Charles Guignebert, Professor of History of Christianity in the Sorbonne, says in his book, *Jesus,* written in French in the 1920s: *"This is another very strange episode. First, we have no other evidence beside our Gospels for this astonishing custom. It is incredible that no other Jewish writer should speak of this outrageous privilege that a criminal must be released if the people should claim him."* In order to explain this custom and particularly the words of the narrator: "now at the Festival the Governor was accustomed to release a prisoner for the crowd..."

the reader is entitled to ask: which Festival is the narrator talking about? Clearly not Roman and equally clearly not Jewish. The only other source of such a Festival is to be found in Greece.

During the spring (Passover also always falls in the spring), purification ceremonies were celebrated throughout the Greek world and their purpose was to prepare the Earth and to promote fertility for the coming summer. Jane Harrison, Fellow of Newnham College, Cambridge, in Chapter 3 of her book *Prolegomena* cites the following places where the purification ceremony involving the driving out and the possible killing of two miserable creatures from the community (one for the men and one for the women): Marseilles in France; the Charila at Delphi, the Bouphonia, the Septarion, the Kallynteria, the Plynteria and, possibly the most famous of all, the Thargelia in Athens on the sixth day of which, Socrates was born. This explains why Pontius Pilate is made to say that at this time of the year a second criminal is chosen for the purification ceremony and in some ancient books he is called "Jesus Barabbas" and is quite possibly an alter ego for the Jesus who was to be crucified. The name Barabbas does not indicate any particular person in Hebrew because it simply means "son of the Father" and might well be a way of saying the equivalent of 'A N Other' in English. The ceremony to herald in the first fruits only incidentally involved human sacrifice. Its object was the physical and spiritual purification of the population by evicting **two** miserable wretches though it may be they frequently died in the process. The purpose of the Greek festival was to despatch a human scapegoat out of the city carrying the sins of the city.

After he had been condemned to crucifixion the soldiers took him and gathered the whole cohort before him, stripped him of his clothes and put a scarlet robe on him. They then twisted some thorns and put it on his head as a crown, put a reed in his right hand, and a man knelt before him and mocked him, saying: "Hail King of the Jews!" Then they spat on him and took the reed and struck him on the head.

The beating with a reed was a characteristic of the ceremony of purifying the pharmakos himself because he had to be clean before he could purify anyone else. Beating the devil out of him is an expression that lasted, possibly, to the present day with recalcitrant children in harsh schools. The reed which is spoken about for the beating could have been up to 1 inch in diameter from the Nile, the Jordan or the Euphrates depending on where the story was told. The insults were to drive the pharmakos out of the city. Jesus is insulted from the meeting with the high priest to his death on the cross and is one of the most pointed references to driving out the scapegoat. It is in this sense that he died for the whole city. The idea that Jesus died for many, like the Pharmakos, is supported by the Letter to the Hebrews 9.28 (author unknown) which says:

'And just as it is appointed for mortals to die once and after that the judgment, so Christ, having been offered once to bear the sins of many, will appear a second time, not to deal with sin, but to save those who are eagerly waiting for him.'

The changing of the clothes to scarlet or purple might be a reference to Simon bar Giora and John emerging from the sewers dressed in the colours of royalty. It is most unlikely that two Jews who took leading roles in the rebellion against Rome would be commemorated in this way. It is more likely to be copying the treatment of the pharmakos who was appointed at the Thargelia every year in Athens and, apparently, in other Greek colonies. Sir J G Frazer in his book *The Golden Bough*, Volume 9, describes such a ceremony in Marseilles:

"When ever Marseilles, one of the busiest and most brilliant of Greek colonies, was ravaged by plague, and man of the poorer classes used to offer himself as a scapegoat. For a whole year he was maintained at the public expense, being fed on choice and pure food. At the expiry of the year he was dressed in sacred garments, decked with holy branches and led through the whole city the while prayers were offered that all the evils of the people might fall on his head. He was then cast out of the city or stoned to death... The Athenians regularly maintained a number of degraded and useless beings at the public expense; and when any calamities such as plague, drought, or famine, befell the city, they sacrificed two of these outcasts as scapegoats..."

The points of similarity are that Jesus too was decked out in a scarlet robe, a crown of thorns was placed upon his head, about which, more later, and he was led through the city to his death. There are other instances of a similar procedure recorded by Frazer, the purpose being always to purify the inhabitants from disease. It will be noted that the unfortunate creatures do not have to be killed necessarily, merely driven out and, in Athens, two were required, one for men and one for women though the Pharmakoi to be stoned or driven out could both be male.

Compare with this the treatment of the mock King of the Sacaea as it is described by Dio Chrysostom:

"They take one of the prisoners condemned to death and seat him upon the King's throne, and give him to the Kings raiment, and let him Lord it and drink and run riot and use the Kings concubines during these days, and no man prevents him from doing just what he likes. But afterwards they strip and scourge and crucify him."

The Sacaea was a festival celebrated in Babylon and associated with the goddess Anaitis, the Syrian war goddess, and identified with the Greek goddess Athena. It was characterised by drunkenness and licentious behaviour in which the masters served their slaves and a Mark King was appointed who was later crucified as a surrogate for the real king. When Babylon fell to Alexander in 331 BCE it became part of the Seleucid Empire and this festival was adopted by the Greeks particularly as it permitted licentiousness and drunkenness. It could never be confused with the Passover ceremony which Jews celebrated in the Temple. As evidence that this was still known to the Greeks there is a story which has come down to us via Philo, the Jewish philosopher: When Agrippa I was appointed by the Emperor Caligula to become King in Judaea in 39 CE, he disembarked in his journey from Rome, at Alexandria, and processed through the streets of Alexandria dressed in his royal robes. He did this on the instructions of Caligula but it so incensed the Greek inhabitants of Alexandria that a Jew could process through their city dressed as a King, that they rioted and fighting broke out between Jews and Greeks. During the course of this fighting, Philo records, quoted by Frazer, the following incident:

"Among other things they laid hold of a certain harmless

lunatic named Karrabas who used to roam the streets stark naked, the butt and laughing stock of urchins and idlers. This poor wretch they set up in a public place, clapped a paper Crown on his head, thrust a broken reed into his hand by way of the sceptre, and huddled a mat about him instead of the royal robe about his naked body, and surrounded him with a guard of bludgeon-men, they did Obeisance to him as to a king and made a show of taking his opinion on questions of law and policy..."

And this is where the Crown of thorns is significant. For example, on outstandingly unlucky days the spirits of the dead rise from the Earth and from early morning the Greeks used to chew buckthorn and anoint their doors with pitch. Buckthorn is known to botanists as *Rhamnus cathartica* and, when chewed, purged the system by vomiting. The Athenians believed that such plants have the power of keeping off evil spirits or even ejecting them when they are in possession of the sufferer. In order for the Pharmakos to purify the community he has to be purified himself and that, it is suggested, is the purpose of the crown of thorns. In Europe buckthorn has a hard wooden spike as depicted in the many paintings of Jesus after his trial, but this genus of buckthorn is completely unknown in Judaea where buckthorn has no more than a prickle and is not an emetic. It is known to botanists as *Rhamnus lycioides*. The idea of a crown of thorns is clearly an importation into the story by a Greek hand.

As has been alleged above, the trial of Jesus is the most extraordinary version of a trial. It is neither Jewish nor Roman nor Greek but might possibly be a mixture of myth and the Greek form of trial which is familiar from the trial of Socrates. The first point to consider is that someone who is not a Roman citizen does not merit a trial at all. Whilst there is no doubt that Jesus, like thousands of other Jews, was crucified, all the detail, Barabbas and the Jews crying out is fiction added by or for a Greek congregation.

There were large Greek communities in the first century between Syria and Egypt dating from the conquests of Alexander the Great in the 4th century BCE[170]. He left behind the Seleucids who ruled from Syria and the Ptolomies in Egypt. The famous Cleopatra, Cleopatra VII, owned land in Israel in the days of Herod the Great.

As has been demonstrated earlier, Jews were still writing and adding to the story of Jesus until after the destruction of the Temple in the year 70CE. Indeed it could have been longer than that because Matthew 2.12 indicates that Jesus was born under a star. In a sense, he was the son of a star. Bar Kokhba, who was thought by Rabbi Akiba and others to be the Messiah, led another rebellion against Rome in the 2nd century, and had the nom de guerre, Bar Kokhba, which means 'Son of the Star'. His real name, discovered in the 20th century, was Simon bar Kosevah. Equally possible is that the star story was derived from Numbers 24.17: 'There shall come a star out of the East.' Both possibilities appear to be later Jewish additions.

A more cogent proof that the gospels were being written in a haphazard way over a period of approximately 400 years is found by comparing the Codex Sinaiticus, presently in the British Library, with

---

[170] *Religions and Trade*, Ed Peter Wick and Volker Rabens.

the Gospels presently in use today. The Codex is the earliest version of the Gospels in Greek ever found, and could not have been written earlier than 325CE because it is divided into the Eusebian Canon, nor later than 360CE.[171] In an abbreviated form, the omissions go as follows:

Mark 16.9-20. The long ending containing the resurrection.

Matthew 6.9-13: 'For thine is the kingdom the power and the glory. Amen'.

John 8.3-11: The woman caught in adultery.

Luke 24.51: Ascension to heaven.

Mark 1.1: 'Son of God'.

Luke 9.55-56: 'The Son of man...is come to save men's lives.'

Mark 1.41: 'Compassion'.

In addition, the parchment contains additions and corrections which have been dated between the 4th and the 12th centuries. The omissions listed above contain allusions to Jesus rising to heaven. This is Greek myth rather than Judaism. Jews lie in their graves until the apocalypse and then pious Jews rise from the grave to dwell in peace on earth (Matthew 27.52-55). The Greek myth of Dionysus symbolises the perpetual renewal of life by saying his mother, Semele, is the clouds, Dionysus is the rain which falls from the clouds and then rises as vapour back into the clouds again. It was in this way that life was renewed. The Codex also contains two parables: the Shepherd of Hermas and

---

[171] Wikipedia quoting Bruce Metzger.

the Epistle of Barnabas, neither of which were included in the Christian Canon.

At the time, there were other notable people with the name 'Jesus': A Galilean, Jesus of Sapphias, described as a bandit, and Jesus of Hananiah who predicted the destruction of the Temple in Jerusalem and who was thought by some to be the Messiah and by others to be no more than a madman. Even Albinus, a harsh man, thought he was a harmless lunatic, flogged him and released him. Jesus of Hananiah was finally killed by a rock from a Roman catapult during the siege of Jerusalem.[172] The identity of James is further confused by the discovery by Eusebius (260/265-339/340) of a document written by Hegesippus attributed to 170CE in which James was killed by the Scribes and the Pharisees by precipitating him from a high point at the Temple, then stoning him while still alive and, finally, beating him with a fuller's staff in order to kill him.[173] Eusebius was the librarian at Caesarea and, it is suspected, was not above adding to the documents under his control to provide Christianity with a historical basis. He wrote an obsequious biography of 'The Blessed Emperor Constantine' (306-337) who conquered the Rhineland tribes and the Britons inspired by a cross of light in the sky[174]. This at a time when the Western Empire was disintegrating and all Constantine's campaigns were against his fellow

---

[172] Richard A Horsley with John S Hanson, *Bandits, Prophets and Messiahs*.

[173] Roberts and Donaldson translation on the Internet.

[174] Sun dogs which appear to the right and left of the sun close to the horizon sometimes have a cruciform shape. They are caused by the rays of the sun refracting of clouds of ice crystals.

Romans to try to keep them under control rather extending the Christian faith. It is most likely that the Jesus referred to was the bandit, Jesus of Sapphias, the sort of man who could be tried by the Sanhedrin.

It would be an easy matter to retain the historically justifiable part of the story and retain Jesus' wisdom and his position as a hero of the poor. In 2011 Pope Benedict tried to clear the Gospels of a charge of racism by saying that the only Jews involved in the death of Jesus were a 'Temple aristocracy'.[175] Unfortunately the Church, both Catholic and Anglican, seem to have ignored what he said (he was not writing in his Papal capacity). Nevertheless the reference to Temple Aristocracy is close to the truth. The people who bear the whole responsibility for the death of Jesus were Joseph Caiaphas and Pontius Pilate, both appointed by Rome.

8d Homosexuality

The earliest reference to an antipathy to people of the same sex making love is to be found in the Bible, in Leviticus verses 18.22 and 20.13, which says that if a man lies with a man he shall be killed. The reason is not far to find because in chapter 18 it brackets homosexuality with other sexual practices which do not result in procreation. Women are not mentioned in this respect though lesbianism is a very common and open in the liberal society of today. One can imagine that lesbian women can bear children once they are inseminated either consensually or by force. These provisions in Leviticus might have made some

---

[175] Pope Benedict XVI, Volume Two of Jesus of Nazareth.

sense 3,000 years ago when, very approximately, the population of the Middle East might have been in the order of half a million people.

The Bible is full of references to divine promises made to the Jews that the number of their people will be like the sands on the seashore. In spite of this Israelis, like most secular societies, have completely liberalised their attitude to homosexuality in the 20th century. Britain made it legal between consenting adults in 1967. Formerly it had been a criminal offence. Homosexuals were hunted down by the police and even the secret services because they might be a security risk among prominent people. For centuries it did not occur to the legislature that the illegality and religious opprobrium attached to this completely harmless practice not only caused unnecessary guilt and pain but exposed homosexuals to blackmail and coercion. The real reason for this aversion was purely emotional. The great black mare of our emotions which carries us all along, should form no part of our decision making in a modern, highly technical world. Skill and brains should be the only criteria of value in making logical decisions. And yet they are not. Every decision has, at least, an emotional element.

Some of the Abrahamic faiths continue to refer to sex between men as 'sodomy' and as late as 2005 Pope John Paul II condemned homosexual unions, accepted as an alternative type of family life, as morally evil in his book *Memory and Identity*. Following Leviticus, a sexual union between two women has never been condemned by the church or by Judaism.

According to *A Natural History of Homosexuality* by

Francis Mark Mondimore, homosexuality is as old as the human race and is as widespread as the human race. It has been observed among the Greeks and among the Native American tribes such as the Navajo, the Illinois, the Arapahoe and the Mojave. In addition to this (p.12 et seq) there are Spanish accounts of homosexuality not only among Spaniards themselves but among the pre-Columbian tribes they encountered in the New World. In pre-Christian Rome sexuality and sexual orientation was a purely personal matter. There was no need to preach or to legislate either for or against sexuality of any kind. With the spread of Christianity, homosexuality was designated "sodomy" and was declared to be a sin against God. St Augustine found it necessary to remind novices that the love they brought to each other should be spiritual rather than carnal and warned them against "shameful playing with the each other". Mondimore records a rather touching poem written by a young nun to her temporarily absent friend:

What is my strength that I should bear it.

That I should have patience in your absence?

Is my strength the strength of stones,

That I should await your return?

I, who grieve thee ceaselessly by day and night

Like someone who has lost a hand or foot?

Everything pleasant and delightful

Without you seems like mud underfoot.

I shed tears as I used to smile, And my heart is never glad. When I recall the kisses you gave me,

And how with tender words you could caress my little breasts

I want to die because I cannot see you.

What more can I say? Come home sweet love! Prolong your trip no longer, Know that I can bear your absence no longer.

Farewell. Remember me.

In spite of the circumstantial evidence that homosexuality in both men and women was a completely natural phenomenon, various attempts in the 19th and 20th centuries were made to depict it as a mental illness. The leading writer of this school was Kraft Ebbing who wrote *Psychopathia Sexualis* in which he described certain subjects as though they were sick patients and described many aspects of normal attraction as fetishism such as kid gloves, lace handkerchiefs and velvet dresses, including parts of the human body such as breasts, feet and legs. In spite of himself Kraft Ebbing demonstrates that the homosexual is born with his sexual orientation in him at birth and ready to manifest itself. He gives the example of 'P':

"P" attempts to suppress his sexual interest in other men, marries and fathers a child. He is unable to maintain the facade and is found having sex with a young man in a public park.

Alfred Kinsey carried out a survey of the sexual orientation and habits of human beings both male and female. In the first result published: *Sexual Behaviour in the Human Male* Kinsey set out a scale in which he implied that many people were bisexual. Men tended to be either heterosexual or homosexual with not many shades of sexual desire in between.

Women, on the other hand showed a more complex reaction in expressing their sexual orientation. There can be no doubt that many people attempted to conform to the norm and tried to become heterosexual and, in the recent past, married but gained little or no satisfaction from heterosexual activity. Young girls as they approached puberty and who feel themselves to be more attracted to other girls, are under such social pressure to become heterosexual that they begin harming themselves in order to alleviate the pain. A young man of the author's acquaintance found himself trapped between his homosexuality, his faith and his parents' expectations and took his own life.

In his book: *Gay, Straight and the Reason Why,* written in 2011, Simon LeVay sets out the scientific evidence for saying that homosexuality and lesbianism is a matter of physiology. On page 11 he sets out the scientific investigation which supports the idea that sexual orientation is a question of physiology:

1. Homosexual behaviour exists among nonhuman animals. In a few species, individual animals have a durable preference for same sex partners.

2. Both in childhood and during adult life, gay people differ from straight people of the same sex in a variety of mental traits that fall under the general label of 'gender'.

3. Evidence suggests that the levels of sex hormones circulating during fetal life influence these gendered traits. [This is a mere probability but there is a tendency for the mother to allocate more foetal testosterone to the first-born child with dwindling amounts for subsequent births so that first-born girls

and last-born boys might possibly tend to be homosexual.][176]

4. Evidence suggests that genes influence sexual orientation and other aspects of gender.

5. Structural and functional differences exist between the brains of gay and straight people. To judge from animal experiments, these are caused by differences in pre-natal hormone levels or in the way that the brain responds to hormones.

6. Differences exist in the structure and function of the bodies of gay and straight people.

7. Birth order influences sexual orientation in men and this influence appears to operate through biological mechanisms rather than social ones.

In order to place some credence in the writings of Sigmund Freud it is necessary to postulate that in the case of men who are mainly gay or mainly straight then, if their natural sexual orientation is frustrated, they might resort to the other outlet. This seems to have been the case with a British television presenter called Jimmy Savile who, caught between his faith and not wishing to shame his family, resorted to criminal measures, using the bodies of children. He was a seventh child and might have thought that sexual release using the bodies of little girls was not a sin because they were female. One child reported that he pushed her into a chair while she was in hospital, inserted his penis and then wiped the surplus sperm off the chair with his white coat. Revealingly, he then said: 'You'll be all right now,' as though he had

---

[176] Added by the author.

bestowed some benefit on her. When the child complained, she was ignored because Savile raised so much money for the hospital without which they could not manage.[177]

Following the detailed argument of LeVay it becomes evident that to be gay or lesbian is no more reprehensible than being born with blue eyes but the social expectancy on people to be "normal" places a burden on them which, in some cases, they cannot bear.

Some men who are unable to express their homosexuality feel diminished, with a hole in their self-esteem. A substantial minority try to restore their feeling of wellbeing and try to relieve their sense of failure by adopting a racist stance and raise their damaged self-esteem by making downward social comparisons and vilifying people of what they regard as a weaker race or gender. The target race of such feelings is frequently the Jews who have been singled out by Christianity over 2,000 years. Such a person was the brilliant poet, TS Eliot.

Eliot, acknowledged to be one of the greatest if not *the* greatest poet of the 20th century, was born into a middle-class American family who, at the time of his birth, lived in St Louis, Missouri. His father was a businessman who was president and treasurer of the Hydraulic Press Brick Company in St Louis. His

---

[177] John McShane in *Savile the Beast: The Inside Story of the Greatest Scandal in TV History*, records that on two occasions, when he was a teenager, somewhat older girls attempted some sort of sexual activity with him but to no avail. Dan Davies in *In Plain Sight. The Life and Lies of Jimmy Savile*, records his criminal behaviour in some detail.

mother was a poet. Eliot was the sixth or seventh child and his late birth would probably give rise to a complex sexuality. He obtained a bachelor's degree from Harvard College in 1909 and moved to Paris from 1910 to 1911. In Paris he met the great love of his life, Jean Verdenal. Verdenal reciprocated his love but it can be supposed from his poetry that the affair was never consummated. Verdenal entered the army in 1914 as a doctor and died tending a soldier on the beach at Gallipoli in 1915. That same year Eliot published a poem called The Love Song of J. Alfred Prufrock which contains the following verse:

And the afternoon, the evening sleeps so peacefully!

Smoothed by long fingers,

Asleep... Tired... Or it malingers,

Stretched on the floor here beside you and me.

Should I, after tea and cakes and ices,

Have the strength to force the moment to its crisis?

But though I have wept and fasted, wept and prayed,

Though I have seen my head (grown slightly bald) brought in upon a platter,

I am no prophet – and here's no great matter;

I have seen the moment of my greatness flicker,

And I have seen the eternal Footman hold my coat, and snicker,

And in short, I was afraid.

Even the name: J Alfred Prufrock, is redolent with his self-disgust. The triviality and lack of depth of women is conveyed in the lines:

In the room the women come and go Talking of Michelangelo.

The whole poem is filled with despair.

Elliot was very unsettled and went from Paris to Harvard and from there to Merton College Oxford and from there to Birkbeck, University of London. Whilst punting at Oxford he met Vivienne Haig-Wood, a Cambridge governess. They were married at Hampstead register office in 1915, the same year that Jean Verdenal died on the beach at Gallipoli. The marriage was a disaster because Elliot had no particular feelings for women other than contempt or even, possibly, disgust. Vivienne tried affairs with other men including Bertrand Russell, but the poor woman was unable to establish a sexual relationship on a long-term basis with anybody and it gradually unhinged her. Eliot on the other hand started writing anti-Jewish poetry which has gained considerable notoriety. Most of his anti-Jewish poetry was written in the years 1917-1922 and followed the death of Jean Verdenal, and by his training as an Anglo-Catholic in what has now become known as "Christian anti-Semitism". Even his marriage, one supposes, was prompted by the Christian faith and the book of Leviticus. The poor man was trying to become 'normal'.

In 1920 he published "a cooking egg" which contained the lines:

I shall not want Capital in Heaven

For I shall meet Sir Alfred Mond:

We two shall lie together, lapt

In a 5% Exchequer bond.
I shall not want society in heaven,
Lucretia Borgia shall be my bride;
Her anecdotes will be more amusing
Than Pipits experience could provide

This poem contains the essence of Eliot's worldview. That the corruption of modern society is due to Jewish capital and women poison a man's life. He never resiled from this view. The parallels with Jean Verdenal and his marital life are fairly evident.

In 1920 he published the poem "Girontion" which contains the lines:

Here I an old man in a dry month,
Being read to by a boy, waiting for rain.
I was neither at the hot gates
Nor fought in the warm rain
Nor knee deep in the salt marsh, heaving a cutlass,
Bitten by flies, fought.
My house is a decayed house,
And the Jew squats on the window sill, the owner,
Spawned in some estaminet of Antwerp,
Blistered in Brussels, patched and peeled in London....

Another poem of the 1920s was "Burbank with a Baedeker: Bleistein with a cigar":

At a perspective of Canaletto. The Smoky candle end of

time declines. On the Rialto once. The rats are underneath the piles.

The Jew is underneath the lot. Money in furs. The boatman smiles, Princess Volupine extends a meagre, blue nailed, phthisic hand.

To climb the water stair. Lights, lights, She entertains Sir Frederick Klein....

In 1922, Elliot published the wasteland in which "a game of chess" has an allusion to Judaism:

Doubled the flames of seven branched candelabra

Reflecting light upon the table as

The glitter of her jewels rose to meet it

From satin cases poured a rich profusion;

In vials of ivory and coloured glass

Unstoppered, lurked her strange synthetic perfumes,

Unguent, powdered, or liquid – troubled, confused...

In later verses there is an allusion to a conversation with his wife. The wife is speaking:

What shall I do now? What shall I do?

I shall rush out as I am, and walk the street

With my hair down, so. What shall we do tomorrow?

What shall we ever do?...

His wife was found on one occasion meandering the streets of London either unclothed or lacking clothing. The allusion to a menorah is probably to create a contrast in the reader's mind between Passover celebrated by the bejewelled, scented Jewess and the purity of the Last Supper in the gospels. In the summer of 1919, Elliot had had sexual relations with his wife and so the resumption of his ice-cold facade would have been particularly painful for her.[178]

At the end of 1921 Eliot suffered a nervous breakdown and he travelled to Lausanne to put himself in the hands of Dr Vittoz in his sanatorium, leaving his wife to fend for herself in Paris. A psychiatrist called Dr Harry Trosman who, possibly, had never met Elliot, diagnosed his psychiatric illness as:

Depression with exhaustion, indecisiveness, Hypochondriasis, and fear of psychosis. His personality had been aloof and distant and he guarded himself against the intrusion of others with icy urbanity. Compulsive defences enable to him to isolate his emotions. Sexuality was a potent danger not only because of intense conflict but because it's still forces threaten him with loss of ego control and dominance. [179]

Early in 1923 Eliot gave up all attempts at being 'normal' and, in spite of being very short of money, rented a flat at Burleigh mansions in Charing Cross Road where he called himself Captain Eliot. The few select visitors noticed that he had started putting on his face a dusting of green powder. At times he drank very heavily but it was here that he started to entertain a whole series of young men. He had previously introduced into his wife's country cottage a handsome young German who was found to be pilfering the housekeeping money and whom Eliot, in a towering

---

[178] Carole Seymour-Jones, *Painted Shadow*, p.247.
[179] Carole Seymour-Jones, *Painted Shadow*, pp.288-289.

rage, dismissed. Rages are a symptom of depression. When, somebody threatens the remains of their self-esteem, the depressive person has difficulty with modulation and management of the angry feelings and fantasies that the threat engenders. The rage itself, like racism, brings a sense of control to a suffering soul.

At about this time Elliot's anti-Semitic references in his poetry stopped but his anti-Semitism in which he saw Jews as underlying the commercialism of modern society and opposing the decency of chivalry never deserted him. In 1933 he gave a lecture to the students of Harvard University which was published under the title "After Strange Gods". His lecture was quietly racist and talked about the values of tradition in which the landscape has been moulded by numerous generations of one race and in which the landscape in turn has modified the race to its own character. It is more important to have a unity of religious background, and reasons of race and religion combine to make any large number of freethinking Jews undesirable. There must be a proper balance between urban and rural, industrial and agricultural development and spirit of excessive tolerance is to be deprecated.

From 1946 to 1957, Elliot shared a flat with his friend John Davey Hayward who collected and managed his papers, giving himself the title of "Keeper of the Eliot Archive". When Eliot married Esme Valerie Fletcher at the age of 68 the Hayward household broke up. Miss Fletcher was 30 years old at the time and has dedicated herself to preserving his legacy. She died in 2012 at her home in London. Eliot himself was cremated in 1965 at Golders Green crematorium. The few extracts of his poems given in this pamphlet are a very pale shadow of his genius. The only shadow over his character is his first wife Vivienne, who died in a sanatorium at the age of 58 in 1947 of a heart attack. When he heard the news he buried his head in his hands and said, "Oh God! Oh God!" She had a tragic life but the draconian homophobic laws of the land must take part of the blame.

His remorse at the way he treated his first wife is evident but, equally evident, is the need to have someone to look down on in order to restore his feeling of self-worth and disparaging remarks about Jews fulfilled this need. There seems to be no evidence that Eliot knew any Jews but he intellectualised his need to look down on another race. In a lecture he gave in 1933 to the University of Virginia:

The population should be homogeneous; where two or more cultures exist in the same place they are likely either to be fiercely self conscious or both become adulterate. What is still more important is unity of religious background and reasons of race and religion combine to make any large number of free thinking Jews undesirable. There must be a proper balance between urban and rural, industrial and agricultural development.[180]

Of course without his frustrations and prejudices, the world might have lost one of the greatest writers in the English language.

At the time of writing, homosexuality is considered, psychologically, completely normal and same-sex marriage has been recognised in the mainly Protestant

---

[180] *After Strange Gods*, pp.19, 20.

countries of the world. The remainder are holding out against it with the exception of Argentina, Mexico and Israel. The latter will recognise same-sex marriage providing the ceremony has been performed abroad.

CHAPTER 9

EXAMPLES OF INTELLECTUAL RACISTS

The definition of the racist form in the 21st century is someone who would never kill a fellow human being but who would look the other way when an injustice is done to them, from making them wait longer than other customers in a shop to sending them to the gas chambers on the instructions of their cognised superiors. There is a whole range of social injustice. An elderly Belgian lady once said to the author: 'We watched them being loaded in to lorries but, of course, we did not know they (the Germans) were going to kill them.' For this lady, an extremely kind, well-meaning person, loading people of a different, inferior race into lorries was a regrettable but understandable thing to do. She herself was born in the 1920s and was a nurse during the war. The racial pantheon she had imbibed from childhood placed white, Christian, male heterosexuals from Northern Europe at the top of the tree with the rest of human race graded off below them depending on how closely they resembled the ideal. Such a person is a racist follower and we all have to be vigilant not to descend into the same mental state because we could all end up supporting someone who fed our prejudices rather than pursuing a course for the benefit of the general good.

Casual racism still exists. A black woman celebrity walked into a Swiss boutique and asked to see a handbag behind the shop assistant's head. The exact words used are difficult to ascertain but the shop assistant decided the bag she was interested in was too expensive ($38,000) and showed her a cheaper one ($22,000). The logic of what the assistant did is difficult to comprehend but it can only be an assertion of her right to be superior to a black woman. Nothing more is known about the assistant.

What follows is a description of three famous men who gained comfort or relief and restored their defective self-esteem by holding up people of another race to hatred and contempt. Because of the way they are treated in Europe, British Muslims feel more anti-Semitic than the general population because to have an, allegedly, inferior race to look down on is a comfort. In an ITA poll carried out for a documentary: 'What British Muslims Really Think', 25% of Muslims thought that Jews were responsible for most wars whilst only 6% of the general population thought the same. Neither group had any evidence of what they were saying. The overwhelming majority of people answering the survey would not hurt anyone but they would stand silently by and might even applaud when someone else did the hands-on killing. They would not do it themselves.

The lives of the three men who follow demonstrate how perceived defects in their self-esteem are repaired by disparaging statements about people of a different race, in their case, Jews, they all being products of Christian anti-Semitism.

9a Martin Luther

Luther was born in 1483 in Saxony, now part of Germany but in those days, part of the Holy Roman Empire during the Renaissance of classical art and Protgoras' saying: Man is the measure of all things. It also involved a break from the narrow legalism of Roman Catholicism. A schism led by Luther called the Reformation in the same way as Jesus led a schism from Judaism.

He was born to, originally peasant, but rose to burgher-class parents, Hans and Margarethe Luder, which they later changed to Luther. Hans was a leaseholder of copper mines and smelters[181] and decided that Martin should become a lawyer. He went to a school run by lay brothers which taught grammar, rhetoric and logic, 'the trivium', and sounded like the PPE of its day. Luther's mother was a member of the burgher social class and Hans was elevated to mining industrialist and town councillor. Martin Luther seems to have become something of a snob, making clumsy, heavy-handed jokes about the peasantry, from which his family sprang, and denouncing the farmers for not bringing food into Wittenberg during plague. As a member of the burgher class social prejudice was part of their way of life.[182] At Erfurt University he broadened his mind

---

[181] Martin Brecht referred to in Wikipedia Martin Luther.
[182] Michael A Mullett, *Martin Luther*, p.23.

and studied Aristotle, gaining his MA in 1505. He suffered from early mood swings, losing the love of Jesus and gravitating away from religion towards the more humanist works of the renaissance. He began a study of law as his father wished but in his reading of the Bible he saw a parallel between Hannah in the book of Samuel and his mother having a son dedicated to God. This might be rationalising his decision to follow the rule of St Augustine and become a monk.[183]

The life of a monk was marred by periods of severe depression. One episode in the choir he fell down, shouting, 'I am not, I am not!' His depression, it is supposed, was related to fasting and his severe ascetic regime, but on another occasion he confessed to 'really serious sins' though what they were is not known, but not women.[184] His sins might have been of a homosexual nature. Celibacy is a burden for many people including some priests.

In 1517 he began to have severe doubts about the sale of indulgencies, the raising of money to build St Peters in Rome. He preached against it but he was ignored, and he describes himself as the little brother who was despised even though he wrote to the Bishop of Mainz. He finally nailed his 95 theses to the door of All Saints Church in Wittenberg. They were printed in German in 1518. He also denounced transubstantiation, saying it remained real bread and real wine in a sermon of 1519. In 1521 Pope Leo X excommunicated Luther. In 1523 he smuggled 12 nuns out of Nimbschen Cistercian convent and in

---

[183] Mullett, pp.33-37.
[184] Mullett, p.44.

1525 he married one of them, Katharina von Bora. She was 26 and he 41.

In 1523 he entered a pragmatic period denying the cult aspects of Catholicism. It was rumoured that he said that Mary was a woman who had many children and Jesus was the son of Joseph, but he later denied having made this statement. However, he did so quite light heartedly, even wittily. In the same tract he goes on to cut across one of the tenets of Catholicism of his day, i.e. that the Jews had killed the Christian Saviour and indirectly reaffirm that Jesus was a man born of woman:

When we are inclined to boast of our position we should remember that we are but Gentiles, while the Jews are of the lineage of Christ. We are aliens and in-laws; they are blood relatives, cousins, cousins and brothers of our Lord. Therefore, if one is to boast of flesh and blood, the Jews are actually nearer to Christ than we are...[185]

This surge of understanding and benevolence is easy to explain. Luther had met Katharina von Bora and he was in love. They had six children. Their eldest daughter was called Magdalena, a child to whom they were naturally devoted.

By 1525 his benevolence disappeared and his burgher nature reasserted itself. In the Peasants War, a time when the aristocracy broke with Rome to save paying tax, confiscated property and applied taxes to enrich themselves all under the slogan 'German money for a German church', resulted in peasant revolts. The peasants got no sympathy from Luther:

---

[185] Council of Centers on Jewish Christian Relations.

You have to answer people like that until [blood] drips from their noses. The peasants would not listen; they would not let anyone tell them anything, so their ears must now be unbuttoned with musket balls till their heads jump off their shoulders.

In 1527 he developed roaring tinnitus in his left ear, vomiting and vertigo symptomatic of Meniere's disease of the left ear which pursued him for the rest of his life until he died in 1546 of a coronary thrombosis.[186] However, in 1542 his beloved daughter Magdalena, aged 13, died in his arms after a long illness. The account of her death in Wikipedia is very moving and Luther's grief would have been terrible.

A year later, in 1543, he wrote his 65,000-word diatribe against the Jews, 'On the Jews and their lies', in which he says their prayer books should be destroyed, synagogues and schools set on fire, rabbis forbidden to preach, homes burned and property and money confiscated. They should be shown no mercy or kindness, afforded no legal protection, and these "poisonous envenomed worms" should be drafted into forced labour or expelled for all time. In the classic manner, he was projecting his misery on the Jews, the alien race of his day.

Sporadic outbreaks of the Black Death in Germany acted like the death of Magdalena and drove the anguished Germans to attempt to regain control by genuine hatred and expulsion of Jewish communities. Luther's words have been accused of rationalising the behaviour of the Germans in the Holocaust. The words of Luther might have given

---

[186] H Feldmann, in United States Library of Medicine.

some support but it has to be said that the Jews would still have been transported to death camps whether Luther had lived or not and in 1938, the synagogues would still have burned.

9b Richard Wagner

Wagner was one of the greatest musical geniuses who has ever lived. He had enormous and deserved musical success by the end of his life but his life was greatly influenced by his sexuality. He relied on a fetish for silk and satin in order to become sexually aroused and it was something of which he was ashamed. The generally accepted view over the acquisition of a fetish by a human being is that the material which stimulates the sexual appetite of a man or woman is related to an experience of pleasure during childhood. Sigmund Freud, and nobody seems to disagree with him, said that a fetish can be acquired as early as five years old. He mentions the child looking up women's skirts. The attraction of silk and satin is that they are soft and cool and remind the fetishist of a woman's skin. This does not mean, initially, that the material itself will give sexual satisfaction, but the sight of a man or woman wearing the material will enable the fetishist to become aroused. Joanne Entwhistle in her book *The Fashioned Body* describes a fetishist, a girl in 1914, who had transferred the sexual satisfaction she got to the silk and satin itself and, presumably, because she could not find a human being wearing these materials she transferred her attention and need to the material without the need for a human being. She stole quantities of it and was imprisoned. Her case was reported by Willheim Shekel in 1930. So far as men are concerned, it might be thought that the sight of a woman not wearing silk or satin under clothes would be very rare but in the 19th century it was common for women to wear a cotton shift. When the fetishist discovers that he or she cannot find another human being wearing the necessary material then he transfers his erotic arousal to the material itself. Dr Morris North in his book *The Outer Fringe of Sex* gives many examples mostly relating to rubber. A young married couple had no children because the man could not get an erection. At the end of one session he remarked, in passing, that if his wife were wearing rubber, he would have no difficulty. The girl he had married, very naturally, had never considered wearing a rubber nightdress but when it was put to her, frankly, that if she required children this was what she had to do, then she did it and became pregnant shortly afterwards. The Can-Can left nothing to chance and was danced in a silk dress, cotton shifts, and then nothing more.

Richard Wagner was a silk and satin fetishist but it is not clear why one of his two wives could not help him in the same way as the young lady who wore rubber. He was wearing his trademark large silk cravat and wide velvet collars in 1840 when he was 27 and so it might be supposed that his fetish was already in place.

When he was in danger of being exposed in the German press, he and his wife, Cosima, were prepared to emigrate to America to avoid the shame of exposure. This gave him the sort of unstable self-esteem which obtains relief from active downward social comparisons and denigrating people of a different race. Unfortunately, almost to the point of boredom, Christian anti-Semitism has done such a good job that he chose the Jews as the object of his vocal deprecation. So far as is known he never physically harmed a Jew but used them to project his own shame and gain comfort thereby.

Richard Wagner was born in Leipzig in 1813 and became one of the greatest composers the Western world has ever heard. He was the ninth child of Carl Friedrich Wagner who was a clerk in the Leipzig police service. His mother Johanna Rosine was the daughter of a baker. Wagner's father, Carl, died of typhus six months after Richard's birth and Johanna went to live with Ludwig Geyer, an actor and playwright. A few months later in 1814 they probably married. Being the ninth child and male, Wagner had a complex sexual life. Wagner's sex life, over the years, became more and more dependent on his fetishes and his need for women's silk and satin under clothing and stockings which broke into the press in 1877. This in no way reduces his stature as a great composer. As Nietzsche once said: If you have a god you must clothe him. He was, at the time, out shopping on behalf of Wagner for silken knickers.

In 1836 Wagner married an actress called Minna Planer who left him for a man called Dietrich about one year later. Minna, at the age of 16, had been seduced or raped and had a child, Nathalie, who was brought up as her sister. In 1838, he and Minna started living together again but in 1839 they had such large debts that they had to flee their creditors and go to Paris where they lived until 1842. Their lives were bedevilled by lack of money and during a large part of this period they were helped, professionally, by the Jewish composer Meyerbeer. In 1842 he left Minna in Paris and pursued his career in Dresden though he continued to support her financially. His reliance on silk and satin grew steadily throughout his life as he required more and more stimulus.

Wagner explained his need for silk and satin clothing by saying that he suffered from erysipelas, a rash which normally appears on the face and has clearly defined borders. It is not uncommon and was known as St Anthony's fire. In the 19th century the treatment was doses of iron and quinine plus dabbing the face with a tincture of opium suspended in lead water. Ice water was also used, if it could be obtained, to counteract the inflammation.[187] There is no record of silk and satin having any remedial effect on this particular dermatological problem, nor that Wagner suffered from it.

In 1849, Wagner's involvement with left-wing politics caused him to have to flee Germany and take refuge in Switzerland. In 1850 he was existing on a small pension paid to him by Julie, the wife of his friend Carl Ritter. This may have been augmented by another woman called Jessie Lasso but Wagner himself ruined this by starting an affair with her, following which her husband terminated any involvement with him. At this very low period in Wagner's life he became an anti-Semite and wrote his famous pamphlet "Judaism in music". It contained expressions of general loathing for Jews such as:

---

[187] The description of Wagner's fetishism is given more fully in Laurence Dreyfus, *Wagner and the Erotic Impulse*, pp.137-147.

"Here, then, we touch the point that brings us closer to our main enquiry: we have to explain to ourselves the involuntary repellence possessed for us by the nature and personality of the Jews, so as to vindicate that instinctive dislike which we plainly recognise as stronger and more overpowering than our conscious zeal to rid ourselves thereof." And: *"...The cultured Jew appears in our society; his distinction from the uncultured, the common Jews, we now have closely to observe. The cultured Jew has taken the most incredible pains to strip off all the obvious tokens of his lower co- religionists: in many case he has even held it wise to make a Christian baptism wash away the traces of his origin. This zeal, however, has never got so far as to let him reap the hoped for fruits: it has conducted only to his utter isolation, and to making him the most heartless of all human beings; to such a pitch, that we have been bound to lose even our earlier sympathy for the tragic history of his stock."*

In the 22 pages of the pamphlet there are many such statements to such an extent that the label "anti-Semite" has stuck to him until the present time. In 1862 Wagner met the wife of Hans von Bulow, Cosima von Bulow.

She already had two daughters when her husband granted her a divorce and she and Wagner were married in 1870. By then he had, and maintained, an entire boudoir of silks and satins with roses and perfume where he liked to sit and be on his own. We must assume that it was a very happy period of his life because in 1868 he wrote his only comedy 'Die Meistersinger Von Nurnberg'. It is unlikely that he was bisexual. Ludwig II of Bavaria wrote him at least one passionate love letter but it is clear from Wagner's reply that he did not reciprocate any similar passion.[188] Wagner's great love was Matilde Wesendonck, a very pretty woman, who reciprocated his feelings, but their love affair was never consummated. After completing Parsifal, based on the Passion of Christ, Wagner died of a heart attack in Venice in 1883.

In 19th-century Germany, Jews were exposed to the most unmerciful ridicule. An actor called Albert Wurm appeared on stage in silk pretending to be a pretentious nouveau riche Jewish woman who spoke ungrammatical German with the odd word of Yiddish thrown in to expose her complete lack of understanding of German culture. In a pretentious accent she attempts to recite Schiller, bringing the house down in helpless laughter. This was not lost on Richard Wagner who described Felix Mendelssohn's music as being like a Jew attempting to recite Goethe in Yiddish. Wurm's act came to an end when it was disclosed that he was, himself, a homosexual, and by the distasteful standards of those times, as despised as being a Jew. The Jewish satirist and journalist, Daniel Spitzer, published 16 of the letters between Wagner and his various milliners over a period of several years. The Wagners were exposed to ridicule in the satirical press with a cartoon appearing in Puck in 1877. The Wagners were so humiliated that they considered emigrating to America but in the end they decided to weather the storm because Wagner himself was such a massive figure in the world of music and his fetishism was, quite rightly, put to one side when measured against his genius.

The matter cannot have been put entirely to one

---

[188] Laurence Dreyfus, *Wagner and the Erotic Impulse*, p.198.

side because the ongoing shame of relying on fetishism for sexual stimulus, though not uncommon, exposed him to ridicule, and ridicule reduced his self-esteem and feelings of self-worth. Under these circumstances, like any common racist he buoyed up his self-worth by denigrating people of another race. He made sneering remarks about Jews though he had a number of individual acquaintances who were Jewish, notably his conductor, Hermann Levi, who admired him. He also had professional relationships with Bruno Walter and Otto Klemperer. They all admired him as a musician, there can be no doubt of that, but, possibly, not as a man. What is certain is that he was a genius and it is impossible to put him in a box with a label.

9c James Joyce

James Joyce was born in February 1882 in Rathgar, Dublin, of middle-class parents, into a Catholic family in social decline due to his father's drinking and total lack of control over the family finances. James was a brilliant student and went to two Jesuit schools, Clongowes and Belvedere. The Catechism current among Jesuits at that time was the Maynooth version of 1891 which was quite virulent on the role of the Jews in the death of Jesus. He completed his education at University College, Dublin, and became one of the leading writers and poets of his generation.

His major work was *Ulysses*, the experiences of Jew, Leopold Bloom, as he meanders around Dublin on the 16 June 1904, still celebrated as Bloomsday. Joyce records Bloom's inner thoughts and the anti-Semitism which surrounds him from the thoughtless racism of the Irish people. The odious figure of the teacher Mr Deasy exemplifies the anti-Jewish racism which existed in 1904. Deasy is an Anglophile while the Joyce family admired Parnell.

He raised his forefinger and beat the air oddly before his voice spoke.

"Mark my words Mr Dedalus, he said. England is in the hands of the Jews. In all the highest places: her finance, her press. And they are the signs of a nation's decay. Wherever they gather they eat up a nation's vital strength. I have seen it coming these years. As sure as we are standing here the Jew merchants are already at their work of destruction. Old England is dying... Dying, he said, if not dead by now."

Stephen Dedalus points out that merchants, in the nature of being merchants, buy cheaply and sell at a profit but Mr Deasy will have none of it: *'They sinned against the light, Mr Deasy said gravely. And you can see the darkness in their eyes. And that is why they are wanderers on the earth to this day.'* [189]

Far from being a racist, Joyce and Stephen Dedalus, who speaks for him, deplores the Deasy character and the others expressing similar prejudices, and identifies with Bloom burdened by his unfaithful wife, Molly. Joyce himself met and went to the continent with, a domestic servant called Nora Barnacle who offered him the sort of sexual satisfaction he needed. In one of his letters to her he says: *'It was you who slid your hand inside my trousers and pulled my shirt softly to one side and touched my prick with your long tickling fingers, and gradually took it all, fat and stiff as it was, into your hand and frigged me slowly until it came off*

---

[189] Minerva Edition, pp.35, 36.

through your fingers, all the time bending over me and gazing at me out of your quiet saintlike eyes.'

There is a similar example of lust by which Bloom's wife, Molly, secured him:

'Must have been the morning in Raymond terrace she was at the window watching two dogs at it by the wall of the cease to do evil. And the sergeant grinning up. She had that cream gown on with the rip she never stitched. "Give us a touch Poldy. God I'm dying for it." How life begins.'[190]

There are other parallels in this effort to show that Joyce himself identified with his character, Bloom; that is, Joyce felt like a Jew. People were sneering at him behind his back. The following involves his wife, Nora, and is an episode out of his life and the need he had for sexual stimulus:

They were soon in bed engaged in what Joyce called 'the ecstasy of combat'. The glove which had kept Joyce satisfied this far was finally discarded. Nora's sexual enthusiasm was evident, and, as her biographer puts it, 'she needed no tutoring'.[191] She often initiated their love-making and encouraged James with whispered obscenities, which would not have been out of place at Bella Cohen's Monto.[192]

Molly Bloom has a long, beautifully rendered, erotic daydream in the section known as 'Penelope'. Spelling mistakes and unpunctuated, stream, dreaming of the men she has brought to climax and her need for more men.[193]

A closer parallel to Bloom can be found in Joyce's

[190] Minerva Edition, p.93.

[191] Brenda Maddox, *Nora*, p.79.

[192] Gordon Bowker, *James Joyce*, p.135.

[193] Minerva Edition pp727-777.

obsessive need for the smell of urine and his need to hear a woman urinating. Whilst this need is fairly common and is found in erotica and pornography[194] it is generally found repulsive by the general public. In Joyce's own life he recalls:

By his fourteenth year, the intense devotion to religion which had marked Joyce's first two years at Belvedere was under threat from the onset of puberty and its fleshly temptations. He told Stanislaus that his firs sexual experience had occurred at around this time. It involved a nursemaid, who, out walking with him, had retired behind a hedge to relieve herself. The sounds of the girl urinating had so excited him that he had an erection leading to orgasm...he was amazed that one of Dante's thunderbolts had not struck him dead.[195]

Nor did this predilection with the sound of female urine leave him in later life. There are regular references to it in his later work. In a letter dated 16 December 1909 to Nora he says: *Fuck me on the stairs in the dark...murmuring into his ear dirty words and dirty stories that other girls told her. And dirty things she said, and all the time pissing her drawers with pleasure and letting off warm quiet little farts behind...*[196]

This fixation with urine is bestowed upon his fictional character, Bloom, leaving the impression on the ignorant that this is how all Jews behave. Far from it. This is how Joyce behaves and it is the reason why he feels shunned and laughed at, like a Jew. He has substituted Bloom for himself but that does not make him a racist.

---

[194] See for example *My Secret Life* by 'Walter' Volume I, Chapter VIII.

[195] Bowker, p.52.

[196] Tribe James Joyce's Dirty Letters on the Internet.

The last question is why did Joyce choose the name Ulysses and not the heroic Odysseus? After all, Ulysses is reviled and appears in the eighth level of Dante's inferno as the man who gave false gifts (a wooden horse) and brought about the downfall of Troy. He is being burned in hell because Aeneas escaped from Troy, became the first of the Alban kings who founded Rome. That being the case, Ulysses is a wicked man. Joyce himself supports this view:

'I find the subject of Ulysses the most human in world literature. Ulysses didn't want to go off to Troy; he knew the official reason for the war, the dissemination of the culture of Hellas, was only a pretext for Greek merchants, who were seeking new markets...Before Troy the heroes shed their lifeblood in vain. They want to raise the siege. Ulysses opposes the idea. [He thinks up] the stratagem of the wooden horse. After Troy there is no further talk of Achilles, Menelaus, Agamemnon. Only one man is not done with; his heroic career has hardly begun: Ulysses.'[197]

Joyce lived in Zurich during most of the First World War and that was also the period when he was writing Ulysses. He was close to events and must have been aware of the slaughter of German, French, British and Colonial troops. It was the greatest loss of life the world had seen up to that time. The traditional view of the hero in war was completely overturned. The traditional ode:

---

[197] Joyce cited in Richard Ellman's James Joyce. Quoted in Notes on James Joyce on the internet.

Let the boy toughened by military service
Learn how to make bitterest hardship his friend
And as a horseman with fearful lance
Go to vex the insolent Parthians

Spending his life in the open, in the heart
of dangerous action. And seeing him from
the enemy's walls, let the warring
tyrant's wife, and her grown up daughter, sigh

'Ah don't let the inexperienced lover
Provoke the lion that's dangerous to touch
For whom a desire for blood sends raging
So swiftly through the core of destruction.'

It's sweet and fitting to die for one's country.
Yet death chases after the soldier who runs.
And won't spare the cowardly back
Or the limbs of peace loving young men.[198]

This image of war was replaced by the mouthless dead of Charles Sorley who was born in Aberdeen in 1895, volunteered and served in the Suffolk Regiment from 1914 to 1915 when he died in the Battle of

---

[198] Part of Horace, ode Dulce et Decorum Est Pro Patria Mori, translated by AS Kline.

Loos, a captain, from a sniper's bullet to the head:

When you see millions of the mouthless dead
Across your dreams in pale battalions go,
Say not soft things as other men have said,
That you'll remember. For you need not so.
Give them not praise. For, deaf, how should they know
It is not curses heaped on each gashed head?
Nor tears. Their blind eyes see not your tears flow.
Nor honour. It is easy to be dead.
Say only this, 'They are dead.' Then add thereto,
'Yet many better one has died before.'
Then scanning all the o'ercrowded mass should you
Perceive one face that you loved heretofore,
It is a spook. None wears the face you knew.
Great death has made all his for evermore.

CHAPTER 10

GENOCIDE

Following an economic recession, for example, many people find it harder to make ends meet and some of those people become racist in order to regain control and have the comfort of sharing a common enemy with many of their own race. The loss of self-esteem might be imposed by society as in the cases of TS Eliot and James Joyce. The loss of self-esteem might be imposed by economic mismanagement either personal or national. Fear for one's life might be imposed by plague or famine, in which case the population is ready to believe that their misfortune has been brought about by immigrants who speak their language with a foreign accent and/or wear different clothing or have a different appearance. In other words, some of the population become xenophobic and a leader who offers control by supporting the culpability of foreigners will get a sympathetic hearing from many without presenting evidence and, in extreme cases of widespread suffering, he can get them to kill.

The first case of national racism recorded was in Hecataeus of Abdera in his *Aegyptiaca*, now lost but an excerpt survived in Diodorus Siculus' *Bibliotheca Historica*:

When in ancient times a pestilence arose in Egypt, the common people ascribed their troubles to the workings of a divine agency; for indeed with many strangers of all sorts dwelling in their midst and practising different rites of religion and sacrifice, their own traditional observances in honour of the gods had fallen into disuse. Hence the natives of the land surmised that unless they removed the foreigners their troubles would never be resolved. At once, therefore, the aliens were driven from the country and the most active among them banded together and, as some say, were cast ashore in Greece and certain other regions; their leaders were notable men, chief among them being Danaus and Cadmus. But the greater number were driven into what is now called Judea, which is not far distant from Egypt and was at that time utterly uninhabited. The colony was headed by a man called Moses, outstanding both for his wisdom and his courage.[199]

Little credence can be placed on the names mentioned. The two Greeks are mythical and Moses comes from the Hebrew bible. Nevertheless, the circumstances surrounding the eviction of foreigners ring true because human beings faced with misfortune do the same thing today. The 'pestilence' was no more than the trigger for this behaviour.

Edward I (Longshanks) 1239-1307 took the country to war on an almost constant basis. He had wars with the Scots, the Welsh and went on a crusade with the predictable result that he ran out of money. Money was owed to the Jews but because the king virtually owned the Jews, he could tax them without

---

[199] Translation from Peter Schafer, *Judeophobia*, pp.15,16.

restraint. Jews started to leave for other places and the king formally expelled them in 1290. This was probably little more than window dressing. With the start of the Hundred Years War the drain on money in both England and France became intolerable and the kings of both countries defaulted on their loans The Italian moneylenders, the Riccardis, were made bankrupt. Coinage was being debased, silver content reduced, more coins went into circulation. The resulting inflation caused prices to outstrip wages and the peasantry under the rigid rule of the landowners, suffered great hardship[200]. The arrival of the Black Death in Europe caused the absolute conviction among the 'common people' that the Jews were poisoning the wells and, as a consequence, Jews were massacred. The trigger which caused the transition from expulsion to killing was the prolonged period of hardship suffered by the population of France and England brought about by war and wholesale inflation.[201] The Jews paid the price.

10a The Rwandan Massacre

In 1994, this shared many of the characteristics of any other piece of prejudice though, tragically, was much more deadly.

The earliest inhabitants of Rwanda were groups of pygmy hunter-gatherers called the Twa who migrated there in about 8000 BC. They were followed thousands of years later, in about 700 BC, by Bantu groups migrating from West Africa who came to be called the

---

[200] David Hackett Fischer, *The Great Wave*, p.23 et seq.
[201] James Carroll, *Constantine's Sword*, p.226 et seq.

Hutu. The final migration was that of the Tutsi who arrived after 1500 CE and might have come from the Nile Sahara area. The Hutu were largely agricultural whilst the Tutsi were cattle herders. In spite of their long residence in the country, during the massacre, the Tutsi were always referred to as 'immigrants' in order to depersonalise them.[202]

Though a minority, the Belgian colonial power favoured the Tutsi who were taller, more graceful possibly and of a rather more European bone structure. In the 1930s the Tutsi chiefs seized land, Hutu agricultural land, and turned it into grazing for their cattle. Even so, there was a considerable racial intermixing and intermarriage took place, not frequently, but on a regular basis. In 1935 the Belgians introduced identity cards which defined the holder as being Twa, Hutu or Tutsi so that the holder's race was fixed for the rest of his life. In the case of mixed marriages the children were given the race of the father so that from that day on a homogeneous society was not possible.[203]

After the Second World War movements began to render power to the Hutu. In 1957 a group of Hutu scholars wrote the Bahutu manifesto which called for a transfer of power from Tutsi to Hutu based on what was called statistical law. In 1959 there was an outbreak of violence at Kigali airport and the Belgian administration changed sides and began to favour the Hutu. In 1960 the Belgians arranged midyear elections which overwhelmingly returned a Hutu majority. The King was deposed and a Hutu republic created; the

---

[202] Fergal Keane, *A Season of Blood*, p.15.
[203] Fergal Keane, *A Season of Blood*, pp.16,17.

country became independent in 1962. Tutsi began fleeing as Hutu purges drove them out. In 1963 Hutu militias murdered 10,000 Tutsis. In 1967 there was a further outbreak of violence. Tutsis fled Rwanda and settled in Burundi, Uganda, Tanzania and Zaire where they formed armed groups who launched attacks into Rwanda. In July 1973, in the midst of terrible economic hardship in Rwanda, Juvenal Habyarimana came to power in a coup d'état and remained in power without a convincing mandate, winning elections by a scarcely credible 98% of the vote, unopposed, and remained in power until his plane crashed in 1994. During that period he gathered around himself a group of kleptocrats whose one aim was to remain in power. With their mania for democracy, Western powers recognised Habyarimana as an unelected dictator and he was forced to move towards democracy by agreeing the Arusha Accords. His followers saw this as a threat to their positions in government and, according to Fergal Keene in his book: *A Season of Blood*, his own followers were heavily implicated in the missile attack that brought down his plane in 1994.

The foundation for the massacre of 1994 was economic failure. In 1990 when, on IMF advice, the Rwandan franc was devalued and the agricultural subsidies removed, the effect of this was a sharp rise in imported foodstuffs and the public debt and the cost of servicing it, doubled in two years.[204] In addition to this the World Bank advised that state enterprises should be privatised with the result that public services collapsed. Child malnutrition increased

---

[204] Gerard Prunier, *The Rwandan Crisis*, p.159.

and malaria, in particular, increased by 21% in 1991. In 1992 there was a further devaluation and an increase in the production of coffee at a time when coffee prices were falling. Joseph Oppong in his book, *Rwanda*, lays the blame for the massacre squarely on the economy:

Rwanda's economy experienced severe difficulties in the 1980s. When world coffee prices plummeted by more than 50%, Rwandan farmers were crushed, as was the country's economy. Widespread famines erupted. Between 1989 and 1993, when Rwanda began to implement structural adjustment, life was extremely difficult. Many changes imposed by the World Bank shocked the economy. Trade was liberalised, and many state businesses were privatised. Government subsidies on health and agriculture were removed. Many government employees were laid off. Rwanda's currency was devalued. Immediately, the Rwandan franc last half of its value, inflation skyrocketed, and public services collapsed. Forward shortages emerged, particularly in the oral areas, and an outbreak of malaria swept the country. Despite soaring domestic prices, coffee prices remained at the low 1989 price. [205]

Hatred which the Hutu felt for the Tutsi reached boiling point under the impetus of poverty. The Tutsi, whose capital was in domestic livestock, could ride the inflation. The reason why the average Hutu in the street supported or turned a blind eye to the killing was because of the economic privations he had suffered. None of this was the fault of the Tutsi but they as 'immigrants' were made to pay with their lives.

---

[205] The weakness of Western loan agencies is that, having made a loan, their main concern is the introduction of austerity measures which ensure its repayment with less regard to political stability.

As early as 1989, a million machetes had been ordered from China and the removal of the remaining food subsidies in 1993 seems to have been sufficient to goad the poorest section of the population to murder.

There was intense fight training of Hutu militia; the radio station Mille Collines started broadcasting programmes urging the Hutu population to attack the Tutsi and the preparation was so obvious that many human rights organisations started evacuating themselves and their families from Rwanda. Immediately after the plane crash Rwandan Armed Forces and Hutu irregulars set up roadblocks and went from house-to-house killing Tutsi and moderate Hutu politicians. Thousands were killed who had no authority to do otherwise and who were stationed in rural areas stood by. The exiled Tutsi military force, RPF, launched a major offensive on Kigali. On 21 April UN forces started to evacuate. On 30 April, the UN Security Council passed a resolution condemning the violence but omitting the word "genocide" so that no action was obligatory. The killing of Tutsis continued until July 1994 when the RPF defeated the Rwandan army and the Rwandan government fled to Zaire. This allowed the UN troops from Ethiopia to take control of Kigali and the RPF set up an interim government. The Hutu slaughter of Tutsi was merciless and one account by a child will have to suffice to demonstrate how pitiless they were:

"The Interahamwe came to our house and asked all who were inyenzi (cockroaches) to step outside. They knew we were Tutsi, these people, because some of them are our neighbours. *When we did not come out they broke down the*

door. We were inside and could hear them shouting. And then they came through the front door and I followed my parents and brothers and sisters out into the fields at the back and we ran. But they ran fast and caught us and they killed my family members and they thought they had killed me too. They hit me with the machetes and clubs and then they threw all the bodies together so that I was lying under my mother who was dead. But I was not dead and that night I crawled away and hid in the fields where the grass was very high. Then after a while the soldiers from the RPF came and they helped me and brought me here.'[206]

There was a widespread material reward. The Hutu women cooked meals, plundered their neighbours' houses, took their clothes and, in many cases, gathered in Tutsi cattle for slaughter. They enjoyed the clothes of the Tutsi women and they enjoyed the Tutsi food as long as it lasted. The identity cards were extensively used at roadblocks to identify Tutsi and murder them.

Finally, following the murder of approximately 800,000 Tutsi in Rwanda, the Times, on August 30, 2010, published details of a United Nations report giving accounts of revenge murder by Tutsi of Hutu civilians. The report is nearly 600 pages long and was completed in 2002, stating that the majority of the victims were children, women, elderly people and the sick who were often undernourished and posed no threat to the attacking forces. Most were bludgeoned to death so that they cannot even be accounted for as part of the hazards of war or collateral damage. The refugee camps in eastern DRC (Democratic Republic of the Congo) and Zaire were ransacked to find Hutu

---

[206] Keane, p.59, supports this account.

and kill them. The bodies were buried in four large mass graves and there are accounts of refugees being burned alive, and 370 refugees were said to be thrown into the latrines at the Luberezi camp. There are other accounts of similar horrors. The Times records that in a letter to the UN secretary general, Louise Mushikiwabo, Rwanda's Foreign Minister, denounced the report as "fatally flawed" and "incredibly irresponsible".

Economic recession with the resulting quest for control causes many to vote for a strong figure who will restore national control and make their country great again. Those who maintain their own internal control are more cynical and do not require such reassurance.

10b The Massacres of Armenians

In the declining years of the Ottoman Empire which probably began with the Viennese bank failures of 1873 and the beginning of the Long Depression which lasted, in most countries, until 1879. In Britain, it probably lasted until 1893 before stagnation lifted. The length of economic stagnation varied throughout the world from country to country. The cause has been generally assigned to printing too much money to finance warfare, post-war inflation and the subsequent struggles to return to sound money and restrict the money supply. The American Civil War produced massive inflation in the Confederate states. It was 'solved' by reducing the coinage in circulation and issuing only gold coins.[207] A similar but self-inflicted oversupply of money was imposed by Prussia who exacted reparations from the French after winning the Franco-Prussian War. Otto von Bismark too introduced gold marks in 1873. It was this downturn in world trade which caused the Viennese stock market to crash. Many small investors blamed the Jews.

The situation in the Ottoman Empire, an agricultural economy in need of industrialisation, was that it attracted a flow of capital from the industrial world simply because the rates of interest obtainable on bonds issued by the Ottoman government were higher than those obtainable in the more industrialised nations of the world.

Ottoman economists propose that during periods of recession in the industrialised countries which have moved on to a gold standard, capitalists will take the risk of buying the bonds of peripheral agrarian economies and, over a period of time, export the oversupply of money to them.

This is what happened in the 19th century in the Ottoman Empire and began modestly in 1854 with a purchase of £3 million bonds by Britain, but escalated in accumulated unpaid debt to more than £253 million in 1866 which was more than ten times the nation's estimated income, with 70% of the amount

---

[207] The Coinage Act 1873. The difficulty of imposing a sudden reduction in the money supply by going onto a gold standard is that the shock to the economy results in widespread.
unemployment. It is for this reason that the monetarists of the Chicago School advocated rises in interest rates until inflation came under control.

owed to the British and the French. In 1877 the Ottoman government defaulted and announced it would suspend interest payments. As a result the debtor nations took over the direct administration of the debt to ensure they got paid. This seems to have been done effectively and the value of Ottoman bonds rose steadily in Paris until 1903.[208] The money was invested in infrastructure in the main with 63% going on building railways, and must have been so beneficial that the nationalist government of the Young Turks, which came into power in 1908, continued to cooperate with the debtor countries.

At the same time as incurring substantial debts with the aim of industrialising the country, a series of reforms were announced starting in 1839 to annul the poll tax paid by non-Muslims and grant equality to the Christians of the Balkans. This was slow coming and after a series of rebellions independence was granted to Serbia 1878, but in the meantime Russia declared itself to be the defenders of Christians in the Balkans. The Christians/Russia became the enemies in the minds of the Ottoman peasantry.

Drought in 1873 and floods in 1874 produced widespread famine. The increasing debt burden, mentioned above, increased taxation which was more than the people of both the Balkans and the Ottomans could bear. In 1877 Russia declared war and gained independence for Serbia, Romania and a divided Bulgaria, united in 1895.[209] This was seen as a major defeat for the Ottomans and a triumph for

---

[208] Murat Bridal p62.
[209] The European debtors removed £90 million from the national debt.

Christianity. A series of anti-Christian pogroms broke between 1894 and 1896, tapering off in 1897, about which Abdul Hamid did nothing until put under pressure by the Christian nations. The brunt of the killing fell on the Armenians living in the Ottoman Empire who had always been considered foreigners in spite of having lived there since the 9th century and under Turkish rule since they were defeated at the Battle of Manzikert in 1071.

The Ottoman government had been watching impassively, the murder and looting in Armenian towns because Armenians were taken to be less than a Muslim and, possibly, less than a human being. The outrages became more bloody as the power of the Ottomans diminished. At Diyarbakir: along the walls of the Gregorian cemetery lay 321 bodies of dead Armenians which had been mutilated post mortem with faces smashed in, heads nearly severed and arms ripped off or skinned.[210] This mutilation indicates the degree of hatred felt by the Turks who did it. At Urfa, Ottoman soldiers set fire to the cathedral with thousands of Armenians inside it. Whilst not creating this merciless horror, Abdul Hamid allowed it to happen in order to instil terror in the Armenian population: *'as Abdul Hamid's private secretary wrote in his memoirs "..decided to pursue a policy of severity and terror against the Armenians, and in order to succeed in this respect he elected the method of dealing them an economic blow...he ordered that they absolutely avoid negotiating or discussing anything with the Armenians and they inflict upon them a decisive strike to settle scores."'*

The killings continued into 1897, at which stage

---

[210] William Sachtleben in a letter to the Times 1895.

the Armenian Question was declared closed. The Armenian Question was the diplomatic urging of the great Christian powers of Europe to prevail on the Muslim powers (Persian and Ottoman) to treat their Christian minorities as equals. Unfortunately, this was undermined by Russia who treated the Christian minorities as potential traitors to assist Russia against the Ottoman government in their struggles for global influence.[211] This emphasised the role of the Armenian as the enemy.

The killing of Armenians continued sporadically: In 1896 in relation to an attempted occupation of the Ottoman Bank by Armenians. In 1909, 20,000 Armenians were killed in the course of what came to be known as the Adana massacres. In 1911 there was an outbreak of xenophobia directed at Christians and both Armenians and Greeks were murdered.

In 1914 the Turkish Government sold £20 million worth of bonds to the French[212] and dedicated to 'floating debt', and in November of the same year, joined Germany in the war with the Entente Powers. The hope evidently was that, in the event of victory, the debt could be unilaterally cancelled. Their first act, in the dead of winter, was to send an army under Ismail Enver into Russia with the eventual field commander, Hafiz Hakki. The 3rd Army consisted of three Corps, IX, X, XI, totalling 118,000 fighting men. The Russian Army which opposed them, the Caucusus Army under Nikolai Yudenich, had to send half their force to reinforce the Prussian front after

---

[211] For example, in 1827 Tsar Nicholas I sought Persian Armenian help in the Russo-Persian War 1826-28.
[212] Bridal Table 3.1 p.89.

the defeats at the Battles of Tannenberg and Masurian Lakes between August and September 1914. Among others, Count Vorontsov-Dashkov recruited 'Russian' Armenian volunteers who were warmly clad and knew the land and the tracks. The Russian Army occupied a front more than 1200km long in front of the rail terminal at Sarikamish.

From the start, the Turkish 3rd Army had inadequate clothing for the harsh conditions, inadequate rations but, above all, inadequate communications so that an elaborate plan to envelope the Russian Army could never have achieved success. On 23rd December, the Turkish 31st Division fired on the Turkish 32nd Division for four hours before the error was recognised.

By 25th December the Turkish troops were exhausted after marching for 14 hours in thick snow. The next day the X Corps came under heavy fire. Enver ordered a night attack and then proceed with the plan at a time when the army was dying from hypothermia and those in shelter were still 30km from the front. The soldiers themselves, on both sides, including the Russian-Armenian volunteers who fought as skirmishers, behaved with courage, but the Turks had been given an impossible task.

Hafiz Hakki died at the front of typhus at the age of 36, while Ismail Enver survived and explained the failure on Armenian traitors.[213] The number of Turkish soldiers who died in the battle is not known but estimates vary up to 76,000, a disaster for many families, and the publicised reason was 'Armenian

---

[213] Wikipedia, The Battle of Sarikamish.

traitors'. There is a grim video from Pathe News showing dead bodies lining the Sarikamish Road after the Turkish retreat, men who had presumably died of cold and hunger. A mass grave being dug by prisoners of war. Pictures are available of bodies being collected in a cart and thrown into the snow, a dog eating a body lying in the snow and the whole being supervised by warmly dressed Russian soldiers.[214]

So far as the general public were concerned, who knew no better, the Armenians were responsible for the disaster in the Caucasus and any measures taken against them was not only acceptable but necessary. Some Turks took retribution into their own hands with or without orders from their officers and thousands of Armenians were massacred in Anatolia, the rural East of Turkey.

The Armenian population of Istanbul was extremely wealthy, including people of the Amira class. They were rich in spite of Armenians being treated like the mud on their boots by the Turkish population.[215] In the subsequent death marches and killings Armenians lost their wealth and property without compensation. And a decree was issued to all financial institutions to hand over all Armenian-owned assets to the Turkish government to the extent that there is what might be a partisan view that the present Republic of Turkey could be responsible for paying reparations though the present generation has no moral responsibility.[216]

---

[214] Available on the Internet. Corpses on Russian Front, 1914-1918.

[215] After William Ramsay writing in the late 1890s.

[216] Henry Theriault writing in the Armenian Weekly, 6 May 2010.

The motive of acquiring Armenian property was reinforced in September 1915 by the passage of 'The Temporary Law of Expropriation and Confiscation'. In April 1915, the deportation of the Armenian population began starting with the richest and most affluent families. They were made to walk until they died and those who survived were put into concentration camps on the Syrian border. It is estimated that between one million and two million Armenians perished. The reason for the government action must have been to finance the war and avoid paying their very substantial debts to Britain and France. As it was, Turkey was financially ruined after the war, areas of its empire were reallocated and financial reparations were cancelled. For some reason, they were treated more rationally than the Germans from whom reparations were exacted with disastrous results. The racial reasoning which brought about the massacre was that the sin of the Russian Armenians in fighting against Turkey could be visited on Turkish Armenians who had had nothing to do with it. This is the lack of intelligence visited on Jews and Muslims in the present day.

10c Adolf Hitler and the Holocaust

The Holocaust, a deranged slaughter instigated when the German people voted for and installed in power a deeply flawed individual called Adolf Hitler. Numbers are so immense that there is only some consensus over the orders of magnitude of the ranges of the numbers who were murdered in cold blood. Hitler and the people around him considered themselves, in various ways, polluted, and they attempted to purify themselves and the German nation by ridding themselves of the inferior races. This sort of dementia exists in many people as a neurosis. They will not kill in the conditions which exist today except certain exceptional individuals. The recent case of the murder of Jo Cox brought to light one such individual.[217]

When economic conditions are conducive to violence, many more such people come to the fore, ready be armed and kill. The races who were murdered by Germans and their allies were primarily Jews followed by Soviet POWs, Ethnic Poles, Serbs, the disabled, Romani, Freemasons, Slovenes, homosexuals, Jehovah's Witnesses, and Spanish Republicans.[218] They were all undefended civilians, whose race was considered impure by the Hitler hierarchy. The bombing of London or Dresden can be taken as acts of war because the bombers were opposed by ground fire and fighter planes whereas the bombing of Guernica in Spain was unopposed.

The road to this genocide was long and possibly started in the 19th century with reparations paid after the Franco-Prussian War in 1870, an influx of cheap money which gave way to inflation followed by deflation, and the recession caused by the Viennese bank failure of 1873. A Jew called Henry Bethel Strousberg left a string of bankruptcies and became a symbol of the 'Jewish swindler' in spite of the fact that by far the great majority of Jews were behaving in a perfectly sober fashion. During a recession, the

---

[217] Guardian 18 June 2016. The suspect gave his name as 'Death to traitors, freedom for Britain.'.
[218] The list is from Wikipedia, The Holocaust, p.37.

people suffering the most hardship find comfort in righteous indignation and blame the whole race if one of that race is blameworthy. A more sinister side of human character emerged with the recession and those who suffered most from the downturn – small shopkeepers, teachers, artisans, clerks, minor civil servants and small traders – began to reject modernity and take to *volkisch* beliefs.[219]

Volkisch has no direct equivalent in English but some translate it as ethno-nationalistic with overtones of 'race' or 'tribe' with its roots in a sentimental look back to Germanic folklore. It clearly is intended to exclude anyone who cannot produce an ancient place in the land from which they sprang. There was a horror of modernity, liberalism and the desire to return to a German way of life. The depression of the 1870s was laid at the door of Jews who had exploited the Germans. Wilhelm Riehl labelled Berlin the *Reich of the Jews* rather than a German city. In 1879 Wilhelm Marr published the Victory of Judaism over Germandom explaining that the modern anti-Semitism was racial rather than religious.[220] In 1881 Eugen Duehring, an economist, taught his students that Jews were inherently inferior and corrupt.

In 1890 the Kaiser accepted Bismarck's resignation much to the latter's surprise and from thereon, the Kaiser acted without a restraining influence. Right-wing and reactionary though Bismarck undoubtedly was, he did have some sense of proportion in international matters and, without him, Wilhelm was

---

[219] Alexandra Richie, *Faust's Metropolis. A History of Berlin*, Loc 6401.
[220] Richie, Loc 6575.

something of a loose cannon. Increasing alienation grew between Germany and Britain, France and Russia with increasing talk of war. At a session in the Reichstag the Socialist August Bebel said:

There will be a catastrophe....sixteen to eighteen million men, the flower of different nations, will march against each other, equipped with lethal weapons. But I am convinced that this great march will be followed by a great collapse (at this moment many in the chamber began to laugh)-all right, you have laughed about it before; but it will come...What will be the result? After this war we shall have mass bankruptcy, mass misery, mass unemployment and great famine. Are you denying this?

He was drowned out by laughter in the chamber. Finally from a right wing bench came the self assured reply: 'Herr Babel, things always get better after every war.' [221]

In the Boer War (1899-1902) and the Boxer rebellion, 1900, which was a right-wing movement which took power in China after a series of natural disasters and expressed the aim of ridding China of Christian foreigners, in 1904, Britain signed a convention with France and in 1907, an entente with the Russians. With violent unrest in the Balkans, war came closer and Berlin society looked forward to it and longed to get into uniform, but real power lay in the hands of the Kaiser, the Junkers and the industrialists. English and Russian names disappeared from both businesses and people and the Schliefen plan, a plan for certain victory, was widely discussed among the cognoscenti.

Every face looks happy. We've got war! Bands in the cafes and restaurants play Heil dir im Siegerkrantz and Die Wacht

---

[221] Richie, Loc 6801.

am Rhein without stopping and everybody has to listen to them standing up. Ones food gets cold, ones beer gets warm: no matter-we've got war! People line up to offer their motor cars for service...Soldiers at the railway stations are offered mountains of buttered sandwiches, sausages and chocolate. There's superabundance of everything: of people, of food, and of enthusiasm.[222]

Germany, acting on the acknowledged wisdom of Count von Schlieffen, set about destroying France before turning on Russia. They offered Belgium a deal whereby they would be granted full independence after the war with some territory taken from France providing they did not resist a German invasion. Having obtained no reply on the 4 August 1914, Germany declared war. The blame for the war was placed squarely on the shoulders of Serbia and Russia. There were scenes of wild excitement and cheering as Germany fought for freedom and its very right to exist. There was some dismay as Britain, acting on the insistence of Sir Edward Grey and Winston Churchill, entered the war on the side of France. Asquith came very close to lying to the House. Stones were thrown through the windows of the British Embassy and the British were labelled 'traitors', though to what is difficult to discern.[223] English became a forbidden language and even Americans had to be careful to wear a badge.

Thus the murder of warfare began. At the first German victory over the Russians at Tannenberg the Russians were herded into two large lakes to drown. Those who struggled in the water were shot. There

---

[222] The actress Tilla Durieux quoted in Richie, Loc 7076
[223] Richie, Loc 7094 et seq.

were scenes of Gothic horror. One witness said he would never forget the shrieks and cries of dying men and horses.[224] On the Western Front there was stalemate with increasing armament production on all sides during 1916 to achieve a breakthrough. In Britain quality control was lessened and, partly because of the soft ground, significant numbers of shells failed to explode and failed to destroy the German front line at the Somme. British troops came out of their trenches and walked into a wall of machine fire. Some 20,000 died on the first day.

Rosa Luxemburg, a young Jewish socialist and co-founder of the Spartacist league with Karl Liebeknecht, a peace activist, wrote: 'Gone is the ecstacy and gone are the patriotic street demonstrations...No more do trains filled with reservists pull out amid joyous cries from enthusiastic maidens. No longer do we see laughing faces smiling from train widows.'

Little by little the British RNVR blockade of the North Sea began to take effect. Alcohol, chocolate and sausages disappeared. In 1915 ration books were introduced and Gerard, the American ambassador, recalls seeing queues to buy meat and watery soup and turnips became common fare. Meat, flour, eggs and milk were all rationed and to bake a cake was a criminal offence. In 1916 butchers' shops were closed for weeks and people danced what was known as 'the Bitter Polonaise' as they moved from queue to queue searching for food.

In 1917 the potato harvest failed and rats were killed for meat. Food riots became common. The

---

[224] Richie, Loc7194 n120.

black market flourished and freezing temperatures kept goods from being unloaded as late as February 1917. In December 1917 coal was so scarce that the magazine Vorwarts suggested that you had to know someone who knew where coal was to be unloaded in order to get any. Thousands died each month from hunger and cold. Princess Blucher, an Englishwoman, recalls black-clad figures on the point of death gliding through the streets of Berlin. Tuberculosis among young women grew more prevalent.

As early as 1916, Berlin became a cold and brutal place as Georg Grosz recalls when he came back. He drew soldiers without noses, a one-armed soldier saluting a heavily bemedalled lady who had just passed him a biscuit, a drunken colonel, his flies wide open, embracing a nurse, and a hospital orderly pouring human parts down the drain. A human skeleton as a recruit taking his medical. At the front, the crippled brigade, disfigured but still able to work, were used to bury the dead. When Grosz was sent back to the army in 1917 he tried to drown himself in a latrine.[225]

The Russian Revolution began in 1917 engineered in part by Germany transporting Lenin out of Switzerland. In 1918 Ludendorff gave the last throw of the dice with 750,000 men from the Eastern front together with 6,000 artillery pieces, but they were repulsed thanks to the dogged resistance of troops and the arrival of fresh American soldiers. Ludendorff advised his government to sue for peace. A major factor in destroying German morale were letters from the home front telling the German troops to end the war because life at home was intolerable. This became

---

[225] All quoted more fully in Richie, Loc 7319 et seq.

the myth of the 'stab in the back'. Even in 1918 the Berlin theatres were still showing patriotic plays like Fifi – The Daughter of the Regiment, and Der Hias which glorified the sacrifice of war. Newsreels showing successful German actions, blowing up bridges and taking prisoners, Germany did not lose the war but was betrayed by the civilians on the home front. Republicans, socialists, communists and Jews were all guilty of betraying the German army. The interim Chancellor, Ebert, who took over when Wilhelm was advised to flee to Holland, told the homecoming German army that they had not lost the war. These were things the Germans wanted to believe. In reality the German army had had its day. A tank attack from Amiens had destroyed six divisions of the German army resulting in 50,000 German prisoners, but the Germans were still fighting and large numbers of British, Australian and French soldiers lost their lives. The American guns pounded the Meuse Argonne front, taking guns and prisoners of war but with terrible loss of American and French life: 122,063 American dead and wounded; 70,000 French dead and wounded. With increasing food shortages even the army rations were cut down. German officers, seeing the war was lost, ordered their men to surrender.[226] Certainly, the casualties suffered by the Entente Powers do not indicate a German army who had totally lost the will to win.

On the 29 September 1918, all political parties were summoned to the Reichstag expecting to hear news of victory only to be told the war was lost. So carefully had the truth been concealed. An entire generation of

---

[226] Alexander Watson. *Enduring the Great War.*

young men had been sacrificed for nothing and the Kaiser had had to run for his life. There was fear of a revolution as had happened in Russia the year before. The Russian émigré presence in Berlin was large and growing. By 1924 it had reached 300,000. Lenin had hopes of Berlin as the focal point of a world revolution and had opened an embassy with a staff of 300 political agitators.[227] A revolution did indeed break out, called the Spartacus Rebellion, and led by Rosa Luxemburg, who was Jewish, and Karl Liebknecht, both of whom, via their paper Rote Fahne (Red Flag) called for strikes, equal rights for women, damned Britain as an exploiter of black and brown workers and called for a class struggle. Rosa, in particular, was a pure communist theoriser who had never committed a violent act in her life.

The workers were becoming restive after years of futile war and lack of food. From 1917 major industrial undertakings were given police protection and the army coming home from the Eastern front were suspected of having been turned by bolshevism. Starvation and low morale caused people to pass out on the pavement, rifle for garbage and scavenge upon dead horses. On top of this, or because of it, the flu epidemic struck. Philipp Scheidemann, the Social Democratic politician, said: 'It was now hopeless to shore up civilian morale: It is a question of potatoes, We no longer have any meat...misery is so great that one poses a riddle when one asks oneself "What does North Berlin live on and how does East Berlin exist?"' [228]

---

[227] Richie, Loc 7529.
[228] Richie, Loc 7713.

The British blockade of the North Sea was a major factor in winning the war which was, in effect, a siege and starvation, and from ancient times, is one of the traditional siege weapons. Hindenburg made the mistake of not keeping labour back to maintain the home front. It was a mistake that Lloyd George, the British Prime Minister, did not make. Hindenburg threw everything into the gamble of achieving 'The Breakthrough'. It is estimated that 763,000 German civilians died of starvation. Britain refused to lift the blockade for eight months after the armistice was signed and an estimated 100,000 more Germans died. In Kiel Admiral Scheer decided to take the fleet to sea to die gloriously for the honour of Germany and, on 4 November 1918, the fleet mutinied. They had no intention of fighting, they wanted a quick end to the war.

Berlin was now in a state of chaos, with demobilised shock troops running around looting. The armaments manufacturers began to lay off large numbers of workers. The Spartacus rebellion began on 5 January 1919, was led by Rosa Luxemburg and Karl Liebkenecht. Processions of sparcacists and Social Democrats made their way through Berlin, both waving red flags and declaring a general strike, and on 6 January 200,000 joined the strike. The next day, violence broke out and Ebert called on the army to put down the mobs in the streets. All this time, gaunt, unshaven men in their steel helmets were marching back from the front. After tens of thousands had died for the Fatherland, far from cheering crowds and maidens waving and throwing flowers, they were asked to face and put down rioters: *Edmund Dreeling describes them as weary beings, stunned by defeat and dazed by the new situation: "The unshaved faces beneath the helmets are haggard, wasted with hunger and long peril, pinched and dwindled to the lines drawn by terror, courage and death."*[229]

These men became the Freikorps, Hitler's shock troops. With Ebert's approval they were organised into paramilitary groups and put down the riots with the utmost brutality, shooting anyone who came near them. The enemy was recognised to be 'The Communists' which was a way of saying 'Jews'. No German would behave in this manner unless their patriotism and integrity had been corrupted by Communists or Jews. Armed fighting broke out and the Freikorps, tragically, had to face death yet again to maintain Ebert's version of law and order. Liebknecht and Luxemburg were seen by their supporters as not being brutal enough and it was thought they could be replaced by someone harsher in the future. Both Luxemburg and Liebknecht were apprehended and released only to be clubbed and murdered by the Freikorps. Other corpses followed them, floating in the canals of the city. *The formidable military machine, which seemed to be crushed forever, has risen again with astounding rapidity. Prussian officers are stalking the streets of Berlin, soldiers marching, shouting and shooting at their command. Indeed Ebert and Scheidemann very likely got more than they bargained for.'* [230] Indeed, the politicians had created a force with a mind of its own, a Frankenstein.

Berlin became awash with violence, drugs, prostitution and pornography. Then the influenza

---

[229] Richie, Loc 7909.
[230] The Manchester Guardian, 15 January 1919, quoted in Richie, Loc 7984.

epidemic broke out and the population, in their weakened state, died in their thousands. The Freikorps became a symbol of wartime camaraderie to which unemployed soldiers flocked and which represented to many right-wing Germans the last bastion against the revolution, bolshevism, the Poles in Upper Silesia, the blood-red women, the Bolshevik Whores. Ernst Junger, a company commander during the war, demobilised in 1923, advocated total mobilisation for the modern state for which democracy was ruinous. On the Jewish Question he advocated assimilation or emigration to Palestine and the creation of a society run by warrior-worker-scholars. He was subsequently adopted by the Nazi Party though, at the time, he distanced himself from them, refusing to allow his writings to be published by them.[231]

The moral decay in Berlin was personified by Ellie the Slut in Walter Mehring's *The Fortune Teller* who has a filthy abortion and is murdered for her money. Alexandra Richie claims that men, fresh from killing in the streets, went straight to the cabarets to dance with blood still on their hands.

Berliners began to create a myth of the 1914 war being forced upon them by Russian aggression and by the threat of allied encirclement. They forgot their enthusiasm for the war and the invasion of Belgium. They thought the war should be put behind them and forgotten. The Versailles Treaty, really a Diktat, thoroughly disabused them of this idea and reparations had to be paid. John Maynard Keynes, the British economist, warned that such a policy would be a disaster and would ruin the economies of both donor

---

[231] Wikipedia.

and the recipient nations. This proved to be the case. France, in particular, wanted what they felt was due to them for the dead, the pain and the suffering they had endured, and invaded the Ruhr to get by force what was due to them under the 'Treaty'. The Weimar government printed money to pay the reparations which resulted in inflation. Between 1921 and 1922 the inflation ran out of control and paper bills were required in barrow loads to buy a loaf of bread. A new Chancellor was appointed, Hjalmar Schacht, a recognised, brilliant economist, who discarded the old currency and invented a new currency secured, he said, on the value of German land. The personal savings of millions of Germans disappeared and they were the people who voted for Adolf Hitler, the strong leader Germany had been waiting for, who promised to make Germany great again.

It seems he really did use this worn-out phrase: *'Adolf Hitler, out of prison took advantage of the groans. He told people that he would make Germany "great" again. He blamed Jews, socialists communists and others for the troubles in the land.*[232]

'Nationalism and Socialism had to be redefined into one strong new idea to carry new strength which would make Germany great again[233]

These sorts of phrases are the pure pathos which carry populists to power.

To the surprise of the rest of Europe, who should

---

[232] Green Bay Press Gazette, January 4 1934. Part of a series on Modern Leaders of Men syndicated across the USA.
[233] Speech by AH February 24 1940. Both were posted by Scott Novak 2016.

have been keeping an eye on the situation, Germany and the Soviet Union signed the Treaty of Rapallo on 16 April 1922. This cancelled all war indemnities between them and included a secret protocol allowing Germany to build weapons and train troops on Soviet soil. This was in contravention of the Treaty of Versailles which, in order to placate the French, took a fairly vindictive line. It was not a fair peace and Europe paid dearly for it.

Germany, like any other Christian nation, had upsurges of anti-Semitism whenever they lost a war or the economy went into recession. This was particularly so after the Great War which Germany lost due to famine and the timely arrival of American power in 1917. Towards the end of the war, there were comments such as: The Jews have not earned enough, that is why the war has not yet ended.[234] References were made to 'saboteurs, the gangsters, the war profiteers, the Socialists and Jews who populate Berlin'. These were the people, so the myth ran, who stabbed Germany in the back. General Schulenburg is on record as saying as early as 9 November 1918: 'Our men will claim... that they were stabbed in the back by their comrades in arms, the Navy, together with Jewish war profiteers and shirkers.'

Walter Rathenau was murdered in 1922 for being a Jew, an intellectual and a November criminal. Post-war misery and inflation caused by Jews and Bolsheviks. There are hundreds of such references as the French humiliated Germany, demanded reparations and chancellor after chancellor struggled

---

[234] Jurgen Kocka, Facing Total War, p.123 from Richie, Loc 7287.

with the economy and took short cuts with democracy time after time.

The German economy, after reparations were virtually cancelled by the Dawes Plan, prospered on short-term loans from foreign banks, notably American. In 1929, the American economy crashed. Wall Street shares were booming and ordinary people were borrowing money to buy shares, using as collateral shares they had bought earlier and upon which they had borrowed money. The banks who were doing the lending had also invested and bought the bonds of Latin American nations. When these governments defaulted on their bonds, it left a hole in the balance sheets and in an attempt to repair the gap, they started calling in unsecured and short-term loans. Banks went into liquidation and private investors were left bankrupt as the banks were left holding worthless pieces of paper upon which they had lent money.

Banks started to call in loans all over Europe. Britain went onto the gold standard in order to control inflation which only served to deepen the recession. Unemployment in Germany spiralled as the trading conditions all over the world worsened. In Germany, in 1929, unemployment had been 1.5 million but by 1933 it had reached six million and young men were scratching a subsistence as casual labourers, beggars or opening car doors for a tip. They even resorted to petty crime. As unemployment got worse, support for the National Socialists and Adolf Hitler grew and by 1932 there were 230 members of the Nazi Party in the Reichstag. Their behaviour was such that no business could be conducted. Chancellor Bruening asked and obtained powers to ban the SA and the SS, Hitler's 400,000-strong private army, who took orders only from him. In a Byzantine power struggle between Bruening, who was the least culpable, Franz von Papen who briefly became Chancellor, and General Kurt von Schleicher who wanted power and tried to use Adolf Hitler as a pawn, this showed a foolish lack of judgement and Hindenburg was forced to make Hitler Chancellor in 1933 in spite of the fact that the Nazi share of the vote had declined to 33.1% in November 1932.[235] The road-building programme was putting Germans back to work and the need to find a racial scapegoat was lessening. Race and war was all the Nazis had to offer. A minority government was put in charge of the country but backed by 400,000 armed men they soon made Adolf Hitler a dictator and Europe paid the price.

Adolf Hitler was one of the most flawed characters ever to take office and be given power. It is hard to think of anyone so lacking in education, integrity and normal empathy other than a criminal psychopath. Hitler's father, Alois, was the illegitimate son of a 42-year-old domestic servant called Anna Schickelgruber born in 1837 in Strones, Dollersheim, Austria. She married a Herr Hiedler in 1842 and they all became 'Hitler' shortly afterwards. Anna died in 1847 but Alois's upkeep was contributed to by a Jew called Frankenberger until the boy was 14 years old. Anna herself said that he was being kind because she was poor, not because he or his son had fathered the child. Alois went up in the world and became a minor customs official with a uniform on the

---

[235] For a more detailed account see The History Place: 'The Rise of Hitler'.

Austrian/German border. Alois married the boss's daughter but had no scruples about sleeping with the housemaids, both of whom he married in turn. In addition to this he had a child by another woman. The second housemaid, Klara Poelzl, who was pregnant when they married, was also his first cousin once removed and became the mother of Adolf to whom she was devoted. All the Hitlers were Catholic so that divorce was out of the question. Klara, in particular was a devout Christian and she and the children attended church regularly.

Klara had six children and Adolf was the fourth. Sadly for her, the first three, Gustav, Ida and Otto, died in infancy. She had two more: Edmund who died young, and Paula who survived. As modern research predicts, there is a tendency for later births to have little or no feelings for heterosexuality and Adolf seems to have been conscious of the same preference. When he was eleven he rebelled against his father's wishes that he should go to technical high school and said he wanted to go to art school. Furious fights broke out between them, so violent that his mother had to place her body in the way to shield him.

It must be remembered how abhorrent homosexuality was to the general public. Now, it is difficult to understand, when all forms of sexuality are not even remarked upon providing they are carried out with consent. In Austria-Hungary it was illegal until the 1960s and it was the same in Germany, though widely tolerated until the Nazi Party came to power. The Roman Catholic Church has always been most condemnatory towards active same-sex relationships, describing them as an intrinsic moral evil and gross depravity. Klara was a devout Catholic and Adolf was devoted to her. He must have thought he was betraying her, at least in thought and then, in deed.

Like others who feel a failure, in order to preserve their self-esteem, they only do the things they are good at so as to avoid failure. Hitler stuck to art and history but went one further and blamed his teachers for not attempting any other subject, saying that his teachers were mentally defective.[236] Hitler carried on frittering his time away and spending the small amounts his family could give him, his father having died in 1903. When in Vienna he lived with a childhood friend, August Kubizek, with whom he might have been in love but whilst August admired him, there was no intention of having a physical relationship with anyone other than the woman he married and with whom he had three children. However, Kubizek provided companionship and was considered by Hitler inferior to him and so bolstered his, Hitler's, feeling of self-worth. He was quite dismissive when Kubizek told him he had got into the Music Conservatory (I had no idea I had such a clever friend) and irritable whenever Kubizek discussed his studies.[237] Kubizek must never be his intellectual equal. In his day-to-day conversations with Kubizek he portrayed himself as above lust and was fit only for the ideal union with the perfect German woman like Stefanie, to whom he had never spoken.[238] The idea of Stefanie in his mind was that she an unattainable

---

[236] Siobhan Pat Mulcahy, *The Peculiar Sex Life of Adolf Hitler* Loc 197 and *Hitler Speaks*, 1939.

[237] Mulcahy, Loc 926, and *The Young Hitler I Knew* 1953.

[238] Mulcahy, Loc 1010 and Kubizek. After the war, Stefanie was located and was amazed that Hitler held her in such esteem.

ideal which he could never reach. He professed a similar feeling for Helene Hanfstaengl in the 1920s. From a sexual point of view there was nothing physical between him and Kubizek, but Hitler displayed jealousy when Kubizek, who was a student of music, took on a girl pupil and gave a display of rage when Kubizek got his call-up papers.[239] Hitler, much later when he was Chancellor, also financed Kubizek's three sons at the Anton Bruckner Academy in Linz which might be an indication of wanting a proxy family by the man he loved.

In about 1909, Hitler moved into a doss house behind Meidling Station after he had spent several nights living on benches and had eaten nothing. He fell in with a man called Reinhold Hanisch who guided him away from utter destitution and suggested he obtain a share of the orphan's pension to which he was entitled. He started painting and the paintings were sold. This was a period when Hitler is said to be slightly more opulent. There has been a suggestion that he was working as a male prostitute.[240] But it must be remembered the information available surrounding this period is very unreliable. There seems to have been little or no sexual activity by Hitler until he joined the German army, the List Regiment, in 1914. The main source for this information is Hermann Rauschning, 1887-1982, who was brought up in the Prussian military, served as a lieutenant in the Great War and became leader of the Danzig Land League with the intention of rejoining Danzig to Germany. He seems to have joined the Nazi Party in 1933 but was not

---

[239] Mulcahy, Loc 1100.
[240] Mulcahy, Loc 1374.

made a minister and left shortly afterwards. In 1942, he emigrated to America. He certainly had many conversations with the Nazi hierarchy but his knowledge could be overstated. Nevertheless, Trevor Roper, the Hitler historian, thought there was certainly some truth in what he said though the extent was difficult to ascertain.

Rauschning claims that Hitler's military record shows him to have been guilty of 'pederastic practices' with an officer.[241] This was why, in spite of four years' active service, he only rose to the rank of Private First Class or Corporal. His commanding officer once described him as 'neurotic'. It is difficult, today, to understand the opprobrium in which homosexuals were held in the early 20th century. Even today, the Roman Catholic Church is highly critical of active homosexuality and Hitler would have been betraying his mother's love, she being a devout observant Catholic.

There were other claims of active homosexual affairs on the part of Adolf Hitler: 'Hans Mend, a fellow WWI dispatch runner [interviewed by member of German resistance, Friedrich Alfred Schmid-Noerr, in December 1939] said Ernst Schmidt and Adolf Hitler had a sexual relationship which lasted for almost six years from 1914 to 1919.' But Mend felt that Hitler had cheated him of royalties after he had written a piece of hagiography praising Hitler's 'brave exploits' during the war, and promised he would let the world know what Hitler used to be. This, he

---

[241] Mulcahy, Loc 1654, and *Hitler Speaks* 1939. His military record has either been tampered with or destroyed in order to preserve the Hitler myth.

seems to have done in 1939.[242] Ernst Schmidt and Hitler were discovered in a hay barn making love, again from Hans Mend.

Hitler seems to have been loyal to his old comrades in arms and preserved their silence by keeping them close to him and giving them good jobs in the Party. Max Amann, a sergeant in his regiment, was given the best paid job in the Party, either because he was a lover or because he knew too much or both. Karl Lippert, a Jew who served with Hitler, was given a job as a clerk in the Party office and was declared not subject to the race laws.

This was not the case with people he could not buy. On 14 October 1918, there was a mustard gas attack and Hitler was put into Pasewalk Military Hospital under a psychiatrist called Edmund Forster, where Hitler was suffering from blindness. On the face of it, this seems perfectly reasonable except that there seems to be no record on the British side of a mustard gas attack on that day. In a letter dated April 1943, published on Monday September 19 2016 in the Mail Online, from Foster Kennedy MD to Dr Victor Gonda, it is said that Dr Edmund Forster had told him that Hitler's medical record showed him to be suffering from hysterical amblyopia. In 1934 the record had disappeared. On September 11 1933, Dr Forster was found dead in his bathroom using a pistol nobody knew he owned and the circumstances surrounding his death make one suppose he had been given the pistol and told what to do with it,

---

[242] Mulcahy, Loc 1553, 1554.

presumably to protect his family.[243]

After the war, Hitler was found to possess a mesmeric gift for oratory and it was this that made him the vehicle for the upsurge of German nationalism and its close relation, racism. The years of humiliation at the hands of the Kaiser, followed by generals and defeat, hyperinflation and global bank failure had made the lower middle-class German ready to accept a Hitler as a saviour, in some cases, in a religious sense. At the Nuremburg rallies up to a thousand uniformed men, women and civilians stood in excited expectation listening to Goebbels, a brilliant rabble rousing speaker in his own right, and others, warming the crowd up. Then, suddenly, like a clap of thunder, the lights came up, hands were raised in salute and a roar of HEIL HITLER came from the crowd. There stood the man himself, a figure of power and control.[244] Hitler had always had a mesmeric presence.

Michael Fry, in 1934, listened to Hitler speak: *'The first time I heard Hitler speak in public, I spent ten minutes repeating to myself "What a comedian-what a comedian!" as the Pope said to Napoleon many years ago. Twenty minutes later I felt like cheering. The passionate conviction, the fire of invulnerable patriotism, and above all, the wholehearted sincerity put Hitler far beyond the little tricks of the mob orator. Every one of his words comes out charged with a powerful current of energy, at times it seems as if they are torn from the very heart of the man, causing him indescribable anguish. When he speaks of the Fatherland, when he describes*

[243] There are a number of articles on the Internet.
[244] The author remembers hearing an eye witness speak at Harrogate Town Hall in about 1944.

the sorry state of demoralisation which has set in, his eyes flash with anger, his voice rises to a shriek of fury-he is inspired. That is what the masses believe-that Hitler is a prophet directly controlled by the Powers above-and can quite understand it. There is a magnetic fluid emanating from Hitler which seems supernatural. [245]

Dr Hanfstaengl who escaped when he became aware of a 'joke' to throw him out of an aeroplane, had the same reaction when he heard Hitler in a bierkeller upon his arrival in Germany from America:

'...Then Drexler introduced Adolf Hitler. He didn't look very impressive standing there in repose. That is until you noticed his eyes. He had clear blue eyes and in them there was neither guile nor fear. Ther was honesty, there was sincerity, there was a hint of scorn.

Then he began to speak. More of a musician than anything else. I could only interpret his speech musically. He spoke mezzo voice, quietly, soothingly at first. His hands never stopped moving and they fascinated me-as the hands of Fritz Kreisler had fascinated me. He had all the effectiveness-but none of the tricks-of the trained orator. Within three minutes I felt the man's absolute sincerity and love for Germany. Within ten I had forgotten everything else but the words the man was quietly dropping into the consciousness of everyone present-words which burned all the more for their softness; words which lashed us as men who had failed a great responsibility...He completely mesmerised that audience-witout paralyzing it. [246]

It will be noticed that the effect on the two men was purely emotional. Neither could say they were won over by the logic of his argument. He had only

---

[245] Michael Fry, *Hitler's Wonderland*, p.105.
[246] Dr FS Hanfstaengl, 'My Leader', *Colliers,* 1934. Internet.

two main arguments: When speaking to the masses and the faithful of his party, the Jews were the villains. The Jews were particularly bent on destroying Germany and every opponent of Hitler's ambitions was an instrument of the Jews. When speaking to the Industry Club in Dusseldorf he adopted a rather more sophisticated line. We are a strong nation who cannot be dictated to by world recessions and by the Treaty of Versailles. More sinister was the emphasis on the inner strength of the German people and the inherent strength of their genetic makeup. 'We rose after the 30 Years War and we shall rise again'.[247]

Behind all this was the fact that he was baptised and raised a Catholic and in being a homosexual, he was committing a sin, so that he was himself not genetically sound. A catechism published on the internet and supported by the book of Leviticus (18.22) and 1 Corinthians (6.9) with two extracts from Genesis states the following:

Homosexual acts are unnatural, and are not open to life, and are outside of marriage, and are between persons of the same gender. To be moral, sexual relations must be natural and open to life and within a marriage and between a man and a woman. Homosexual sex offends against all these moral imperatives which God has placed in the natural law and in Divine Revelation and in the very nature of humanity. Therefore, homosexual acts are much more gravely disordered and much more sinful than heterosexual acts outside marriage. The greater the disorder, the greater the sin. The more moral principles an act violates, the more sinful that act is.

---

[247] Max Domarus, *The Complete Hitler. A Digital Reference to his speeches and Proclamations 1932-1945.*

Whilst it is probable that Hitler had embarked on homosexual affairs while he was in the army, he went on describing himself as a Catholic until 1933. In spite of his bravado and outward air of absolute confidence, there must have been a feeling, squirming inside him, that he was betraying his mother's faith. One of his many peculiarities was that he put a photograph of his mother in every bedroom of his Munich apartment.

His gift for rhetoric and his feeling for drama, together with the economic chaos essential to make xenophobic right-wing parties national in extent, transformed the National Socialist Party into one of the most popular movements in Germany. It attracted some of the most emotionally disturbed people any political party has ever seen. *Konrad Heiden, in his book 'Der Fuherer (1944) described Hitler's Munich circle in the 1920s as a collection of misfits, hunchbacks, sexual outlaws, moral degenerates, decadent aristocrats, ex-cons and occult con men. He said they were "Fascist Libertines" who spent their free time in the Cafe Heck and Osteria Bavaria, stuffing themselves with pasta and pastries while pimps scoured Munich schoolyards to supply boys for SA chief, Ernst Roehm's predatory appetites.*[248]

There have been a number of allegations that Hitler continued to have casual homosexual encounters as and when he required them from bisexual bodyguards or drivers whom he paid by giving them jobs in the Party. Lothar Machtan (*Hidden Hitler*, 2001) said that Lotte Bechstein told her husband that she and Hitler had never had sex because: '*He could not kiss. His fixation on his own sex was*

---

[248] Mulcahy, Loc 1738.

too strong and his self imposed heterosexuality too dependent on an effort of the will. All his attempts to start a love affair with a woman had come to nothing.' If she is right about him trying to become a heterosexual, in must have been after he left Landsberg prison in 1924. The girls he tried with were all young because he did not have the confidence to attempt sex with a fully grown woman unless she was prepared to play the part of a dominatrix. Mimi Reiter was 16 and was, finally forced to make a sworn deposition that she had no relationship of any kind with him. But she told Der Spiegel that in 1931 she spent the night with him during which she let him do whatever he wanted with her. What that was must be left to the imagination but the phrasing of the statement probably rules out 'Making Love' as it is commonly understood.

Angela 'Geli' Raubal (1908-1931) was the daughter of Hitler's half-sister Angela, and Geli was, therefore, his half niece. She was 15 when he met her and 23 when she died. Hitler doted on her, buying her clothes and jewellery, but their relationship was not to her liking. She told several people that he made her do 'disgusting things'. She had to squat over his face so that he had a plain view of her genitalia and urinate over him, possibly defecate, on his face while he masturbated.[249] While he was in Munich he controlled every aspect of her life but when he was away, she managed to have assignations with other men.

Walter Langer and others, all psychiatrists, who carried out an analysis of the available material on Hitler in 1973 said: *'In her description of sexual experiences with Hitler, Geli stressed the fact that it was of the utmost*

[249] Mulcahy, Loc 3372.

importance to him that she squat over him in such a way that he could see everything...From a consideration of all the evidence it would seem that Hitler's perversion is as Geli has described it. The great danger in gratifying it, however, is that the individual might get feces or urine into his mouth...[250]

His other source of sex was his photographer Hoffman's parties which attracted starlets and demi-mondaines who were perfectly happy to provide sex for a price. Hitler seems to have been looking for something darker than what was available from men or women. A number of teenage girls ostensibly committed, or attempted, suicide. It is to be doubted that he was a paedophile in the usual sense of the word. He was strongly attracted to them and they were young and malleable enough to be persuaded to do what he really wanted of them.[251] A Catholic priest, Father Bernhard Stempfle, asserted that, in 1929, Hitler wrote Gelli a letter confirming his masochistic perversion, but the letter was never sent, though Ernst Hanfstaengl and Carl Anton Reichel had read a letter along those lines. The letter was finally bought by the Rehse collection (Nazi memorabilia) and is now in the Library of Congress.

Hitler would not have indulged in masochistic orgies on a regular basis but only when he was driven by lust. The girl had to be equipped with outstandingly fine examples of male fixation. Legs, hips, breasts and hair. They had to be very young and of a low class. When he met such a girl, he grovelled

---

[250] Walter Langer, *The Mind of Adolf Hitler*, p.168.
[251] Robert G L Waite, *The Psychopathic God: Adolf Hitler* (1977), pp.223-243.

at her feet in a disgusting manner.[252] Her response to his grovelling would either encourage him or reject him. It is to be doubted whether he ever saw the girl as a human being. Their very attributes would reify them and reduce them to objects who could be killed without regret. Freud would have said that Hitler had an Oedipus Complex made more convincing by the fact that he had an undescended testicle. His defence was the adoption of the characteristics of his father. Very male, confident, domineering and brutal but under that, he had a sexual appetite which his mother would not have understood. Hitler was so demented that he might have been attracted to coprophilia and urophilia in order to have sex with a woman.

In the case of Renate Muller, an actress, who spent the night at the Chancellery, her director, Zeissler, asked her what was troubling her. She said: '*that the evening before she had been with Hitler and that she had been sure he was going to have intercourse with her; that they had both undressed and were apparently getting ready for bed when Hitler fell on the floor and begged her to kick him. She demurred, but he pleaded with her and condemned himself as unworthy, heaped all kinds of accusations on his own head and grovelled in an agonizing manner. The scene became intolerable to her and she finally acceded to his wishes and kicked him. This excited him greatly and he begged for more and more, always saying it was better than he deserved and that he was not worthy to be in the same room with her. As she continued to kick him he became more and more excited.*' [253]

In another account Renate beat him with his whip, called him obscene names and he started to

[252] Langer, p.171.
[253] Langer, p.171.

masturbate. She had other sadomasochistic episodes with him and he showered her with gifts. While in London, on a visit, he put agents to follow her and found she was having a proper affair with a Jewish lover called Frank Deutsch. She had affairs with other men and after a visit to Paris, he had her apprehended and forcibly brought into his presence after hours of waiting. He screamed with fury and broke a chair in his rage. She started taking drugs and threw herself from the hospital window when she saw below the SS coming to get her. Sadomasochism was his way of making love to a woman and when she was unfaithful to him, it was a blow to his already diminished self-esteem and, rather than losing her to another man, which would be another defeat, she had to die.[254] This was in 1937 and she was 31 years old; one of the most beautiful and potentially talented women in German cinema.

Hitler had read and imbibed the racial work of Houston Stewart Chamberlain which placed great weight on the purity of blood:

Race and purity of blood are what constitute a type, and nowhere has this been more carefully preserved than among the Jews... History show us no single example either among men or beasts of a prominently noble and distinctly individual race which is not the result of mixture. Once the race is established it must be preserved. The English constitute a race.

The leitmotif which runs through the whole book is the assertion of the superiority of the Teutonic race.

---

[254] Mulcahy, Loc 3907.

The line of argument is absurd:

Horses and especially dogs give us every chance of observing that the intellectual go hand in hand with the physical, this is specially true of the moral qualities: a mongrel, very clever, but never reliable morally; morally he is always a weed.

What is the use of detailed scientific investigations as to whether there are distinguishable races? Whether race has a worth? And so on. We turn the tables and say: it is evident there are such races: it is a fact of direct experience that the quality of race is of vital importance; your province... not to deny the facts.

Julius Wellhausen (1844-1918), the biblical scholar, expresses himself thus: '*In the case of the Jews...there is no inner connection between the good man and that which is good. The action of the hands and the desire of the heart are severed.*

Sin is to the Hebrew every action that puts a man in the wrong with one who has the power to punish him for it.

Far away in Asia, behind the great mountain fastnesses of India...there dwelt a race of white men...They were called Aryas...from them are descended the dominant caste of India, the Persians and the great nations of Europe.

There are, of course, no Aryan people. It is a language group and there were various regional groups who spoke it. The Aryan race was invented in a book of essays by self-styled Count Arthur de Gobineau in 1848. With regard to the rest, some mixing of race is essential to arrive at a great race like the English. But in the event of blood mixture like the formerly Teutonic Slavs who have now become un-

Teutonised[255] the Jews, on the other hand, have kept themselves pure which makes them decadent because there is no blood mixing in their makeup. There seems in these muddled statements some homage to Darwin's Origin of Species and the survival of those species who adjust most successfully to a changing environment. Chamberlain never talked about nationality but only about 'race' and for this he used the word 'Teutons'. This again is merely a language group: The Germanic branch of the Indo-European languages which include, among many others, German, English and Yiddish. In modern society Chamberlain would have been a joke but not in the Depression-ridden Europe of the 1930s.

The Poles and Lithuanians liberated Prussia when they defeated the Teutonic Knights in 1410 at the Battle of Tannenberg. Instead of hailing the Poles and Lithuanians as their liberators they hailed a victory over the Russians in 1914 at Tannenberg, when a Russian army was driven into the lake while the Germans watched them drown, as the revenge for the defeat of the Teutonic Knights in 1410.

Hitler, like many others absolutely believed this racially inspired nonsense because it restored his feeling of self-worth. He was, after all, a masochist filled with self-disgust whose only way of getting an erection was to have a woman urinate and defecate over his face. It sometimes happens, according to letters on the internet, that in a loving relationship, women are prepared to do this, but had this been known in Germany at the time his fate would have

---

[255] Houston Stewart Chamberlain, *The Foundations of the Nineteenth Century*, Kindle Ed, Loc 987.

been sealed together with the Nazi Party and it may be no coincidence that seven young women 'committed suicide'. In addition to this there was a strong rumour that one of Hitler's grandfathers was a Jew called Frankenberger.[256] According to racial theory his blood was polluted, like the Teutonic Slavs, and thus rendered him unfit to lead. He flew into a rage when he found that a plaque had been erected at his father's birthplace.[257]

Hitler was very preoccupied by his own blood and was always having it extracted, in childhood by leeches and in adulthood by the syringe of Dr Morell. He also had his head measured because, according to racist theory, the cranial shape would indicate the extent of a person's Jewishness.[258] One of the antidotes for this feeling of racial and sexual inadequacy was to become a great warrior. According to the opinion of the great Hitler historians these real and imagined defects in his character are irrelevant. So they would be in any normal society, they would be in the mind of a powerless man. But Hitler had been elevated to a position of enormous power, backed by a personal army which owed allegiance directly to him and further backed by a group of intellectually maimed characters devoid of Judeo-Christian integrity. He had indeed been given enormous power.

Hitler's outstanding inadequacy as the leader of a nation could never be allowed by him to enter his conscious mind and he erected defence mechanisms

---

[256] Waite, p.126.

[257] Waite, p.130.

[258] Waite, p.128.

to protect himself from the truth. In his early days he inflated his ego with the wild cheering of the crowds depicted, albeit flatteringly, in Leni Riefenstahl's 'Triumph of the Will' but later, this was not sufficient.

Langer (p.183) writes: '*Hitler's outstanding defense mechanism is one commonly called projection. It is a technique by which the ego of an individual defends itself against unpleasant impulses, tendencies or characteristics by denying their existence in himself while he attributes them to others....*

From a psychological point of view it is not too farfetched to suppose that as the perversion developed and became more disgusting to Hitler's ego, its demands were disowned and projected upon the Jew. By this process the Jew became a symbol of everything Hitler hated in himself. Again, his own personal problems and conflicts were transferred from within himself to the external world where they assumed the proportions of racial and national conflicts.'

Hitler then was trying to rid the world of the impurities which existed in him. His manner of doing it has been well recorded and has disgusted the whole of the Western world and one can now only record a roll call of those who were murdered, gassed or starved to death:

Jews	5.93 million	Lucy Dawidowicz [259]
Soviet POWs	2-3 million	Michael Berenbaum [260]
Ethnic Poles	1.8-2million	Franciscek Piper and Holocaust Encyclopedia. Polish Victims[261]
Serbs	300,000-500,000	Croatia Yad Vashem in PDF
Disabled	270,000	The Danish Centre for Holocaust and Genocide Studies[262]
Romani	90,000-220,000	Holocaust Encyclopedia and Ian Hancock[263]
Freemasons	80,000-200,000	Chris Hodapp, My own Masonic History
Slovenes	20,000-25,000	Institute of Contemporary History. Ljubliana
Homosexuals	5,000-15,000	Marilyn J Harran[264]
Jehovah's Witnesses	2,500-5,000	William L Shulman[265]
Spanish Republicans	7,000	David Wingate Pike[266]

---

[259] *The War Against the Jews* p.403.

[260] *The World Must Know: The History of the Holocaust* as told in the United States Holocaust Museum.

[261] Piper Polish Scholar and chief historian at Auschwitz.

[262] Euthanasia The 'Mercy Killing' of disabled people in Germany.

[263] Genocide of European Roma Hancock Romanies and the Holocaust: A Reevaluation and Overview. In Dan Stone. *The Historiography of the Holocaust*, pp.383-396.

[264] *The Holocaust Chronicles: A History in Words and Pictures*, p.108

[265] *A State of Terror: Germany 1933-1939*.

[266] *Spaniards in the Holocaust: Mauthausen, the Horror on the Danube*, p.11.

This tragic list is taken from the Wikipedia article The Holocaust. When the British Army entered Belsen, Richard Dimbleby, the BBC correspondent, was with them and gives a small sketch of the scene he saw:

Here over an acre of ground lay dead and dying people. You could not see which was which...The living lay with their heads against the corpses and around them moved the awful, ghostly procession of emaciated, aimless people, with nothing to do and with no hope of life, unable to move out of your way, unable to look at the terrible sights around them...Babies had been born here, tiny wizened things which could not live...A mother, driven mad, screamed at a British sentry to give her milk for her child and thrust the tiny mite into his arms...He opened the bundle and found the baby had been dead for days. The day at Belsen was the most horrible of my life. [267]

In the same vein the humiliated Germans were prepared to go to war to show they were a warrior nation. The savagery unleashed by that war has never been matched, in terms of dead, anywhere in the world since: 4.2 million Germans; 2.3 million Japanese out of a total 8.2 million on the Axis side. On the allied side the numbers, quite apart from the gas chambers and starvation killing of civilians, are so huge, they are still being estimated, but in the Soviet Union, an estimated 20 million died and in China, at the hands of the Japanese, an estimated 10 million died. In Poland, the death toll was largely civilian, and is estimated at 5.8 million. The estimated total loss of life on the allied side was nearly 40 million dead.

Hitler could not order a ceasefire because to give

---

[267] BBC News 15 April 1945 "Liberation of Belsen".

in would have been a further blow to his self-esteem. This is a common characteristic of the racist whose essential defence mechanism depends on having races inferior to him, or her and craving success and adulation. Because of inner unhappiness, the racist is always seeking control. It is worth remembering, however, that previous German administrations had handed him the tools with which to inflict this bloodbath on the world, notably the Great War, the Freikorps, unemployment, secret rearmament in Russia and the muzzling of the freedom of speech so that the Germans voted and fought for a dangerous psychopath.

10d Anti-Black Prejudice in the USA

Anti-African-American prejudice in the USA seems to have been learned and passed on, remorselessly from generation to generation and from father to son. Based on the abysmally small social status of the black community, so that, particularly for those with poor achievement performance, to have even a black neighbour was an insult to their sense of well-being.

In the 17th century, in Europe, there was a pervasive use of physical punishment to maintain public order. Whips and the stocks were common, the nobleman beat his servants and the gentlemen of the village beat the poor. The dons at Oxford and Cambridge beat the undergraduates and the city companies beat the apprentices. Thieves were whipped, branded with the letter T, pilloried in the stocks or transported to America. Hundreds of immigrants arrived in the colonies and between 1650 and 1700 the population of

Virginia tripled but during that period the supply of indentured labour and poor European migrants actually declined, so that the requirement for cheap labour became paramount. The reason for this was simply that the rise of farm wages in England exceeded 10% in real terms over that period and labourers found it increasingly easy to find a living. The demand for labour in the colonies was satisfied by slavery from Africa. Slaves had the advantage for their owners when compared with indentured servants: they were owned permanently and did not have to be freed after three or four years when their contract of indenture was completed. Nor, because they could be easily identified, did black slaves succeed in escaping with the regularity of white labour. Millions of Africans were transported from the West Coast of Africa in the 18th century in the most appalling conditions. There is a description by Alexander Falconbridge, a doctor, which goes as follows:

Some wet and blowing weather having occasioned the portholes to be shut and the grating to be covered, fluxes and fevers among the Negroes ensued. While they were in this situation, I frequently went down among them till at length their rooms became so extremely hot as to be only bearable for a short time… The floor of their rooms, was so covered with the blood and mucus which had preceded from them in consequence of the flux, that it resembled a slaughterhouse… Numbers of the slaves having fainted they were carried up on deck where several of them died and the rest with great difficulty were restored.[268]

These people were ripped by slave dealers from their homes. It is quite wrong to think of Africa as a

---

[268] Quoted in *American Slavery* by Peter Kolchin, p.21.

primitive, primeval country. Some areas were nomadic and some agricultural. Every area had a political and social organisation. With regard to the latter, some were matriarchal and some patriarchal. They had religions based mainly on the spirits of their ancestors.[269] To take civilised people like these and subject them to the conditions in the slave ships naturally led to death in preference to life under those conditions Falconbridge continues.

The conditions were so bad that many of the Africans chose suicide by jumping overboard; others suffered from what was called "fixed melancholy". They became morose, moody and unresponsive. They refused food and, from time to time, took their own lives. They were not regarded as human beings but as chattels to be bought and sold. The profits to be made in the slave trade were so big that the tragic death of these people both by plague and taking their own lives could be treated as wastage. As an example, general trading by William Davenport of Liverpool brought him a profit of 10.5% but, because of the longer voyage brought in 8.1%. This was an average based on the gross inefficiency of Mr Davenport's operations. At times he delivered only 55% of his human cargo and made a loss. Even this did not seem to inspire ship owners to provide more humane conditions. [Percentages taken from a paper by David Richardson of Keele University]

The tragic aspect of slave labour is the belief that still persists in Britain in 2016, that cheap labour is economical. Even in the 19th century free, not slave, labour provided prosperity.

---

[269] John Hope Franklin, *From Slavery to Freedom*, Chapter 2.

'Texas had a valuable German element in its population that cultivated cotton with free labour. At Mainz in the Rhine Valley a group of noblemen headed by Prince Carl of Solms Braunfels formed a ...society which in 1844 sent over large numbers of their countrymen to settle in Western Texas... They founded thriving villages such as New Braunfels...San Antonio, Fredericksburg and Sisterdale which was called a "Latin Colony" on account of its learned inhabitants. [270]

There were regular slave revolts which started in the 17th century and continued until emancipation. Upon the outbreak of the American War of Independence in 1775-1783, Washington was reluctant to allow slaves to fight because he knew that a man who fights for his country must be a free man if he survives. In the event, many blacks fought for American independence but only the slave owners of Virginia were moved, in the main, to do the honourable thing. Washington himself remained populist and it was not until after he died that his wife Martha freed his slaves.

The very big slave population of America was kept in thrall to the white immigrants by fear and violence. There was violence meted out by the owners of the slaves and violence meted out by the slave courts that existed mainly in the southern colonies. The punishments included branding, nose slitting and amputation of toes and fingers. Occasionally hands and feet were amputated but since this reduced the value of the slave it was done quite infrequently. It was known for slaves to be castrated but not frequently because this would reduce the increase in the slave population, and again, occasionally, burning

---

[270] Clement Eaton, *The Growth of Southern Civilisation* p.46.

at the stake. These punishments were considered by any right-thinking person to be vile even when measured against the Corporal punishment of the 17th century. One overseer said: "*Some Negroes are determined never to let a white man whip them and will resist you, when you attempt it; of course you must kill them in that case*".

There are descriptions of women being whipped. They usually screamed and prayed that there was always a few that never made a sound. It seems to be no different if the woman was pregnant. She was whipped just the same. Sometimes a metal collar was put on a slave to remind him of his wrongdoings. These collars were heavy and had protruding spikes to make it difficult to live and to sleep. Women were raped and subject to sexual abuse. Even the freeing of a slave was forbidden unless it was by deed and even that was forbidden after 1820.

One of the great iniquities of the slave trade was the splitting up of families. '*William Reynolds the itinerant merchant, witnessed in Memphis the sale of twenty three slaves at auction, which he described in his journal: "One yellow woman was sold who had two children. She begged and implored her new master on her nees to buy the little girl (about five years old) but all to no purpose, it was truly heart rending...*"[271]

White women turned a blind eye to the sexual abuse of black women. The southern culture of America treated all women, black or white, as property or chattels. Against this background of rape a number of stereotypes and fictions were invented to relieve the man of guilt. For example, southern

---

[271] Eaton, p.50.

women, white women, were put on a pedestal of purity and were treated as dependent and submissive. This in part explains why black women were consigned to a life of sexual exploitation and a stereotype was invented of the black woman who lusted after sex with any man and who enjoyed being raped. Andrew L Williams in 2001 wrote: "perhaps she remembers her great great grandmother who wanted to protest but only rolled her eyes willed herself not to scream when the white man mounted her from behind." Henry Bibb's master forced a young black woman to be his son's concubine and, when sold, Bibbs's own wife was forced into prostitution. The image of the black woman devoted to satisfying male lust persisted well into the 20th century. In the racist film, The Birth of a Nation, one character of mixed race is the mistress of a senator and is depicted as savage, corrupt and lascivious and uses her femininity to corrupt a white man.[272] The most well written and striking portrayal of the beautiful black woman in thrall to her own lust is to be found in DuBose Heyward's description of Bess in his novel *Porgy* written in 1925. Bess comes across her old lover, Crown, during a picnic on Kittiwar Island. It leaves no doubt as to Bess's animal nature which will eventually bring her down. The following exchange between her and Crown takes place:

"I know yuh ain't change," he said

"with yuh an' me it's always going to be de same. See?"

He snatched her body toward him with such force that her

---

[272] Both extracts quoted by Dr David Pilgrim, *The Jezebel Stereotype* published by the Jim Crow Museum.

breath was forced from her in a sharp gasp. Then she inhaled deeply, threw back her head, and sent a wild laugh out of the clearing.

Crown swung her about and threw her face forward into the hut.[273]

In an extension of the female stereotype, another frequently used one was the invention of a very fat very black woman who was a household servant and whilst being very cheerful and willing to work, she was not very intelligent. In most cases she was the equivalent of a household pet but she could do simple domestic tasks. Fairly frequently, she could cook. One historian is quoted as saying:

"*Records do acknowledge the presence of female slaves who served as the right hand of Plantation Mistresses. Yet documents from the planter class during the first 50 years following the American Revolution reveal only a handful of such examples. Not until after emancipation did black women run white households or occupy in any significant number the special positions ascribed to them in folklore and fiction. The mammy was created by white southerners to redeem the relationship between black women and white men within the slave society in response to the anti slavery attack from the North during the ante-Belum period. In the primary records from before the Civil War, hard evidence for its existence simply does not appear.*'[274]

This caricature underlines the belief that black

---

[273] Dubose Heyward, *Porgy,* p.137.

[274] Catharine Clinton, *The Plantation Mistress: Woman's World in the Old South* pp.201-202. Quoted by Dr David Pilgrim on the Jim Crow Museum website.

women were only fit to be domestic workers and therefore supports the white view that an African-American could never be given any position of responsibility. DuBose Heyward extended this character when he invented "Maria". Black and fat she may be, but she is in reality an avenging angel. She is not a churchgoer but she knows good from evil and deals, temporarily, with Sportin' Life, a drug peddler who brings about Bess's final downfall. Having equipped herself with a brick from under her stove, Maria acts:

With frightful deliberation, Maria swung her long arm back; then, like the stroke of a rattler, it shot forward. The brick caught the mulatto full on the side of the head. He crumpled among his gaudy habiliments like a stricken bird.[275]

The actress, Hattie McDaniel, played the faithful black house servant in the popular film Gone with the Wind and was portrayed as the only character who could talk sense and was listened to by the wilful heroine, Scarlet O'Hara. She won an Oscar for her part in the film as best supporting actress. She died in 1952 and was denied her wish to be buried in Hollywood because she was black. In spite of her excellent portrayals of an increasingly intelligent and outspoken black servant it has to be remembered that the entire character is fictitious and a caricature. Such a caricature does not represent anyone and certainly not the average black woman in the street. Nor, at that time, the treatment of the average black woman in the street. A visitor to Charleston in 1816 saw this contrast in the way house servants were treated in comparison with the savagery meted out to field

[275] *Porgy*, p.144.

hands and runaway slaves.[276]

The savage treatment of male slaves was justified by the fiction that they were all very dangerous and brute caricature was invented of an innately uncivilised, animal-like criminal who deserved constant punishment and possibly even death. His other beastly characteristic were that he lusted after white women and was ready to rape them. It will be noticed that this was a projection of the white slave owners' casual habit of raping black slave women and there is no evidence of any such propensity on the part of black men other than in the normal course of things when a black man and a white woman fall in love. However, the image of the black brute lusting after white women was widespread:

When a knock is heard at the door (of a white woman) shudders with nameless horror. The black brute is lurking in the dark, a monstrous beast, crazed with lust. His ferocity is almost demoniacal. A mad bull or tiger could scarcely be more brutal. A whole community is frenzied with horror, with the blind and furious rage for vengeance.[277]

The American Civil War (1861-1865) changed the whole tone of anti-black prejudice in America from a fictional benevolent master with a black

---

[276] Clement Eaton, *The Growth of Southern Civilisation*, p.8. Mr Eaton is trying to counterbalance the image of the white slave owner with something more benevolent and so his evidence is all the more compelling.

[277] Winston GT (1901) The relations of the whites to the Negroes. Annals of the American Academy of Political and Social Science XVII pp.108-109. Quoted in *The Brute Caricature*, Jim Crow Museum Ferris State University.

servant who accepted his inferiority, to a struggle between two equals, both free to be recognised as equals. On the white side, to recognise a black man as an equal, no matter what the law said, would have been an insult to his sense of social standing and self-esteem. This provided the climate for a violent racist response and this is what happened and, according to news bulletins of the police shootings of black Americans, is still happening in 2016.

The southern states, finally the total was eleven, claimed the right to autonomy and to man the forts on southern land with a southern army, they also felt threatened by the northern states removing one of their great capital assets-slaves. The northern states saw the attitude of the South as a threat to the unity of the nation. The South also believed, wrongly, that the threat to cotton production (King Cotton) would bring the European states to their aid. No foreign government recognised the Confederacy. The difficulty for the abolitionists in the North was that the American Constitution, drafted in 1787, recognised slavery. Against the pleas of George Mason of Virginia who objected to slavery on the grounds that it corrupted the society that practised it, it was enacted that in Article 1.2 slaves counted as 3/5 of a person for taxation purposes; Article 1.9 Congress has no power to ban slavery until 1808 and, for the South, independence would solve this legal difficulty.

In the 1860 presidential election, the Republican Abraham Lincoln campaigned for the banning of slavery but in March 1861, in an effort to avert war, he said: *I have no purpose, directly or indirectly, to interfere with the institution of slavery in the United States where it exists. I believe I have no lawful right to do so, and I have no inclination to do so.'* Confederate States were unimpressed and opened fire in April 1861 on Fort Sumter in South Carolina. The war cost the greatest loss of life in the history of the United States and was lost by the Confederacy mainly because, reliant on cheap slave labour, they had failed to mechanise and were still a fairly primitive agrarian society.[278]

The post-war hatred opened in April 1865 with the murder of President Lincoln by John Wilkes Booth, aged 26, and a member of the Booth acting family of Maryland and a vehement anti-abolitionist. Booth was the ninth of ten children and the younger brother of Edwin Booth who achieved great acclaim as an actor. John, as it happens, is only remembered as the killer of Abraham Lincoln. Whether he was moved by the desire to be famous like his brother or because he felt rejected in some way will probably never be known, but his motive was ostensibly racial.

The 13th Amendment, abolishing slavery, was passed by the Senate in April 1864 (possibly to encourage black troops to join the Union army). It was followed, in the ex-slave states, by vigilante groups maintaining white supremacy. The assertion of equality by black people was felt by the whites as an insult. Black people who gave offence, whether real or imagined, were hanged without trial. The name which attached this form of murder was 'lynching', probably after Charles Lynch (1736-1796) who administered rough justice in Virginia. In 1884 the owner of Memphis Free Speech said that over a short period 728 black men and women had been lynched by white

---

[278] Wikipedia, The American Civil War.

mobs, some of them dressed in the white robes of the Ku Klux Klan but by no means all. Photographs of pathetic bodies hanging from trees with a smiling white mob under them, some smartly dressed, stand proudly and without shame. Why should they be ashamed? In their eyes they had proved they were winning their war for the South.

The root cause of this outburst of savagery was the economy of the Confederate states which had been ruined by the war. At the start of the war a Confederate paper dollar was worth 90 cents in gold while, by the end of the war, it was worth 6 cents in gold. By 1900, most of the white population were ruined but the black population were doing rather better. They were wage-earning labour working on railroad building. The whites were losing control of their own country to a formerly slave race. That year, 1900 and then 1901, 214 lynchings took place.[279]

The general rule in the USA is that most states have jurisdiction over criminal cases involving murder, unless the victim is a federal officer. Each state formulates and enforces their own laws regarding the definition and consequences of murder.[280] As a consequence of this the state law authorities were entitled to deal with lynching on the basis of it being justifiable homicide and without bringing the suspects to court. Had there been a trial, then an appeal could have been referred to the Supreme Court. As a result of this, strenuous efforts were made to make lynching a federal offence.

---

[279] Franklin, 8th ed, p.291.

[280] Criminal Law Lawyer Source.

George Henry White, an ex-slave, proposed a bill in 1901 to make lynching a federal offence. He pointed out that in 1899 of the 109 people lynched, 87 were African-Americans. The bill was defeated easily. In 1919, ten black soldiers were lynched still in their uniforms. In 1917 trades unionists were lynched presumably on the grounds, real or imagined, that they were communists.

A closer result was achieved by Leonidas C Dyer, Republican representative for Missouri, who brought in a bill to make lynching a federal offence which passed in the House of Representatives in 1918 but was frustrated in the Senate by Southern Democratic Filibusters. Southern legislators have always frustrated such a bill.

It is because of the acquiescence of US legislators that the murder of black people approaches genocide and is done to compensate white people for loss of social status and failure.

In a report on lynching in 1930 it was stated that 3,724 people were lynched in the USA between 1889 to 1930. Nearly all the lynchers were native white men. In 1933 two men were arrested for kidnapping and murder in California. Facing an angry mob, the Sheriff asked for the National Guard to protect them but the Governor refused and the mob hanged them in the park across the road from the jail. The hanged bodies of Thomas Shipp and Abram Smith, in 1930, had a relaxed crowd of men and women talking animatedly to each other. The Billie Holliday song, 'Strange Fruit' was denounced by Time Magazine as a: A prime piece of musical propaganda for the *National Association for the Advancement of Coloured People.*

Even after the passage of the Civil Rights Act in 1964, lynchings continued. Two young white men grabbed a teenage black boy off the street and murdered him. This did go to court but the Jury found the death was the result of a drug war. There was no evidence to this effect and the black boy's mother refused to accept the verdict and ultimately brought a civil action against the Ku Klux Klan in Alabama in 1987, which ruined them financially but did not close them down. They are still there.[281]

In white eyes the image of the savage black man persists to this day. In 1991, Rodney King, a taxi driver, was involved in a high-speed chase by the police whilst drunk in charge of his motorcar. When he got out of the car he cavorted around for a few moments in a drunken manner at which stage four officers of the Los Angeles Police started to beat him with batons. When he lay insensible on the ground they continued beating him. They took him to hospital where a nurse testified that they were laughing and congratulating each other. Even the presentation of video evidence at the trial did not prevent one jurywoman saying that King was always in charge of the situation. At the trial, all four officers were acquitted of using excessive force. At a subsequent trial two officers were found guilty of infringing King's human rights. The image of the savage black male has not changed since antebellum days.

The black brute lusting after white women persisted in America at least until the 1960s if not longer. When Sammy Davis Jr, a talented black actor and dancer, met Kim Novak, a successful, very blonde actress, in 1957, they fell in love and began an

---

[281] John Simkin, Spartacus Educational, Lynching.

affair. Anti-black prejudice was still rife in America in those days and in 1957 there were still lynchings in Tennessee. News of the affair between a black man and a blonde actress got into the press and threatened the earning power of both Kim Novak and Sammy Davis. The man who made money out of Novak arranged for Davis to have a very serious death threat to end the affair and marry a black girl which, under threat of assassination, he did.[282]

The black brute is again depicted in *Porgy* when Crown kills Robbins:

With a low snarl, straight from his crouching position, Crown hurled his tremendous weight forward, shattering the lamp, and bowling Robbins over against the wall.... Crown was crouched for a second spring, with lips drawn from gleaming teeth. The light fell strong upon thrusting jaw, and threw the sloping brow into the shadow. One hand touched the ground lightly, balancing the massive torso. The other arm held the cotton hook forward, ready, like a prehensile claw.... The end came quickly, and with startling suddenness. Crown broke his adversary's weakening hold, and held him the length of one mighty arm. The other swung the cotton hook downward. Then he dropped his victim, and swaggered drunkenly toward the street.[283]

The indolent black politicians shown in The Birth of a Nation were inspired by another very common caricature known as "the Tom caricature". This fictitious black man is always shown as a faithful submissive servant who is happy with the non-skilled job serving the superior white man. It is intended to

---

[282] Vanity Fair, 3 September 2013.
[283] *Porgy*, pp.20-22.

show that no black man could ever be given a position of responsibility. It has persisted in the white, European mind until President Obama was elected president of the United States. In spite of that, most reasonable people will harbour the suspicion that it still persists. As a piece of prejudice, it is completely without foundation and is discredited by the facts.

In spite of all opposition designed to show that somebody with black skin was not the equal of somebody with white skin, in the 19th century African-Americans were graduates of the universities, owned newspapers, became lawyers, university professors, playwrights, doctors, obtained PhDs. John Willis Menard was elected to Congress in 1868 but not allowed to take his seat. They became graduates of West Point and police officers.

In the 20th century a black woman became president of a bank which finally became the Consolidated Bank and Trust Company of Richmond Virginia; a black woman became a millionaire; there were black composers, and black conductors, black commissioned officers in the United States Army, delegates to the United Nations and, famously, a Secretary of State and now there are Senators and chess masters and one President.

It is possible that at the very highest intellectual levels they fail to attain their full potential. There are only 15 black people worldwide who have obtained Nobel prizes as compared with 115 British and 353 American. This could be proportional to the opportunities provided in these countries.

The last great stronghold of white supremacy was Mississippi where volunteers helped to break down segregation in what was known as the Mississippi summer project in the most totalitarian state in the country. In June 1964 three civil rights activists were murdered. The actual target of the killings was a man called Michael Schwerner who was described by the Klan as Goatee or Jew boy. They first sought to find him at the Mount Zion Church but he was not there. As a result of their disappointment they beat up the black members of the congregation and set fire to the church. In fact, Schwerner, Andrew Goodman and James Chaney were driving back to Meridian in what sounds like a rather beat-up Ford station wagon when they were spotted on Highway 16 by Deputy Sheriff Price, who arrested them and put them in the county jail. They were denied phone calls and in the afternoon when their colleagues made a call asking where they were, their presence was denied by the jailer. Price informed his fellow Klan members of his fortuitous catch and released them at about 10 o'clock at night. He and two car loads of Klan members followed them, kidnapped them and took them down a turnoff called Rock Cut Road where an ex-Marine, with a dishonourable discharge, murdered them at point-blank range. They were buried on a reservoir site on land owned by another Klan member.

The resulting furore in the press made it impossible for the FBI to ignore the murders and, because nobody would talk since they were all involved, Hoover resorted to asking the Mafia for assistance and discovered the whereabouts of the bodies. The man who had ordered the killing was Samuel Holloway Bowers Jr, who styled himself Imperial Wizard of the White Knights of the Ku Klux Klan of Mississippi, who gave orders that they were to "activate Plan 4". Plan 4 was the scheme to murder Michael Schwerner.

Samuel Bowers was a portrait of the racist. His family had once been well-to-do in southern society. His father was the son of a Congressman and his mother was the daughter of plantation owners of several generations of slave owners. Father lost his money in property speculation in Florida, drifted from job to job and divorced his mother when Bowers was 14. Bowers had left school and joined the Navy during the war. When he was discharged he went to university but dropped out without a degree. He was a violent man who was accused of bombing Jewish targets in 1967 and 1968. He ordered, but did not take part in, the murder of the three civil rights activists in 1964. He was a partner in the Sambo Amusement company which manufactured either pinball machines or jukebox machines or vending machines. It is not clear precisely what they did. Bowers never married, was an only child, and seems to have been in and out of prison though he was agile in covering his tracks. At a recorded interview in the Mississippi State Penitentiary he described his family in tones of grandiosity and great dignity. He came from fantastic stock: plantation owners and eminent congressmen. He was very proud of them but he himself relied on the title Imperial Wizard for his respectability and greatness.

After his release from prison in 1976 he worked as a Sunday school teacher. His instructions to his followers included their responsibility as Christians: "As Christians we are disposed to kindness, generosity, affection, and humility in our dealings with others. As militants we are disposed to use physical force against our enemies. How can we reconcile these two apparently contradictory philosophies? The answer of course is to purge malice, bitterness and vengeance from our hearts." In other words, he could justify his murder by seeing himself as a militant priest the equivalent of the soldiers of Islam who kill today. One source describes him as being fascinated by guns and explosives and having "a swastika fetish". If he really was a fetishist then it helped him get an erection when he clothed himself in these symbols of power. He died in the Mississippi State penitentiary at the age of 82 in 2006.

After the emancipation of the slaves in 1863, racial violence erupted throughout the southern states. The main targets were educated black people: teachers, ministers, smallholders and politicians. There were burnings whippings and lynchings. The whites announced their intention of keeping the southern states white and directed their abuse at what they described as uppity Negroes. In DW Griffith's film The Birth of a Nation, indolent black politicians are shown idling their time away with their feet on the desks and presumably all at public expense. An actor is shown, with his face blackened because no black man could touch a white woman, manhandling a white woman with the intention of possessing her body. She resists and runs away.

In the face of abundant evidence to the contrary, the belief in a racial hierarchy persists. Clement Eaton, a historian, wrote in 1961: *Nevertheless, a much closer integration of blacks and whites occurred during slavery days than has existed in this century; indeed, strict segregation was largely a product of the 1890s and the early twentieth century. In the ante-bellum period Negro and white children played happily together. Slave women often nursed the master's children at the breast. Negroes belonged to the same churches as the whites, and joined with their masters in singing hymns. Only after the Civil War did they withdraw, of their own volition, from the white churches. Travelers record numerous instances of Negroes riding in stage-coaches and railroad cars with whites. E S Abdy, the Cambridge don travelling on a stagecoach between Lexington and Frankfort in 1834, found that two of his fellow passengers were Negroes. The Englishman Richard Cobden noted in 1835 that a Southern planter brought his slave, riding on the top of the coach, inside the vehicle when it began to rain and squeezed him between the white passengers, and that the Negro ate in the tavern in the same room but at a different table as the master. On some farms the slave ate at the same table as the yeoman farmer.*[284]

This is an example of a white man's belief, in the 1960s, that there exists a natural racial hierarchy and the black people of America brought segregation on to their own heads. In other words, they had only themselves to blame. These are the words of a Harvard-educated historian used as a text book to educate young people in the 20th century.

---

[284] Clement Eaton, pp.56, 57. Eaton was a standard text book in the 20th century and taught in schools.

CHAPTER 11

XENOPHOBIA

'The term "xenophobia" was invented by the ancient Greeks, to describe a reflexive feeling of hostility or fear for the stranger or 'other'.

Xenophobia, like lust, is buried deep in the human personality and seems almost part of the species survival mechanism. Mankind's closest living relative is the chimpanzee who parted from the human chain some five million years ago and share 98.3% of their genetic material with humans. Oddly, on this basis, they are closer to humans than they are to gorillas with whom they share 96.5%.[285] Like the chimpanzees of Gombe, in East Africa, studied by Jane Goodall, the chimpanzees of the Tai Forest in Cote d'Ivoire, are territorial. They protect territory because it contains a resource and when that resource dwindles their access to fertile females dwindles. When food supply, because of seasonal or climatic change, is reduced, the number of young males drops and the territory shrinks.[286] Chimpanzees protect their territory from incursions by their neighbours of the

---

[285] Christophe Boesch et al, *The Chimpanzees of the Tai Forest*, p.13
[286] Boesch, Chapter 7.

same species by means of patrols of as little as ten males. Occasionally, they are accompanied by two or more females but if there is contact, the females hang back. When entering neighbouring territory, the patrol remains silent and drumming has never been observed. Injuries, when fights occur, do not threaten death and only one war, which wiped out a neighbouring community, has been reported.

If the human race shares one thing with the chimpanzee, it is the desirability of the fertile female. It is instinctive and, like the camel, the more primitive human male will kill to possess a fertile female, regardless of whether he wants children. It is a triumph of lust over 'love'.

'To be reproductively successful, ancestral men had to marry women with the capacity to bear children[287] The way in which a woman of any race displays her reproductive capacity is to have an hourglass figure which shows she is producing oestrogens. Oestrogens develop breasts, hips and thighs and put fat on buttocks. When a woman reaches menopause there is a tendency for the fat to migrate to the waist and abdomen. In spite of being hundreds of thousands of years old and in many ways no longer relevant, this still rules human behaviour and, as a result, there is now a global multibillion-dollar fashion industry. If the human race has inherited this primitive instinct from its animal forebears, and without it or something like it, the human race would not exist, there is no reason why the human race should not share the chimpanzee's territoriality. The possession of a fertile woman is a sign of controlling territory then territory is important.

---

[287] Workman and Reader, *Evolutionary Psychology*, p.94.

Even today the less intellectual man of property wants to marry a second wife who is younger and displays the attributes described above. This is not to say that such a woman is stupid. One ex-career woman who had been married to a very rich man said: '*Women considered trophy wives are both accomplished and ambitious in both their careers and their lives. They have some looks, but are neither, glamorous nor stupid enough to be called a 'bimbo'; they attract husbands who generally see second wives as a kind of reward, but who want more than a pretty face.*'[288]

In the rich West the mythology which they took in by limbic resonance from their parents or their peers governs the way they feel about foreigners. Only those who fought and died for their country had an afterlife in Valhalla. Who were they fighting against? The monstrous wolf Fenrir, the enemy of the gods and the personification of evil who consumed Odin at the final battle of the world, Ragnarok. The wolf's sister was called Hel (Hell. Judaism, for example, has no Hell). The hero then fights evil, the thing that wants to kill all mankind. The hero fights forces that want[289] to deprive us of our homes, our parents, our womenfolk from foreigners. When the Einsatzgruppen were machine gunning Jewish Polish peasants sitting on the edge of mass graves which the victims had dug themselves, the middle-aged Germans who had volunteered to do the killing excused themselves by saying it was an act of war required to preserve the security of Germany. Unfortunately for them these arguments did not prevail before the judges at Nuremburg.

The idea of a warrior being a hero is an ancient

---

[288] William Safire, New York Times, 1 May 1994.
[289] Greg Dawson, Judgement Before Nuremburg.

one and foreigners who were warlike are more acceptable than foreigners who are not. Ancient Romans also held notions of superiority over other peoples, such as a speech attributed to Manius Acilius, *"There, as you know, there were the Macedonians and the Thracians and Illyrians, all most warlike nations, here Syrians and Asiatic Greeks, the most worthless peoples among mankind and born for slavery."* [290]

The idea of the warrior who fights for his nation's way of life and to preserve her borders and therefore the nation's territory, access to fertile women and a food supply, is an idea which goes back to the city states which sprang up in every river valley of the prehistoric world. The Greeks fought incessant wars which finally ruined them, the final blow being dealt by Alexander the Great who mistook gold for wealth. The idea of the heroic warrior persists to this day and an incoming president of the United States' first duty is to go to Arlington Cemetery to pay homage to the heroic dead.

Initiation ceremonies vary throughout the world but they have, in common, the time when a child ceases to be an encumbrance on the tribe and becomes a contributing member of society. As a gross generalisation with many exceptions, this means becoming a warrior and a parent[291]. It might seem extraordinary that many people still live by this archaic standard. There is a rash of people with low self-esteem who endow themselves with a military career and decorations to which they are not entitled.

---

[290] Wikipedia, Xenophobia.
[291] Jane Ellen Harrison, *Epilegomena to the Study of Greek Religion,* p.14.

The onetime Town Crier for Oxfordshire claimed to be a former regimental sergeant major in the Coldstream Guards with a service record in the Falkland Islands, Northern Ireland and other zones of conflict, all of which were complete invention. He had never been in the armed services at all. His fantasy seems to have started with his father who was a pilot in the RAF and took part in the Berlin airlift for which he was awarded the MBE. According to British custom, a medal holder's son was entitled to wear the medal on his right breast but not on the left, nor was he entitled to say that he had won the medal himself. From there, he awarded himself the British Empire Medal and the Imperial Service Medal together with some 15 other decorations to which he may or may not have been entitled as a Town Crier. When he apologised he may, as he claimed, merely have been trying to commemorate the men, including his father, who had fought and died doing their duty for their country.

Since 2013 some 200 imposters have given themselves spurious records in the British Armed Forces and have been outed by a veteran's association. Some are suffering from neuroses and attempting to increase their feelings of well-being by giving themselves a past that they can be proud of. This is an extreme form of boasting, allowing innocent, Walter Mitty daydreams to come to life. In the United States the practice of pretending to have a heroic past caused the enactment of the 2013 Stolen Valor Act whereby it is illegal to impersonate a member of the Armed Forces. Nevertheless, these sad cases bear witness to the regard we have for heroes.

The idea that a man only achieves adulthood when he becomes a warrior like the Norse heroes, is still present. In 2003 the British Prime Minister, in an address to Congress, referred to the men and women who fought and died in Afghanistan as 'heroes'[292]. Many people at the time would have referred to the event as a tragic loss of life in a war to which they should never have been sent. In an essay in the Guardian newspaper, Ian Buruma pointed out that 'Britain is the only European country where war is still associated with glory.'[293] Max Hastings, the journalist and war correspondent, writing in the Telegraph newspaper was warning that cutbacks in the armed forces would leave Britain unprepared for war and commented, quite rightly, that this represented a big cultural change. '*This momentous decision, with all it means for our culture and heritage, has been a long time coming. And it raises an important question: "what are soldiers for in the 21st Century?"*'[294]

This move to more and more technical warfare with drones and robots implies the loss of the front-line soldier and, with it, loss of the definition of 'hero' has indeed left a void. Veterans returning from Afghanistan and Iraq have told the author, in casual conversation, that their colleagues died in vain. However, millions still believe in the dying definition of a 'man' being a 'warrior' is evidence of the belief in a nation state with borders that have to be maintained from the ingress of foreigners. Because trade now is

---

[292] The Guardian, 18 July 2003, Tony Blair's speech to the US Congress.
[293] Ian Buruma, The Guardian, 30 October 2001.
[294] Max Hastings, 'Farewell to Our Warrior Nation', The Telegraph, 9 November 2012.

global, the idea of the nation state with borders is weakening; nevertheless, populist politicians revert to an appeal to the nation state with its own inviolable borders and at times of peculiar economic conditions when many people feel out of control, this appeal is very strong, nor does it have to be argued because it seems obvious as a way of regaining control. This appeal is universal as Karl Mannheim, the sociologist, wrote while working in Germany in 1922 during the period of hyperinflation when pensions became worthless:

Everywhere people are awaiting a messiah and the air is laden with the promises of large and small prophets...we all share the same fate: we carry within us more love, and above all more longing than today's society is able to satisfy. We have all ripened for something, and there is no one to harvest the fruit.

In 1933 the man they thought was the long-awaited Messiah arrived with the message that he was going to make Germany great again.

Since 1973, Britain had joined what became the European Union, one of the tenets of which was the free movement of labour from any Community country to another. This worked well for many years and, by 2016 the rest of the European Union had become Britain's largest trading partner. After the banking crash of 2008, world trade went into decline through lack of commercial confidence and a shortage of credit as banks shored up their balance sheets by being, belatedly, much more cautious in their lending. In Britain a change of government brought in a policy of austerity and a sharp decline in public spending brought unemployment, nationally, to close on 3 million or 12% of the working population. The immediate reaction from the native-born British, of whatever race, was to say that the influx of foreigners were taking 'our jobs'.[295]

Due to lack of funds, the National Health Service was overstretched and could only operate with immigrant nurses and immigrant doctors, nevertheless the cry went out that the reason for this tension was foreigners 'coming here as health tourists'[296]. In addition, there was a cry that immigrants were 'coming here, not to work, but to draw social security'. One National newspaper reported that *'migrants had quickly learned how to work the benefits system...a queue of girls speaking foreign tongues snakes down the road' outside an Inland Revenue Benefits Office '...their buggies and prams crowd the pavement as they wait to sign on for tax credits and child benefits.'* [297]

Roughly half of immigrants came from the European Union with the other half coming from the old Commonwealth countries. Poland was the biggest contributor from the EU and India from the Commonwealth.[298] No evidence was offered for any anti-migrant claim that was made, it was all believed on the basis that foreigners must be to blame. Pressure grew for a referendum to decide whether we

---

[295] British people were also leaving, permanently or temporarily, so that net immigration was never greater than 0.5% per annum of the total population. This is by no means negligible.

[296] A study carried out in 2013 showed that the maximum spent in this way was £300 million per year or 1/3 of 1% of the health budget.

[297] Institute of Race Relations. The New Geographies of Racism: Peterborough.

[298] The Migration Observatory. EU Migration To and From the UK.

should leave the European Union and 'Take control of our borders again'. The government of the day could not resist the pressure for allowing a referendum. The campaign to leave was misleading to say the least. It was claimed that membership of the EU was costing the taxpayer £350 million a week[299]. We have lost our sovereignty. One politician was photographed in front of a huge poster showing a queue of migrants, several thousand strong, trying to leave the Syrian war zone and entering Turkey. Perfectly worthy people were assuring the author that, unless we left the EU, we would have 80 million immigrants in Britain.

All these statements were gross distortions but people were prepared to blame 'immigrants' for their own lack of work and being economically sidelined. No rational argument prevailed against the irresistible appeal of xenophobia. (It has to be admitted that there were exaggerations on both sides of the argument.) On the 23rd June 2016, 17,410,742 people voted to leave the EU and 16,141,241 voted to remain, and as a result a new British government was formed to negotiate leaving the country's greatest trading partner whilst maintaining trade links but not open borders.[300] The 'Leave' campaigners very shrewdly kept using the word 'control' and one poor woman was pictured outside her home, festooned in the British Union flag, almost in tears of relief at the Leave result.

---

[299] The tariff paid into the EU budget for the poorer EU states was £163 million a week or less than 1/3 of 1% of UK GDP.
[300] Fortunately Britain is still a member of the World Trade Organisation so any damage will be limited.

Gary Gibbon, in his monograph 'Breaking Point', stresses that history played a big part in the decision to leave. In 1973, Europeans had clear memories of World War II and loss of life and occupation. British memories were not as stark as that, having suffered loss of life but having avoided occupation thanks largely to the Channel, the Royal Air Force and the Americans and Commonwealth soldiers who gave loans for unstinting aid. '*From the beginning when Britain joined the Common Market, the UK saw Europe as useful but not endearing.*'[301] Nevertheless, xenophobia seems to be an instinctive response to any group of foreigners in any country in the world. As long as there are ills, the native population feel completely justified in pointing to a foreign group, resident in their land, as being the cause of it. Nor will reason or analysis ever be listened to. In 2015 the Economist intelligence unit analysed success or failure among the industrialised nations of the world. They called this the Quality of Life Index taking into account the following factors:

Material Wellbeing. Health. Political Stability and Security. Family Life. Community Life. Climate and Geography. Job Security. Political Freedom. Gender Equality.

Comparing, 1988 to 2015, and adding headline immigration figures, it will be seen that there is no correlation between quality of life and the number of immigrants or membership of the EU.

---

[301] Gary Gibbon, *Breaking Point* p.21.

1988	Pos'n	2015	Pos'n	Comments	Immigrants /Population
USA	1	USA	16	Down 16 places	26%
France	2	France	26	Down 24 places	7-9%
W Germany	3	Germany	16	Down 13 places	4.5%
Italy	4	Italy	21	Down 16 places	8.2%
Canada	5	Canada	9	Down 4 places	1.7%
Japan	6	Japan	25	Down 19 places	1.7%
Hong Kong	7	Hong Kong	10	Down 3 places	Less than 1%
UK	7	UK	27	Down 20 places	11.9%
Sweden	9	Sweden	4	Up 5 places	19.6%
Netherlands	10	Netherlands	8	Up 2 places	11.1%
South Korea	10	South Korea	19	Down 9 places	
Austria	12	Austria	13	Down 1 place	
Switzerland	13	Switzerland	1	Up 12 places	22.8%
Norway	13	Norway	8	Up 10 places	12.2%
Australia	18	Australia	2	Up 16 places	26.8%
Denmark	24	Denmark	5	Up 19 places	8%

It will be noticed that those countries which have improved their quality of life the most have up to 26.8% immigrants per head of population. It is true that the United Kingdom has declined, by global comparison, 26 places with only 11.9% immigrants, but this seems to be due to lack of investment since the banking crisis of 2008 and the lack of research and development of robotics so that Britain could improve her productivity and be less dependent on cheap labour.

One of the Economist leaders put the economic issues relating to immigration in the following words: *'Migrants improve not just their own lives but the economies of host countries. European immigrants who arrived in Britain since 2000 have been net contributors to the exchequer, adding more than £20 billion to the public finances between 2001 and 2011'.*[302] This is about £2 billion a year net which corresponds with a University College London report done earlier.

The campaign for ending immigration is not in the immediate economic national interest. In the United States immigrants contribute an estimated $10 billion a year net to the economy[303] and an even higher estimate can be derived which places the net contribution of immigrants at $20 billion per annum.[304] In spite of this, any politician who says he

---

[302] The Economist, October 1st 2016, p.13.

[303] James Smith, United States Research Council quoted in Wikipedia, Immigration to the United States.

[304] Wikipedia, Immigration in the United States '...the typical immigrant and his children will pay a net $80,000 more in their lifetime than they collect in government services according to the National Academy of Sciences.' Quoted in the Cato Handbook for Congress p632.

is going to reduce or eliminate immigration is greeted as a hero because he is keeping 'foreigners' out. In 2011 the State of Georgia passed HB87 designed to keep immigrants out as a result of which 50% of its agricultural produce was left to rot in the fields.[305] One of the values of an immigrant population is that, in the short term, they will do work which the native-born population does not find attractive.

Historically the main weapon of the trade unions was strike action, and in the American Far West, for example, the strikes were broken by importing poor immigrants to do the work either as strike breakers or cheap labour. They were Irish, Italians, Mexicans, African Americans and, finally, Asians.[306] In Britain, in 1829, Sir Robert Peel urged his colleagues not to condemn Irish labour because he recognised the economic value of cheap labour and their use as strike-breakers.[307] Immigration has been seen for many years as the enemy of the blue-collar worker. It is hardly surprising therefore that many of 'the exploited class' see immigrants as holding down the rate of wages paid for unskilled work. In fact, the emphasis is now on qualifications and in the USA there was a shortage of over 90,000 doctors.[308] The USA has such high standards of qualification that only 7,000 International Graduates were being admitted for training per year. In Britain the reliance on immigrants was more pronounced and 11% of

---

[305] Wikipedia, 'Immigration to the United States' p.16.

[306] Earl Spencer Pomeroy, *American Far West in the Twentieth Century*, p.262.

[307] Robert Winder, *Bloody Foreigners: The Story of Immigration to Britain*, Chapter 13.

[308] Philip Sopher. Article on the Internet, November 18 2014.

NHS staff and 26% of Doctors were not British-born.[309] Even after the referendum in 2016 which was argued on the basis that it was going to exclude foreigners, the Government tacitly admitted that immigration would have to continue.[310]

A further and most important reason for voting to leave the European Union in Britain was the economic inequality in a small country. There is anecdotal evidence that in parts of the North East, with the dearth of heavy industry, unemployment reached 80% while London unemployment was 3.8%. In a revealing article in the Economist Weekly it demonstrated that those who voted to leave the European Union lived in areas where the *increase* in immigration was the highest.[311] Human beings do not like sudden change[312]. They feel they are being swept aside and *control* of immigration became a catchphrase rather than any rational argument. In the United States a populist campaign based on controlling immigration was delivered with great success by a big, powerful man among the richest in the United States.[313] The promise of control from such a powerful figure was irresistible though the candidate was nonplussed when confronted by the parents of a warrior who had died for his country and who was a

---

[309] The Guardian, 26 January 2014.

[310] Rowena Mason, The Guardian, 5 September 2016.

[311] The Economist, July 16 2016.

[312] Robert Cialdini, *Influence: The Psychology of Persuasion*, Chapter 3.

[313] Forbes placed Donald Trump's personal wealth at $4.2 billion and 113th in the United States.

Muslim.[314] The campaign was directed mainly against Muslims and Mexican illegal immigrants. The road to success was assisted by the decline in Median Household Income in real terms which reached a high of $56,896 in 1999 and had declined to $55,775 in 2015 together with two armed conflicts in Afghanistan and Iraq which cost the lives of thousands of Americans.

[314] Captain Humayun Khan went forward himself to investigate an explosive laden car telling his men to stand back. Iraq in 2004.

CONCLUSION

The essence of racism is that it brings solace to an unhappy person by projecting the blame for their unhappiness on someone from another group who is weaker than them. In times gone by, the largest weaker group was women who were, and still are, bullied by unhappy men. The next huge group who have been subjected to discrimination are homosexuals and who are still subjected to humiliating treatment in some societies in the Middle East. A third derided group are those who are economically weaker. In agricultural economies and during the industrial revolution, the male manual labourer was more valuable than the female and this again made women weak and subject to violence. In times of great economic hardship, the wife or daughter sold her body in order to put some bread on the table. While prostitution was vital, at the time, for the family's survival, it brought shame on the head of the household because he was unable to support his family.

The unemployed and the dispossessed in Britain who voted to leave the European Union were protesting and projecting their unhappiness on immigrants who earned less than they did and had no right according to some media outlets to avail themselves of scarce resources like social security and the National Health Service. There were accusations of immigrants being health tourists.

On this basis, racism is akin to bullying when 30% of those who are bullied, become bullies themselves.[315] Young bullies who have been bullied at home arrive in school and, some, become bullies themselves. It is a way of taking back control of their lives. As one 13-year-old boy said:

A Bully's like a king. You rule the playground until someone bullying you takes over. You are deposed.

There are various forms of discriminating against a foreign group but it is heightened when an authoritative finger is pointed at them as being different or having committed some heinous crime. This was regardless of whether the claim of iniquity was true or false, it was believed because it justified the need to look down on somebody. Examples of such mendacious claims are: the Jews killed the Christian saviour; black people are inherently stupid; immigrants are costing £325 million a week; by 2020, Britain will have 80 million immigrants; homosexuality is a lifestyle choice and the fact that it is chosen by an individual is a sign of their inherent wickedness. More recently, ISIS is a wicked movement, which it may well be, therefore exclude Muslims from our country. This sort of non-sequitur is accepted by many people but if one were to argue that the Columbine massacre was carried by two white boys, therefore white people with no religious

---

[315] Adrienne Katz et al, *Bullying in Britain, Testimonies from Teenagers*, Young Voice.

affiliation should be excluded from our country, there would be uproar.

Racism in Britain was heightened by the British vote to leave the European Union because it was seen as a move to exclude foreigners rather than a move to enhance trade for which latter there was no evidence. Generally, the rationalisation of the feeling that foreigners are stealing scarce resources is so close to the racist heart that no rational, evidence-based argument can displace it.

Racist anger is heightened when a person of what is viewed as an inferior race does better economically than the host population. This was horribly illustrated in the USA when African-Americans were emancipated and the Confederate States lost the very bloody civil war. During the reconstruction period blacks in America were earning more than the whites by working on the railroads.

When Gina Miller, born in Guyana, educated at London University and supported by a first-class legal team put the question of whether the Prime Minister could trigger Article 50 relying on the Royal Prerogative and without the authority of Parliament to three Lords of Appeal, in effect, asking whether the Prime Minister's decision to leave the European Union should be ratified by parliament, she received the answer 'Yes.' A grossly unbalanced press reaction said that the appellant, a foreigner, supported by a Spanish hairdresser and helped by a firm of solicitors with a foreign-sounding name together with the three Law Lords who agreed with her, were betraying the British people and delaying the exit from Europe. The British people were persuaded to vote for an exit by a largely xenophobic argument which existed in their minds and which explained their deprivation. The comment in the press emphasised that the claimants were both foreign and rich.[316] It was a frightening example for Britain and a day later the tone of the press comments had become more reasonable, as had the politicians. A right to appeal was granted.

The same syndrome was displayed when a black African objected to the statue of Cecil Rhodes at Oriel College, Oxford. The Guardian, a liberal paper,[317] said she was, effectively, being unreasonable without mentioning that Rhodes made his fortune out of cornering the diamond market over the bodies of thousands of black labourers who died in his mines. This is not a criticism of Rhodes himself but only 3.5% of Rhodes scholars come from Africa and most of those are white.

The racist then, is someone with a burden to bear – real, imagined or imposed by society – feels out of control and seeks to regain at least the sense of control by projecting his source of pain on someone weaker than him, or her, and transfer the pain they feel on to someone else. Like Frankenstein they have created their own monster but are unable to find anyone to love them.

---

[316] The papers found it necessary to mention that she was foreign born, her husband was a hedge fund manager and one of her supporters was a Spanish hairdresser. Also, one of her legal team had a foreign name. BBC 3 November 2016.
[317] 2 February 2016.